THE DEVIL'S ART

Studies in Early Modern German History

H. C. ERIK MIDELFORT, EDITOR

JASON PHILIP COY

the Devil's Art

DIVINATION AND DISCIPLINE IN EARLY MODERN GERMANY

UNIVERSITY OF VIRGINIA PRESS
Charlottesville and London

UNIVERSITY OF VIRGINIA PRESS

Printed in the United States of America on acid-free paper

First published 2020

1 3 5 7 9 8 6 4 2

Library of Congress Cataloging-in-Publication Data

Names: Coy, Jason Philip, author.
Title: The devil's art : divination and discipline in early modern Germany / Jason Philip Coy.
Description: Charlottesville : University of Virginia Press, 2020. | Series: Studies in early modern German history | Includes bibliographical references and index.
Identifiers: LCCN 2019047978 (print) | LCCN 2019047979 (ebook) | ISBN 9780813944074 (hardback) | ISBN 9780813944081 (epub)
Subjects: LCSH: Divination—Germany—History. | Lutheran Church—Germany—History.
Classification: LCC BF1773.2.G67 C56 2020 (print) | LCC BF1773.2.G67 (ebook) | DDC 133.30943—dc23
LC record available at https://lccn.loc.gov/2019047978
LC ebook record available at https://lccn.loc.gov/2019047979

Cover art: "The Fortune Teller and the Lady," engraving, after Jacques de Gheyn II. (The Elisha Whittelsey Collection, The Elisha Whittelsey Fund, 1949, The Metropolitan Museum of Art)

CONTENTS

ACKNOWLEDGMENTS

I first decided to write a book about divination in early modern Germany a decade ago. Searching for primary sources to use in a seminar on the European witch-hunts I was teaching at the College of Charleston, I noticed that many of the most famous—or rather infamous—demonological treatises of the era condemned fortune-telling in addition to witchcraft. Most of the scholarship in the field failed to mention that the era's most ardent witch-hunters were so deeply concerned with fortune-telling, however. Despite the prominence of divination in works by famous demonologists like Heinrich Kramer and Jean Bodin, scholars more interested in witchcraft had largely neglected this aspect of their treatises. As I continued my research, I found that prominent theologians like Thomas Aquinas, Martin Luther, and John Calvin also denounced divination. Learned attacks on popular fortune-telling outlasted the witch hunts, and Enlightenment-era luminaries ridiculed it as an ignorant superstition throughout the eighteenth century. Visiting American research libraries and German archives over the next few years, I set out to answer a number of questions: why were early modern authorities so opposed to divination? Why did Lutheran reformers seem particularly concerned about the popular forms of fortune-telling practiced by the unlearned? Did secular authorities in Germany respond to the clergy's call to eradicate popular forms of divination? Why did Reformation-era reformers and Enlightenment-era intellectuals face such difficulty in rooting out these occult practices?

The research and writing of this book took many years, but finishing it has been bittersweet. While working on this project, I experienced a life-shattering personal tragedy, and its completion is a reminder of how much my life has changed in the last ten years. I began my research with the loving encouragement of my wife, Amy, who had supported my scholarship ever since I was a graduate student. As I was finishing my research for this book, Amy was diagnosed with terminal cancer. She passed away in 2016. We had been happily married for 19 years when I lost her. I felt my life unraveling just as I began a sabbatical year in which I intended to complete the manuscript of this book. With the support of caring colleagues and friends, I threw myself into my writing, and finishing this book provided me with a renewed sense of purpose as I began to rebuild my life. Thus, I am doubly grateful for the many people and institutions who have helped me complete this book, since its completion represents both a milestone in my career and in my own personal healing.

I would like to thank a number of institutions that supported my research for this project. I conducted preliminary research in Duke University's David M. Rubenstein Rare Book & Manuscript Library in 2009–10, research funded by an Eleanore and Harold Jantz Fellowship from Duke. I am grateful for this crucial early support. I also made three summer archival research trips to Germany, with funding support from a 2011 Deutscher Akademischer Austauschdienst (DAAD) Re-Invitation Grant, a 2012 Herzog Ernst Fellowship of the Fritz Thyssen Foundation from the Forschungszentrum Gotha, and a 2013 College of Charleston Faculty Research and Development Grant. This project would have been impossible without these generous research grants. Archivists in Erfurt, Weimar, and Gotha have been crucial during these summer research visits, especially Rosemarie Barthel of the Landesarchiv Thüringen-Staatsarchiv Gotha. I completed and revised the manuscript while on a yearlong sabbatical from the College of Charleston during the 2016–17 academic year, and I thank my home institution for this support. I would also like to thank Berghahn Press for their gracious permission to reprint material from an essay I contributed to a 2014 volume I coedited with Benjamin Marschke, Jared Poley, and Claudia Verhoeven entitled *Kinship, Community, and Self: Essays in Honor of David Warren Sabean*.

I have also accrued a number of personal debts during the years that I worked on this book. A great many friends and colleagues helped me as

I started researching this project and began to formulate my early thoughts on the subject. The director and faculty at the Forschungszentrum Gotha were pivotal in helping me refine my topic during my research in Thuringia, especially Martin Mulsow and Alexander Schunka. Others have provided valuable feedback as I presented early versions of these chapters at conferences over the years. Some, like Tom Robisheaux, Ed Bever, Johannes Dillinger, Michael Bailey, Laura Stokes, and Kay Edwards, have enhanced my understanding of magic and witchcraft in early modern Europe. Others, like David Luebke, Mary Lindemann, Joel Harrington, and Sigrun Haude, have enriched my knowledge of early modern Germany.

My greatest thanks go to those who read early versions of the manuscript, providing me with invaluable advice on how to improve it. My department chair, Phyllis Jestice, busy working on her own study of Ottonian female rulership, met with me every other week during my sabbatical to discuss chapter drafts over expensive craft beers (and usually picked up the tab). She not only provided me with valuable feedback, but also encouraged me to keep writing at a steady pace during a turbulent time in my life. Three dear friends—David Sabean, Jared Poley, and Robert Davis—read through the entire manuscript once it was done and offered me advice on final revisions before I sent it to the press for review. I am grateful for their helpful suggestions. I owe a special debt of gratitude to Erik Midelfort, who supported this project from the very beginning and offered a wealth of sage counsel as I worked to revise the manuscript for publication. The anonymous readers selected by the University of Virginia Press provided me with invaluable advice about how to restructure my manuscript, and they also have my thanks. Finally, I want to thank Leah Worthington for helping me enliven my writing and, more important, for showing me how to be happy again.

THE DEVIL'S ART

INTRODUCTION

The Wise Man of Ohrdruf (1671)

In the summer of 1671, a stranger entered Ohrdruf, a village on the edge of the Thuringian forest. The villagers immediately took note of the "planet book" he carried, an astrological almanac that marked him as a soothsayer. For the villagers, the wise man's strange book promised an opportunity to glimpse into their futures. One of them, Hans Karst, invited the wise man to his house. Many of Karst's neighbors gathered, eager to have their fortunes told. For the price of a mug of beer, the stranger agreed. One by one, he gazed into the villagers' eyes and offered them each a prediction about their future. Mostly, he warned them about threats they must avoid, including the threat of witchcraft. With the region in the grips of a violent outbreak of witch-hunting, bewitchment was a concern on the minds of many Thuringian villagers. One of the women present asked the wise man to read her palm in order to confirm for her neighbors that she was not a witch, but he refused. After the woman left, however, the fortune-teller warned his host, Karst, that she was indeed a witch. He also cautioned that she wanted to harm the villager with her hexes. As a result, Karst began calling the woman a witch in public. Her husband, in turn, sent a letter to the ducal officials in Gotha complaining about the slanderous accusation. With the duchy in the midst of a gruesome witch-hunt, rumors of witchcraft prompted an official investigation that brought the soothsayer's shadowy activities to light.[1]

After questioning a number of the villagers about the episode, the authorities in Gotha failed to uncover evidence of witchcraft and let the matter drop. Although they ordered the villagers to recount all of the mysterious fortune-teller's activities, the magistrates did not even bother to ask his name. And so, the wise man of Ohrdruf slipped away to the next village without ever being questioned, let alone punished. Court records from seventeenth-century Thuringia reveal that the officials' willingness to brush aside divination was not an anomalous oversight, but rather their standard response to these illicit occult activities.

According to the territorial law code in Saxe-Gotha, the wise man of Ohrdruf and his clients should all have been punished. Thuringia's secular rulers prohibited performing divination or consulting a soothsayer and threatened lawbreakers with serious punishment. The region's Lutheran clergy encouraged these efforts, preaching that divination was a sinful form of idolatry and that professional fortune-tellers gained their insights from the devil and deserved to be punished. Nonetheless, despite such clerical disapproval and official prohibition, as the case of the wise man of Ohrdruf shows, the local populace remained eager to consult soothsayers.

When they encountered soothsayers like the Ohrdruf wise man, the region's secular authorities, so keen to hunt witches, usually ignored the clergy's call to punish diviners severely. Their refusal to deal harshly with soothsayers no doubt annoyed, even infuriated, Lutheran officials, but it also went against their own statutes. In practice, secular authorities chose to treat divination as a minor nuisance crime, rather than as a form of demonic sorcery. Thus, amid the dramatic changes of the early modern period, popular fortune-telling stood at the crux of popular culture, religious reform, and official disciplinary efforts, showing the limits of Reformation-era reform efforts and the durability of magical belief.

Divination and Discipline in Early Modern Europe

Divination was ubiquitous in early modern Europe. Clerics condemned it, demonologists denounced it, and princes prohibited it. Yet despite this official disapproval, learned mages and humble villagers alike practiced divination in myriad forms that ranged from learned astrology to popular forms of soothsaying like casting lots, gazing into crystal balls, and reading palms. In the wake of the Reformation, Protestant theologians, pastors, and demonologists worked to stamp out popular forms of fortune-telling, which they viewed as dangerous superstitions rooted in diabolism, paganism, and Catholic error. Consequently, famous reformers and obscure clergymen alike condemned soothsaying, building their arguments upon a foundation of long-standing Christian opposition to the practice. These Protestant theologians and demonologists marshaled all the available sources—biblical, classical, and patristic—in an attempt not only to convince parishioners to eschew popular forms of divination but also to persuade local magistrates and territorial princes to punish soothsayers and their clients. In early modern Germany these efforts culminated in the century after 1550, an era of intense confessional conflict and massive witch-hunts. Soothsaying, however, proved remarkably resistant to these disciplinary efforts, persisting even into the modern era.

This book is about the Lutheran clergy's campaign to eradicate the popular forms of divination employed by common townsfolk and villagers in early modern Germany and why these efforts failed. It examines why popular fortune-telling drew the attention of so many prominent theologians and demonologists and explores the disciplinary efforts their sermons and treatises inspired. In order to explore these issues, it relies on archival evidence from Thuringia, a region in central Germany. Divided into a patchwork of princely territories, imperial cities, small towns, and rural villages, Thuringia was in some respects a microcosm of the Holy Roman Empire itself. Accordingly, it provides an ideal case study for considering the role popular divination played in early modern Germany. By integrating an analysis of the theological debate regarding divination with an examination of Thuringian criminal cases involving the practice, it calls into question the Reformation's impact on popular culture. More specifically, this book shows how the negotiation, accommodation, and resistance that accompanied the era's reform efforts blunted the Reformation's ability to eradicate magical belief. Thus, it also challenges the long-standing notion that the Reformation fostered widespread "disenchantment" in European culture, arguing against the Weberian view that evangelical culture encouraged a more rational worldview that supplanted belief in magic.

Divination was a prominent aspect of European culture in the early modern period, but scholars, more interested in witchcraft, have long neglected it.[2] As a ubiquitous form of magical activity, divination crossed the boundary between literate and vernacular cultures. Learned astrologers at court, illiterate cunning folk in the countryside, and ordinary individuals using customary forms of fortune-telling all practiced it.[3] Common people employed a wide array of divinatory practices handed down through the generations in rural villages and market towns. By reading the movement of a sieve suspended from a pair of shears, the arrangements of beans cast on the floor, or the shape of drops of molten lead dripped into a basin of water, they sought to identify future spouses, mark auspicious days, or find lost or stolen goods.[4] Across Europe, villagers and townsfolk also employed professional fortune-tellers and witch-doctors. Like the wise man of Ohrdruf, these soothsayers made a living wandering the countryside as itinerant seers, identifying thieves and witches, reading palms, and casting horoscopes.[5]

Divination has a long history as a popular practice and as a target of official suppression. People have practiced divination in an attempt to predict the future and uncover hidden knowledge since ancient times.[6] It is properly regarded as a beneficent branch of magic, an attempt to manipulate supernatural or natural forces through occult means. Divination has always been a common magical activity, practiced through the centuries along with healing incantations, charms and amulets, and love spells. The use of magic has always been controversial. From ancient times divergent attitudes toward magic have competed, but authorities and religious elites have usually frowned upon the practice, if not outright prohibited it.[7]

On the eve of the Reformation, this ambiguity continued. Most clerics tolerated at least some forms of learned magic—such as alchemy, hermetic sorcery, or astrology—but condemned the popular magical practices of common people as demonic.[8] As the Reformation spread, clerical opposition to popular magic intensified, with reformers preaching that the myriad forms of folk magic practiced by their parishioners were united by a common link to diabolism.[9] Rulers and secular authorities, who often embraced elite forms of magic, prohibited popular magical practices but rarely punished them severely. Villagers, meanwhile, continued practicing folk magic, and given the secretive nature of these occult activities, it only rarely came to light in court. Defined as diabolical, criminal, or wholly indispensable, divination elicited divergent responses from clerics, rulers, and commoners in early modern Europe.

Throughout the early modern period, divination captured the attention of prominent theologians and demonologists. Their treatises ranged from Heinrich Kramer's infamous *Malleus maleficarum* (*Hammer of Witches*) in the fifteenth century to Heinrich Ludwig Fischer's encyclopedic *Das Buch vom Aberglauben* (*The Book of Superstitions*) in the eighteenth. Many of these famous and influential demonological treatises included exhaustive treatment of popular divination, material scholars usually ignore. Likewise, many of the most important Protestant theologians of the Reformation era—including Martin Luther, Johannes Brenz, John Calvin, John Knox, and Heinrich Bullinger—also condemned divination in their writings and sermons. Even famous witchcraft skeptics like Johann Weyer, Balthasar Bekker, and Christian Thomasius, celebrated for helping to halt the witch hunts, did not doubt that divinatory rites afforded even unlearned magical practitioners glimpses of the future. Accordingly, even they advocated punishment for soothsayers. The fulminations of these famous theologians and demonologists, however, did little to stop the practice of divination in early modern Germany.

Given divination's popularity, theologians working to root out soothsaying found themselves fighting an uphill battle. Lutheran authorities usually condoned the learned forms of astrology that educated elites practiced, while attacking the humbler sorts of divination employed by commoners. In order to convince parishioners to abandon these traditional forms of divination, quotidian practices that served important social and psychological functions, Reformation-era preachers and polemicists sought to persuade them that fortune-telling, just like blatantly malevolent forms of black magic, was inherently evil. Thus, the most persistent attack clerical authorities levied against divination concerned its supposedly satanic basis. These authorities argued that since the Bible and the Church Fathers had excoriated pagan forms of divination as demonic, any knowledge gained through occult means must be derived from a satanic pact. Accordingly, they sought to convince their parishioners that all varieties of folk magic, including forms of fortune-telling that might seem harmless to their practitioners, were sinful and rooted in demonic sorcery.[10]

The Lutheran authorities' efforts to dissuade their flock from practicing divination met with a lukewarm response, as did their efforts to persuade rulers to prosecute diviners. Despite a flood of treatises and sermons condemning divination, Protestant theologians ultimately failed to convince secular authorities that divination was inherently demonic and as such merited capital punishment. In practice, rulers and their subjects alike adhered to the ancient distinction between harmful and benign magic. Accordingly, despite sporadic enforcement of statutes against diviners, the populace continued to embrace divination as a crucial adjunct to official Christianity and as an essential means of mediating conflict. This tension between theology and cultural practice illustrates the limits of early modern disciplinary efforts and demonstrates the extent to which reformers' efforts to inculcate new cultural norms relied upon the support of secular authorities and the acquiescence of parishioners.

The records of prosecution for divination in Thuringia's archives show that these occult activities flourished in rural Germany long after the Reformation, surviving Reformation-era preaching and Enlightenment-era ridicule alike. As I argue, the persistence of divination demonstrates the Protestant Reformation's failure to amend attitudes toward magic in the face of popular opposition, an opposition rooted in a vibrant folk culture that sustained magical belief.

Reformation, Magic, and Modernity

The failure of the campaign to root out divination and the resilience of magical belief in early modern Germany have important implications for our understanding of the legacy of the Reformation. It especially challenges the notion that a radical disenchantment paved the way for modernity. The scholarly debate on disenchantment goes back to Max Weber at the start of the twentieth century. In his classic study *The Protestant Ethic and the Spirit of Capitalism,* Weber famously argued that the Reformation was part of a "great historic process" that led to the "disenchantment of the world," integral to modernity. Weber posited that the Protestant Reformation introduced a rational religiosity stripped of the superstitious and sacramental trappings of medieval Catholicism. Thus, he argued, it paved the way for modern scientific rationality, secular society, and capitalist activity by internalizing religious faith and sequestering the supernatural from everyday experience.[11]

Weber's teleological picture of the Protestant Reformation as the catalyst for modernity cast a long shadow over historical scholarship, and his views dominated the field for almost a century. Focusing on theological change, generations of confessional historians, steeped in Lutheran triumphalism, chronicled the heroic struggles of the Protestant reformers and celebrated the Reformation's contributions to the creation of the modern individual and the modern state.[12]

This teleological understanding of the Reformation has proven durable, and it has continued to influence more recent historical work as well. The most important proponent of the disenchantment paradigm as a way to understand the changes wrought by the Reformation is undoubtedly Keith Thomas. In his *Religion and the Decline of Magic* (1971), Thomas argued that after the Reformation the English populace gradually abandoned the "superstitious" worldview of medieval Catholicism in favor of the rational theology of Protestantism. Thomas's influential work echoes Weber's notion that the Reformation fostered disenchantment by marginalizing the miraculous elements of Catholicism and magical elements of folk culture alike, eventually paving the way for modernity.[13] As late as 1987, Richard van Dülmen also echoed Weber in arguing that the Reformation was crucial to Europe's transition to modernity by demystifying the world and ridding society of magical beliefs.[14]

While the Weberian view of early modern disenchantment remains influential, by the late 1970s revisionist historians had begun to question Protestantism's social impact, including its effects on magical beliefs.[15] Basing their analysis on detailed archival studies, these scholars questioned the link between the Reformation and modernity by demonstrating its failure to establish adequate education and literacy, foster stable, god-fearing marriages and households, or produce viable political institutions in the empire.[16] The most famous, not to mention controversial, study in this corpus is Gerald Strauss's examination of educational reforms in sixteenth-century Germany, which argues that Protestant reformers failed in their stated goal of teaching proper morals.[17] Based on detailed analysis of visitation records, which present a dismal picture of the Lutheran faithful's learning and piety, Strauss's work sparked heated responses.[18] The long-running debate on the Reformation's relative success gradually gave way to more nuanced studies that seek to assess the nature of its effects rather than defend or dismantle the traditional triumphalist narrative. In recent decades, historians have accentuated the role of mediation, negotiation, and accommodation in early modern reform efforts. In this regard, the Reformation's effects on popular magical beliefs remain a fruitful area of investigation.[19]

Analyzing the Reformation's role in fostering cultural change, studies appeared in the 1990s that challenged the Weberian notion that the Reformation fostered a dramatic "disenchantment." In 1993, for example, Robert Scribner challenged the supposed rationality of Lutheranism through an examination of its effects on popular religion and folk customs. He argued that Protestant authorities confronted Catholic survivals and customary folk practices alike with accommodation and modification, showing that the Reformation did not represent a clean break with medieval Christianity and did not usher in a modern, rational worldview.[20] Subsequent studies have drawn attention to the resilience of popular magic and heterodox folk religion during the Reformation. In a recent survey, for example, Ulinka Rublach argued that far from promoting "disenchantment," until the 1650s the Reformation actually fostered a "super-enchantment," marked by intense millenarian expectations, renewed fears of the demonic, and enthusiasm for miracles, portents, and prophecies.[21] Likewise, Robin Barnes showed the centrality of apocalypticism and astrology in Lutheran circles in the era of the Reformation, arguing that pious forms of divination were an essential element of early evangelical piety.[22]

Intellectual historians have also reassessed the impact of the Reformation on magical beliefs. Stuart Clark, for example, used printed demonologies from across early modern Europe to explore elites' continuing fascination with sorcery and the supernatural during the so-called Age of Reason. Analyzing the internal logic in learned magical belief, Clark demonstrates that staunch belief in witchcraft and magic remained an essential component in theological and scientific circles long after the Reformation and well into the eighteenth century.[23]

Reacting to these revisionist challenges, Euan Cameron advanced a modified version of the disenchantment paradigm in 2010 with his comprehensive work, *Enchanted Europe*.[24] Analyzing theological treatises on superstition from the Middle Ages to the Enlightenment, Cameron maintained that the Reformation played a key role in the *eventual* triumph of secular rationality and in the advent of modernity, at least in the context of learned discourse. He credits the Protestant Reformation with diminishing magical belief by redefining the role of ritual in religious life, a conceptual change that helped pave the way for the gradual abandonment of such "superstition" among European elites during the Enlightenment.

While scholars have debated whether or not the Reformation was the catalyst for disenchantment, others have questioned whether modernity itself is even a corollary of the abandonment of magical belief. The master narrative that presents disenchantment as one of the most essential features of the modern world has come under intense scrutiny. A host of studies has demonstrated that popular magical beliefs not only survived in Europe in the nineteenth and twentieth centuries, but that occultism even flourished among educated elites during this period. In light of recent studies of forms of modern Western enchantment like esotericism, mesmerism, and spiritualism, a new consensus has emerged that Weber's teleological disenchantment paradigm is no longer tenable.[25] In the place of the old linear modernization narrative, scholars increasingly argue for a cyclical understanding, marked by succeeding cycles of disenchantment and re-enchantment. Thus, the emphasis on reason and attacks on superstition that marked epochs like the Reformation or the Enlightenment not only harbored vestiges of enchantment but were also temporary. Once the intense emphasis on rationality began to fade, fascination with the supernatural reemerged, helping to explain the interest in the occult that flourished among educated elites in nineteenth- and early twentieth-century Europe.[26]

Analysis of the clerical discourse on divination and official efforts to suppress it in Thuringia from the sixteenth to the nineteenth centuries supports this revisionist challenge to the Weberian notion of disenchantment. The Lutheran clergy's failed attempts to eradicate popular divinatory practices, and the Thuringian authorities' halfhearted efforts to prohibit soothsaying, call into question the success of the Reformation in discouraging magical belief. The cases that survive in the region's archives show the difficulty of suppressing heterodox behavior and inculcating new norms in the wake of the Reformation and during the intellectual revolution of the Enlightenment era. Revealing the dogged persistence of divinatory practices until well into the 1800s, they also challenge the idea that Europe experienced a thorough disenchantment at all.

1

"IDOLATRY AND REPROBATE INFIDELITY"

Divination before the Reformation

The Hammer of Witches (1487)

The infamous *Malleus maleficarum,* written by the Dominican inquisitor Heinrich Kramer in 1487, helped fuel the earliest mass witch-hunts in Europe.[1] In this notorious witch-hunters' manual, Kramer instructed inquisitors on the dire threat posed by witches and how to use torture to elicit the confessions necessary to send them to the stake.[2] Kramer's lurid descriptions of the diabolical crimes of witches, and his rampant misogyny, are notorious. Less well known are the condemnations of divination that he included in his treatise.

In the *Malleus,* Kramer was unequivocal in his condemnation of divination and linked it explicitly with diabolism. Listing prominent forms of divination, he asserted that most were accomplished "through the explicit invocation of demons."[3] Well versed in scholastic philosophy, he sought to convince his readers of the evil inherent in divination by citing a wide array of biblical, classical, and medieval sources. Collecting centuries of elite condemnation of the occult practice, he reinforced the age-old link between divination and the demonic that drove Christian moralists' efforts to suppress soothsaying.[4]

Kramer focused his ire at popular forms of divination, warning his readers that anyone who so much as conferred with a soothsayer would suffer eternal damnation. Invoking Augustine, he cautioned against consulting these ubiquitous magical practitioners, common in every medieval town and village: "None of you should seek the advice of diviners or fortune-tellers or consult them about any matter or situation or illness, because whoever does this evil act will immediately lose the sacrament of baptism and be rendered a sacrilegious pagan. Unless repentance comes to his aid, he will immediately be lost for eternity."[5] Thus, he asserted that those who practice divination or heed its advice were heathens who stood apart from the Christian community. As apostates, they faced eternal damnation. An eager inquisitor, Kramer also ominously warned that only the Church could bring these sinners back to the fold—through correction.

Heinrich Kramer was not alone in condemning popular forms of divination or associating them with the devil. Fortune-telling, condemned by ancient Hebrew, Greek, Roman, and Christian moralists, had a sinister reputation by the late Middle Ages. Medieval theologians and demonologists, concerned with the spread of heresy and witchcraft in their dioceses, attacked divination in strident terms. While some medieval theologians expressed doubts about the reality of soothsaying and sorcery, portraying these magical activities as demonic illusions, religious authorities were united in accentuating their diabolical origins. Nonetheless, despite strict legal prohibition and intense clerical censure, divination was ubiquitous in medieval society.

The efforts of learned demonologists and god-fearing magistrates to eradicate such a popular medieval practice were based upon centuries of Christian condemnation. From its earliest origins, Christianity had formed its identity in part through its opposition to forms of magic prevalent among ancient polytheists. Divination figured prominently in the ancient magical practices of the Persians, Egyptians, Greeks, and Romans, and early Christians helped define their new faith by eschewing these rites. Much of the abhorrence that the Church Fathers felt for the magical practices of their polytheistic neighbors stemmed from traditional Judaic prohibitions against certain forms of magic expressed in the Hebrew Bible.[6]

By the time of the *Malleus,* medieval theologians and demonologists had buttressed their condemnations of popular forms of divination by citing a range of authoritative sources. These sources not only included biblical prohibitions of soothsaying, but also the writings of ancient Greek and Roman authorities, early Christian theologians, and medieval scholastic philosophers. In Kramer's day, the Church prohibited divination and sought to suppress soothsaying among the laity through preaching, penitentials, and punishment. This centuries-old campaign to eradicate divination set the stage for Reformation-era efforts to suppress these popular occult practices.

The *Malleus maleficarum,* appearing a generation before the Reformation, distilled centuries of elite condemnations of divination. These traditional critiques of soothsaying deeply influenced Martin Luther and other Protestant reformers, and exploring these intellectual foundations helps shed light on the impetus behind Reformation-era efforts to prohibit these magical practices. The early Christian and medieval sources Kramer cited in his infamous work associated divination with diabolism, and Lutheran reformers followed suit. The ancient moralists Kramer quoted established a sharp distinction between learned, official, public forms of divination, which they sanctioned, and vernacular, profane, private forms, which they censured and sought to suppress. Lutheran reformers would adopt this attitude as well. As this chapter will show, on the eve of the Reformation the notion that divination was an inherently demonic activity was well established, as was the articulation of a fundamental division between licit kinds of elite divination and illicit popular forms. These ideas would shape efforts to root out soothsaying throughout the Reformation era.

Divination and the Ancients

The Hebrew scriptures are replete with explicit condemnations of divination, rooted in the Hebrews' experience of exile and the gradual development of monotheism, which prompted them to take a harsher stance against magical practices like divination than their polytheistic neighbors. For the Hebrews, polytheistic religious rites, which often centered on the use of divination to ascertain the will of the gods, were an evil magic that God's chosen people must eschew.[7]

The Hebrews sought to preserve their distinctive religious culture by rejecting the religious rites and magical practices of the polytheistic peoples they encountered in Canaan. Thus, the Hebrew Bible demonstrates this revulsion toward the magical and divinatory rites of the Canaanites. For example, in Deuteronomy, God commands the Hebrews to avoid imitating the "abominations" of the Canaanites, divination in particular. He warned that the Hebrews should not tolerate anyone among them "that consulteth soothsayers, or observeth dreams and omens," nor "that consulteth pythonic spirits, or fortune tellers, or that seeketh the truth from the dead."[8] This famous passage shows the Hebrews' distaste for polytheistic magic and the prominence of divination among these forbidden arts. Leviticus even demands the death penalty for soothsayers.[9] The Hebrews' conflation of harmful black magic, sorcery, and various forms of fortune-telling exerted a powerful influence on later Christian attitudes toward divination.[10]

Despite the Hebrews' revulsion at Canaanite magical rites and the severity of biblical prohibitions against divination, the Hebrew scriptures also reveal their ambiguous attitudes about its practice. Saul's famous encounter with a medium, who came to be known as the "witch of Endor," related in I Samuel 28, shows the continued importance of soothsaying in Hebrew culture.[11] Really about a necromancer, rather than a witch, the account fascinated Christian demonologists, and it remained a mainstay in treatises about divination for centuries. The Endor story begins with an account of how the Israelite King Saul, following the Deuteronomic Code, had banished all soothsayers from his realm. Threatened by a mighty Philistine army, Saul prayed to God to send him a sign of his fate, but he did not receive an answer. In desperation, he ordered his attendants to find a seer he could consult about his future. Although Saul had driven all of the soothsayers from the land, they informed him straightaway that such a woman could be found at Endor.

Disguising himself, Saul visited the woman by night and asked her to raise a spirit for him. Wary of the royal prohibition against divination, the necromancer refused until Saul, still in disguise, promised her that she would not be punished. The king asked her to raise the dead prophet Samuel, and when the shade appeared before her, she immediately knew that her client was Saul. The king assured her that she was safe and asked her what she saw. She replied that she saw the ghostly visage of an old man rising from the earth. The shade of Samuel rebuked the king for disturbing him and asked what Saul wanted of him. Saul replied, "I am in great distress. The Philistines are fighting against me, and God has departed from me. He no longer answers me, either by prophets or by dreams. So I have called on you to tell me what to do." The dire news that Samuel delivered did not relieve his distress. The ghostly prophet's words filled the king with dread, as he told Saul that the Lord would "deliver both Israel and you into the hands of the Philistines," and that "tomorrow you and your sons will be with me."

Samuel's words came to pass, and Saul fell in battle the next day, defeated by the invading Philistines. Although Saul had broken the divine prohibition against divination, the passage does not suggest that his fate came as a result of consulting the necromancer. In fact, Saul turned to necromancy only after God refused to answer his queries through prophecy or dreams. Furthermore, the story shows that divination, while illicit, did in fact work. Afraid of royal punishment, but not of God's wrath, the woman at Endor managed to raise the spirit of Samuel, who correctly foretold Saul's fate.

While Hebrew authorities generally condemned divination, other ancient societies embraced it as part of official religious practices. Magic and religion were integrated in ancient polytheism, and divinatory rites played a central role in both. Among many ancient peoples, including the Sumerians, Egyptians, Babylonians, and Persians, divination was central to religious culture as priests sought to ascertain the will of the gods. Priests and commoners alike used it for more mundane reasons as well, telling private fortunes for money. These popular forms of divination, which turned sacred rites to profane purposes, alarmed Greek and Roman moralists.[12]

Many ancient Greek thinkers held in contempt divination performed outside of temples and oracle sites. By the classical period, educated Greeks had come to associate magic with sinister rites they believed had emerged in Persia among the *magoi.* Although surviving inscriptions prove that magical practices were common among the Greeks, many philosophers condemned these occult activities, presenting them as foreign and dangerous.[13] The Greeks believed that the universe was filled with spirits they called *daemones,* who occupied the space between humans and the gods. The *daemones* could be benign or malignant, and magicians and soothsayers could enlist their aid for good or evil ends. A Hellenistic-era philosophical text, the *Pythagorean Commentaries,* describes these spirits and their role in divination. The work regarded it as axiomatic that "the whole air is full of souls. We call them *daemones.*" According to the author, it was these spirits who were the focus of divinatory rites, and he explained that "it is towards these *daemones* that we direct purification and apotropaic rites, all kinds of divination, and the art of reading chance utterances."[14] Throughout Greece itinerant *magoi* and rural wise women sought to contact these spirits in order to read omens and tell fortunes. For strict moralists, the secretive practices associated with such divinatory rites, directed at the *daemones* or the shadowy chthonic gods of the underworld, seemed sinister compared with the public, beneficial rites of the Greeks' polytheistic religion and the prophecies of oracles at Delphi and Dodona it sanctioned.[15]

The distinction between private fortune-telling conducted by commoners and the official divination performed by priests was as important to Roman moralists as it had been to their Greek counterparts. Thus, upright Romans were repulsed by private divination, and leading figures like Pliny and Cicero drew a sharp distinction between the improper use of divination for selfish ends and its beneficial use as part of the Roman civic religion. For these Roman moralists, despite its popularity, the former was the very epitome of "*superstitio,*" the wrongful misappropriation of religious rites that threatened to upset Rome's relationship with the gods. The Roman statesman Cicero, for example, deemed fortune-telling to be a morally corrupting force within society and recorded many examples of soothsayers' faulty predictions.[16] Thus, while the *Twelve Tables,* Rome's earliest written law code, condemned harmful magic, opposition to divination remained largely moral, although instances of official repression began to appear in the imperial period.[17]

Amid the political turmoil of the first century of the Common Era, Tiberius launched sporadic efforts to rid Rome of "*mathematici,* diviners, and astrologers," despite his own faith in the predictions of his personal astrologer, Thrasyllus. According to the Roman historians Tacitus and Suetonius, these efforts were largely political, as Roman authorities blamed profane divination for stirring up rebellion. Cassius Dio also draws this link between fortune-telling and insurrection in his writings. The Roman historian admitted that "divination is of course necessary," meaning the official rites of the Roman state cult, but he had no patience for private divinatory activities. Speaking of soothsayers, he warned that "such men, by speaking the truth sometimes, but generally falsehood, very often encourage numbers to stir up revolution."[18] Thus, Dio accentuates the moralists' distinction between dangerous forms of divination employed for selfish, subversive ends and the necessary and beneficial augury and haruspicy Roman priests routinely performed to ascertain the will of the gods who protected the empire.[19]

Despite such discouragement, penal and moral, a range of magical operations including divination remained widespread in ancient Rome. Magical texts and divinatory practices had proliferated in the Hellenistic period as Greek, Persian, Babylonian, and Egyptian magical traditions fused. Itinerant seers and everyday people carried out all manner of divination, and these practices remained popular in the Roman Empire.[20]

Divination and the Early Church

With the spread of the new faith within the Roman world, a new sort of virulent opposition to divination emerged. Early Christian leaders condemned divination in all its forms more harshly than did their polytheistic Roman contemporaries, associating both official rites and private practices with a diabolic pact.[21] Christian authorities radically redefined the *daemones* of classical polytheism, the spirits at the heart of Greco-Roman divination, asserting that they were inherently evil. For early Christians, these spirits were in fact demons, the embodiments of evil, and thus divination in all its forms was irredeemably wicked.[22] The demonization of all pagan religiosity soon followed. In the late 50s CE, Paul preached that all pagan religious rites—including the sacred augury and haruspicy the Romans used to ascertain the will of the gods—were demonic.[23]

The authors of the Christian New Testament intensified the Hebrews' traditional revulsion toward divination by explicitly linking it with demonic possession. In Acts 16, an account of the deeds of the apostles dating from the second half of the first century CE, the author, traditionally believed to be the evangelist Luke, recounts a confrontation with a slave girl in Asia Minor who was possessed by a "pythonical spirit":

> And it came to pass, as we went to prayer, a certain girl, having a pythonical spirit, met us, who had brought her masters much gain by divining.
>
> This same followed Paul and us, cried out, saying, "These men are the servants of the Most High God, who preach unto you the way of salvation."
>
> And this she did many days. But Paul, being grieved, turned, and said to the spirit, "I command thee, in the name of Jesus Christ, to go out from her." And he went out the same hour.[24]

The episode recounted in this passage subsequently colored Christianity's official attitudes regarding divination. By identifying the entity Paul exorcised as a "pythonical spirit," a reference to Apollo's famous oracle at Delphi, the evangelist associated divination with the supposedly demonic rites of the polytheists and demonstrated the Christian God's superiority over pagan spirits.

The account of Paul's victory over the "pythonical spirit" in Acts 16 also shows the popularity of soothsaying among the Roman populace in the provinces and the ambiguity of official attitudes toward the practice. It is plain from the account that the slave girl's fortune-telling had been popular (and lucrative) and tells how her owners, angry about the loss of revenue, were able to complain successfully to the provincial authorities about the Christians. Paul's interference with the popular divinatory practices of the locals provoked both mob violence and official punishment. According to Acts, "the people ran together against them; and the magistrates rending off their clothes, commanded them to be beaten with rods. And when they had laid many stripes upon them, they cast them into prison."[25] Thus, Paul's opposition to soothsaying, laudable for his Christian audience, earned him the wrath of Roman polytheists and punishment from the provincial officials.

Despite Paul's treatment at the hands of the Anatolian populace after casting out the pythonical spirit, the condemnations of divination penned by Roman moralists, as well as Hebrew ones, exerted a powerful influence on the writings of the Church Fathers. These patristic writers proved particularly hostile to popular forms of fortune-telling, again displaying a sharp distinction between popular and elite practice that endured for centuries.[26] In late antiquity, as Christianity gained prominence within the crumbling Roman Empire, church leaders sought to persuade the emerging Christian community to abandon traditional forms of divination, commonplace rites practiced not only in the context of official Roman polytheism but also in everyday life. Early Christian authorities sought to convince converts that fortune-telling, just like blatantly malevolent forms of black magic, was inherently evil. Hoping to undermine soothsaying's widespread popularity, the most persistent attack the early Church levied against divination concerned its supposedly satanic origins.

Christian authorities argued that since the Old and New Testaments alike excoriated pagan forms of divination as demonic, any knowledge of the future gained through occult means was derived from a diabolic pact. This view, that divination was inherently diabolical, found its most powerful expression in the writings of the great Church Father, Augustine (354–430 CE), bishop of Hippo. Augustine established views of divination and its relationship to the demonic that experienced a strong revival in the scholarly atmosphere of the late Middle Ages.[27] In his *On the Divination of Demons* (*De divinatione daemonum*), Augustine sought to explain how a pagan diviner had managed to foretell the destruction of the temple of Serapis in Alexandria in 391.[28] He argued that since the gods of the pagans were nothing but empty idols, such fortune-telling must be based upon an implicit pact with the devil and charged that diviners entered into alliances with demonic entities out of sinful pride and vanity.[29]

Convinced that divination was accomplished through demonic agency, Augustine warned his readers about the dangers it posed to the Christian soul. He asserted that "by some inscrutable divine plan," wavering Christians with evil desires were allowed to be "deluded and deceived according to what their own wills deserve." Thus, through "superstitious and deadly kinds of divination," demons actually provide these sinners with glimpses of the future, but only "so that as they are caught up in them they may become evermore inquisitive and entrap themselves more and more in the manifold snares of this most deadly error."[30] Augustine clearly thought that, although evil, divination was efficacious. Through forbidden rites and aided by demons, wicked people could foretell the future, and demons were eager to draw the curious into damnation in this manner. Thus, the danger divination posed was essentially spiritual.

Theological opposition to divination shaped official disciplinary efforts in late antiquity, and these efforts show that soothsaying remained popular within the early Christian community. A synod at Ancyra in 314 ruled that diviners were subject to five years' penance, and Christian emperors soon backed these ecclesiastical penalties with their own measures. Thus, fourth-century emperors banned "pagan" magical practices, which increasingly came to be viewed as satanic, and soon brought capital punishment to bear. These efforts were preserved in historical works that survive from the waning days of the Roman Empire. The *Res Gestae* of the Roman historian Ammianus Marcellinus, for example, which survived in fragmentary form in ninth-century Carolingian copies, chronicles such official repression. According to Ammianus, during the reigns of the fourth-century Christian emperors Constantius II and Gallus, anyone who so much as "consulted a soothsayer about the squeaking of a field mouse" was immediately indicted, tried, and executed.[31] Constantius threatened all magicians and diviners with beheading in 357, and Emperor Theodosius II continued these draconian threats, although there is little evidence that they were enforced.[32] In 438, the emperor formally outlawed all magical rites and divination in his comprehensive *Theodosian Code,* and this prohibition was passed on to the medieval Church after the collapse of Roman authority in the West.[33]

Despite these clerical and official prohibitions, enforcement was sporadic in the waning days of the Roman Empire, and divination and other magical practices remained common in late antiquity and in early medieval Europe. Nevertheless, Athanasius of Alexandria (c. 296–373 CE) celebrated the triumph of Christianity and its role in the demise of divination. Complaining that "formerly everywhere was filled with the deceit of oracles," he was pleased to report that "now, since Christ is preached everywhere, their madness has ceased and there is no longer any augur among them."[34] Athanasius was deluding himself, and his confidence in the triumph of Christianity was certainly premature. Folk magic, including divination, remained commonplace within early Christian communities, as surviving magical texts, some employing Christian phrases and iconography, attest.[35] Likewise, church councils repeatedly condemned Christianized divinatory practices, like the *Sortes Biblicae* (the reading of randomly selected Bible passages in an attempt to predict the future), but tacitly permitted their use.[36] Ironically, even Augustine, the great critic of divination, famously described in his *Confessions* how his own use of the *Sortes Biblicae* prompted his conversion.[37]

Given the tenacious hold divination retained on the Christian community, hard-line preachers expressed frustration at their failure to convince their parishioners to abandon these sinful practices. Around 530 CE, for example, the Gallo-Roman bishop Caesarius of Arles delivered a sermon caustic in its condemnation of divination. As its catchy title—"An Admonition to Those Who Not Only Pay Attention to Omens, but, What Is Worse, Consult Seers, Soothsayers, and Fortune-Tellers in the Manner of Pagans"—proclaims, the homily decries the popularity of divination among the pious bishop's own flock. Complaining that his audience had long ignored him, Caesarius reminded them that he had "frequently exhorted you with paternal solicitude, advising and proclaiming that you should by no means observe those wicked practices of the pagans." Echoing Augustine, he warned his flock that they must not consult soothsayers, because if they did they would forfeit their baptism, "becoming at once impious and pagan." Only good works and penance would save these wavering Christians from damnation, and he warned that "unless generous almsgiving together with hard, prolonged penance saves him, such a man will perish forever."[38] Bishop Caesarius's sermon was stern, revealing his frustration at the persistence of these occult practices despite his repeated admonitions. He was not alone in his exasperation. In the end, although Christian authorities set out to eradicate all forms of magic, the continued prevalence of these practices forced them to accept the same compromise that Roman authorities had: punishing harmful magic but tolerating lesser forms of magical activity like divination.[39]

Divination in the Middle Ages

During the tenth century, concerns about the demonic nature of divination resurfaced as medieval theologians articulated a new demonology that confounded magic with heresy. Increasingly, demonologists preached that all magic was based upon diabolical apostasy. Despite such strident clerical disapproval, divination remained popular in early medieval Europe.[40] By the time Regino of Prüm compiled his *Canon Episcopi,* around 906 CE, divination and harmful sorcery had become conflated, linked by their purported satanic origins. In fact, until the twelfth century, theologians writing about magic usually focused primarily or even exclusively on divination.[41] Thus, the *Canon Episcopi* begins with an exhortation to pious clerical leaders to root out occult practices, including both casting lots and casting spells. It ordered bishops and their underlings to "labor with all of their strength so that the pernicious art of *sortilegium* and *maleficium,* which was invented by the devil, is eradicated from their districts." If they discovered any "followers of this wicked sect," local clerics were to "eject them foully disgraced from their parishes."[42] The *Canon Episcopi* took a skeptical stance on the more outrageous aspects of early medieval magical belief, most famously casting doubt on the reality of witches' flight. As this passage shows, however, its author left no doubt that clerics were to be diligent in their efforts to root out divination (*sortilegium*) as well as witchcraft (*maleficium*) owing to their shared demonic origins.

Another medieval bishop, Burchard of Worms, contributed a penitential known as the *Corrector* in the early eleventh century, a work that reveals clerical efforts to suppress divination in the central Middle Ages. Part of Burchard's *Decretum,* the *Corrector* was a guide for the clergy serving his diocese that suggested questions that confessors should ask penitents, including queries about divination. The sixtieth question he advised confessors to ask their charges was: "Have you consulted magicians and led them into your house in order to seek out any magical trick, or to avert it; or have you invited according to pagan custom diviners who would divine for you, to demand of them the things to come as from a prophet, and those who practice lots or expect lots to foreknow the future, or those who are devoted to auguries or incantations? If you have, you shall do penance for two years on the appointed fast days."[43] The inclusion of divination in the questions asked of penitents, and the penance demanded of those who admitted to indulging in it, demonstrates Burchard's intent to eradicate these sinful pursuits. It also suggests that despite long-standing prohibitions, fortune-telling remained popular within medieval parishes. Evidence of divinatory practices is sparse for most of the Middle Ages, but surviving traces show that it remained widespread. Commoners used simple forms of divination, including discerning omens in the call of birds, reading palms, casting lots, or ascertaining lucky days based on the lunar cycle.[44] Despite efforts by medieval episcopal authorities to dissuade soothsayers, their attempts to root out these popular forms of fortune-telling remained ineffectual.

While penitentials like the *Corrector* were aimed at lowly parishioners, it was not only commoners who practiced divination in the Middle Ages, but also their social betters. In fact, divination and other forms of learned magic experienced a remarkable resurgence in the twelfth century. Among erudite elites, astrology flourished. Like alchemy, it was reinvigorated by the reintroduction of classical esoteric texts through Hebrew and Arabic translations from Sicily and Spain.[45] The learned "natural philosophers" who practiced astrology did not consider their esoteric pursuits to be magical, let alone demonic.

While there was considerable disagreement among ecclesiastics on the issue, the most prominent theologian of the age took a hard-line stance against learned and popular forms of divination alike. Thomas Aquinas, the foremost theologian of the High Middle Ages, included sweeping condemnations of divination in his most famous work. In his *Summa Theologiae,* started in 1265 and left unfinished at the time of his death in 1274, Aquinas sought to distinguish illicit divination from permissible forms of prediction and divine revelation. He reasoned that predictions based upon human reason or derived from divine revelation were not to be considered divination. Only when someone "usurps to himself, in an undue manner, the foretelling of future events" did it become "manifestly a sin."[46] For Aquinas the presumptuous vanity that lay at the heart of divination, that a mortal would attempt to peer into the future without divine aid, made it sinful.

Aquinas's wholesale condemnation of divination proved highly influential, disseminated through pastoral works and penitentials. The most popular medieval manual for training clergy, the *Handbook for Curates*, included extensive treatment of divination. Guido of Monte Rochen, a Spanish cleric, wrote the work in the 1330s as a guide for parish priests, and it proved exceedingly popular among the clergy. Hundreds of manuscript copies survive, and the work became a staple of early print culture with 122 editions published in the last four decades of the fifteenth century.[47] Intended to prepare new clergy for their duties, the *Handbook* begins with a discussion of the Ten Commandments. Guido's presentation of the First Commandment—"thou shall not have strange gods before me"—centered on divination.

The Spanish priest sought to convince his audience that divination in all its forms was the ultimate form of idolatry. He lumps all the various types of divination under this blanket condemnation, asserting that the First Commandment prohibits all kinds of soothsaying "however they may be done." Providing an exhaustive list of the forbidden forms of divination parishioners might employ, including pyromancy, aeromancy, hydromancy, geomancy, necromancy, augury, and bibliomancy, he declares that "all divination, whether it is done by the aforesaid means or however else, is prohibited by this commandment and is cursed by God and by holy mother church as so much idolatry and reprobate infidelity."[48] Thus, Guido urged novice priests to teach their parishioners that divination was a grave sin and to use the pulpit to convince them to abandon it.

In the parish, the confessional was the most important means of suppressing divination, and confessors' manuals sought to train new clergy in how to apply the sacrament of penance. One such handbook, written by the fourteenth-century Florentine Dominican Jacopo Passavanti, encouraged parish priests to use the confessional to uncover soothsaying and penance to suppress it. Although Passavanti was convinced of divination's demonic nature, he remained skeptical of its efficacy. Conceding that Satan could predict certain likely events, using his preternatural knowledge of the nature of substances, the influence of planetary bodies, and perception of human emotion, Passavanti reserved true foreknowledge to

God. Admitting that "one finds people who favor the side of the devil and who say that the devil can indeed know random or particular things which have not yet happened," he responded that "they do not speak the truth and they lie, like him whose side they favor, who is, as Christ said of him, a liar, and the father of lies."[49]

In any case, Passavanti prescribed heavy penance for diviners, especially commoners who confessed to using popular forms of fortune-telling. After listing the various forms of learned divination practiced by evil necromancers, he turned to the magical activities of the lower orders. He condemned "persons of low condition, both men and women," who practice divination, but "who do not understand the art and cannot use it, since in any case only a few people know how to use it." Passavanti argues that with the aid of the devil, "who favors every wicked deed," these rustic soothsayers sometimes were able to ascertain glimpses of the future. However, he also warned of fraudulent soothsayers, who "claim that they are enchanters and fortune-tellers out of vanity or some other interest, and by these claims fool many simple people who are prone to believe this kind of thing," asserting that they committed a mortal sin through their deceit and trickery.[50]

Passavanti's treatise distilled Aquinas's dense theological postulations for use in the confessional, but he also introduced ambiguous elements of his own. By presenting divination on the one hand as demonic, and people who practiced it as being "on the side of the devil," and on the other hand as nothing but swindlers' tricks, he departed from Aquinas, who never doubted that it was real. By taking this approach, Passavanti sought at once to prompt confessors to condemn divination as demonic and to convince parishioners to abandon it as unreliable.

As concern with heresy and diabolical magic grew within the Church in the fourteenth century, rising anxieties prompted the development of new inquisitorial procedures, including judicial torture, to deal with the menace. Fifteenth-century theologians and demonologists amplified these concerns by stoking fears of a cult of devil-worshipping witches. In this atmosphere of fear and paranoia, the Church commissioned inquisitors to uncover traces of a vast diabolical conspiracy, and clerics condemned

The frontispiece of Bartholomaeus Anhorn's *Magiologia* equates witchcraft and divination, depicting astrologers and fortune-tellers alongside witches. From Bartholomaeus Anhorn, *Magiologia* (1674). (Yale Collection of German Literature. Beinecke Rare Book and Manuscript Library, Yale University)

divination as demonic in increasingly fiery terms.[51] As the first witches were burned in Europe's alpine regions in the fifteenth century, concerns with divination also occupied the inquisitors.

Encountering a dizzying array of popular magical practices, these inquisitors began to concern themselves not only with demonic magic but also with common "superstitions" like divination. While theologians like Regino and Burchard had condemned these practices in harsh terms, in practice the clergy had long ignored them as harmless folk customs, and secular authorities had done little to stop them.[52] At the close of the Middle Ages, however, as inquisitors scoured remote villages in the western Alps looking for traces of heresy and diabolism, they confronted folk magic and its humble practitioners. For these ardent witch-hunters, quotidian forms of fortune-telling were nothing less than signs of the spread of Satan's kingdom on earth.

These encounters inspired the preacher Bernardino of Siena to deliver a sermon in his hometown in 1427 that reviled diviners. In this caustic homily, Bernardino railed against the prevalence of fortune-telling among the laity, conflating witchcraft and divination. He excoriated faith healers and spell-casters before turning his wrath against soothsayers, complaining that laypeople ran off to consult "the enchanter or diviner if they have been robbed of five cents."[53] Bernardino warned his audience that by consorting with such sinful magicians they were turning against God and falling into the clutches of the devil, bemoaning that "the devil is adored through such a great iniquity."[54] He anguished over the manifest idolatry inherent in these folk customs, exclaiming, "Do you know what you have done? You have caused men to renounce God, and you have caused the devil to be adored."[55] In portraying divination as a form of idolatry that exalted the devil over God, the preacher transmitted centuries of Christian theology to his listeners while trying to stir their emotions.

From the pulpit, Bernardino sought to convince his listeners that all forms of divination were demonic, while acknowledging that many parishioners did not consider fortune-telling to be evil. Reporting that many common people did not see the harm in it, and even believed that the predictions of fortune-tellers had come to pass, he preached that they had been deceived. The inquisitor tried to convince his audience that the devil was using divination to bring them to ruin, asking them, "[H]ave you never comprehended his snares and deceits, how he has always deceived us, and has struggled to do so?"[56] The Franciscan confronted a basic problem faced by centuries of Christian moralists: the faith that the populace placed in the predictions of soothsayers. Forced to admit that the glimpses of the future afforded by divination often seemed true, Bernardino countered with warnings of the devil's deceit.

Turning to scripture, Bernardino drew a parallel between those who consulted soothsayers and Adam and Eve. Pawns of the devil, their shared lust for unlawful knowledge brought them alike to destruction. Attempting to shame his audience, he railed sarcastically, "[Y]ou who have cast lots, what a great evil you do, and how many people have trusted in them and followed them! How well they teach you the truth!"[57] Bernardino's frustration that his flock failed to recognize divination as a grave sin, and continued to dabble with fortune-telling, is palpable. Sixty years later, on the eve of the Reformation, the Dominican inquisitor Heinrich Kramer echoed his concerns. Other concerns that Kramer shared with Bernardino—that divination was accomplished through a demonic pact, that it was a serious affront to God, and that it was a means for the devil to bring wayward Christians to damnation—were in turn echoed in the demonologies, sermons, and ordinances of the Reformation era.

At the close of the Middle Ages, popular forms of divination were under attack from clerical authorities, who warned of their diabolical nature in hopes of dissuading parishioners from relying on the occult. The clerical campaign to root out soothsaying drew its lifeblood from a long tradition of elite condemnations of popular divinatory rites. Preaching against fortune-telling, medieval clerics and early modern reformers alike relied on a rich tradition of Hebraic, classical, and Christian condemnations.

Late medieval efforts to suppress divination within the Christian community also presaged the disciplinary efforts that would accompany the Reformation. At the close of the Middle Ages, clerical authorities relied on the pulpit, the confessional, and the rituals of penance in an attempt to stamp out soothsaying. Heinrich Kramer, for example, certainly advocated punishing diviners, since they drew their powers to foretell the future from the devil. However, like other medieval authorities, he clearly saw witchcraft as a greater threat than divining. Thus, he advocated treating divination and other forms of folk magic as a lesser crime than witchcraft. Although he recognized its diabolical nature, the Dominican saw divination as essentially a victimless crime, explaining that "though all these forms of divination take place through the explicit invocation of demons, nonetheless there is no comparison with acts of sorcery on the part of the sorceress, since the immediate purpose of the former is not to harm men, domestic animals and the fruits of the earth but to know the future in advance."[58] By treating divination as a less aggravated form of demonic sorcery than witchcraft, Kramer was adopting the same compromise solution to magical activity devised by early Christian authorities. Fervent in their desire to stamp out all pagan magical rites, and utterly convinced of the demonic origins of magic, early Christian authorities proved unable or unwilling to uproot centuries of folk tradition that flourished within their communities. Rather, they pursued a pragmatic course, accommodating relatively harmless folk customs and dealing with divination through preaching and penance, while reserving capital punishment for deadly witchcraft.

Heinrich Kramer's call for Christian magistrates to punish witches and other magical practitioners, including soothsayers, met with considerable resistance in his own day. He helped launch witch hunts in the Alps, and inquisitors like him scoured villages in the region for signs of demonic sorcery and divination. However, secular authorities, alarmed at the cruelty of his methods, resisted his efforts. The *Malleus* is a polemical work, meant to convince his readers of the diabolical threat posed by witchcraft and magic and to urge magistrates to support the grim activities of inquisitors. As we will see, the Reformation, and the confessional strife and apocalyptic anxieties it engendered, breathed new life into the call for secular authorities to punish not only witchcraft but also magical activities of a lesser sort like divination. Protestant reformers' attacks on divination echoed ancient and medieval condemnations, as they worked to root out divination. The reformers' zeal, however, was soon tempered by the realities they faced in the parishes.

2

"A HELLISH TRAP"

Divination in Early Reformation Theology

The Erfurt Soothsayer (1537)

In July 1537, Martin Luther received a letter from the reformer Friedrich Myconius, who related the story of a "soothsayer" who had been burned in Erfurt. The fortune-teller had supposedly made a pact with the devil and paid with his life, but not before repenting of his sins. Luther immediately recognized the story's value as a parable of sin and redemption, and he urged Myconius to publish the tale.

In the meantime, Luther shared the story with his disciples in Wittenberg, and it is included in the *Tischreden* (*Table Talk*) where the reformer's students recorded their mealtime conversations with him. Luther's version of the tale began with a tragic account of the devil tempting the desperate man: "In Erfurt a soothsayer (*Warsager*) and sorcerer (*Schwartzkünstler*) was burned, who for many years was sad and sorrowful, because he was very poor and had nothing to eat. One day he encountered the devil, in physical form, who made great promises to him that he would become rich if he would deny his baptism and redemption through Christ and never again prayed." According to Luther, the evil magician accepted the bargain, and "the devil gave him a crystal from which he could soothsay." The man made a fortune working as a cunning man, using the crystal to identify thieves for his clients.

These nefarious activities made him rich, but he eventually learned to his horror that "the devil had cheated him, and he realized that with the crystal he had seen many innocent people and accused them of theft."

The authorities arrested the man, who soon confessed that he had sealed a demonic pact. Luther's tale, however, ends on an inspirational note. The repentant sinner broke his deal with the devil: "Asking for someone to bring a pastor to him . . . he did righteous penance. He instilled the fear of God in many people through his example and died with a glad heart at his execution. So, he beat the devil at his own art and exposed his evil tricks."[1] Praising the soothsayer's last-minute conversion, Luther embraced the tale of the Erfurt diviner as a vehicle for saving souls, as a parable of sin and redemption. The story also reveals, however, the reformer's attitude toward popular forms of divination. Inadvertently, it also shows how eagerly the local populace flocked to the soothsayer in hopes of eliciting his supernatural aid to recover stolen goods.

No record exists in the municipal archives in Erfurt of the execution of a soothsayer or even of a witch in 1537. In fact, only three such capital cases appear in the local records, dating from 1530, 1538, and 1550, and none of those involve a diviner. A letter to Luther from a local pastor named Aegidius Mechler, who claims to have taken the condemned soothsayer's confession on the eve of his execution, adds some weight to the notion that the unnamed diviner was indeed executed in Erfurt around 1537.[2] It is certainly possible that the documents from the case have not survived, but it seems just as likely that the story was apocryphal. Perhaps Myconius heard the tale secondhand or even adapted it from the Faustian legends already circulating in Germany at the time (the *Table Talk* also includes a 1537 story about Luther saving one of his students at Wittenberg from a demonic pact). Thus, the story could represent a sort of "wishful thinking" for these Lutheran reformers, depicting a world where soothsayers came to the clergy and repented of their evil deeds and the secular authorities burned them for their crimes, using them as an example of the wages of sin. In reality, however, Lutheran theologians and demonologists had a terrible time convincing their parishioners to abandon divination or persuading rulers to punish it so harshly.

For Luther, the activities of soothsayers like the one supposedly burned at Erfurt were inherently diabolical. He preached that popular cunning folk, common magical practitioners who told fortunes and identified thieves and witches for money, gained their occult knowledge from the devil. By tempting these pathetic creatures into signing a blood pact, the devil gained their souls and by planting false accusations, he sowed discord and brought innocent people to ruin. Luther's attitude toward popular forms of divination, commonplace practices in early modern towns and villages, reflected and built upon centuries of clerical condemnation of folk magic.

Nonetheless, his fulminations had little effect. Despite the intensity of Luther's condemnation, divination remained one of the most common magical activities in early modern Germany. As they had for centuries, people from all ranks of society sought to foretell the future and avert

Sieve driving, depicted in this eighteenth-century work about popular magical beliefs, was a common form of divination used to detect thieves and witches. A diviner instructed two people to take hold of a pair of shears and to suspend a sieve from the blade and then spoke the names of likely suspects. If the sieve moved as one of the names was uttered, the diviner would declare that person the culprit or the witch. From Heinrich Ludwig Fischer, *Das Buch vom Aberglauben* (1790). (Harold Jantz Collection of German Baroque Literature and German Americana, David M. Rubenstein Rare Book & Manuscript Library, Duke University)

misfortune by consulting astrologers and fortune-tellers, reading prophetic broadsheets and horoscopes, and interpreting dreams and portents. Practitioners used a wide range of methods in their attempts to predict the future, recover lost or stolen property, and diagnose bewitchment, including crystal-ball gazing, casting lots, and palmistry. Divination was an activity that crossed social boundaries; learned courtiers cast horoscopes, unlettered cunning folk told fortunes, and ordinary villagers and townsfolk turned the sieve.

Reformation-era efforts to suppress popular forms of divination echoed centuries of Christian condemnations. However, Lutheran authorities, eager to foster personal piety and enforce godly discipline, focused more attention on popular magical practices than their medieval counterparts.[3] Accordingly, these reformers' theological writings, pastoral efforts, and disciplinary initiatives intensified the long-standing clerical opposition to popular soothsaying, widening the gap between acceptable erudite astrology and the illicit forms of divination used by the unlearned. While popular divination had been discouraged throughout the Middle Ages, Lutheran authorities stepped up efforts to abolish it as part of a broader campaign to inculcate strict evangelical morality and to suppress unruly aspects of popular culture.[4] Given the ubiquity of soothsaying, they met with limited success in the early years of the Reformation.

Astrology and Learned Magic in Lutheran Germany

The ambivalent attitudes that medieval theologians displayed toward divination continued during the early Reformation. Churchmen of the High Middle Ages had generally tolerated learned astrology, while excoriating folk divination as inherently demonic. This divergence intensified during the early decades of the Reformation. Astrology assumed an evermore prominent role in Lutheran areas even as reformers railed with increasing vehemence against the popular forms of divination used by commoners.

Pious forms of astrology were quite popular among early Lutherans, who viewed their struggle against the papacy, portrayed as the "Antichrist" described in Revelation, as a sign of the looming end-times. In fact, a learned astrology informed by evangelical providentialism and early Reformation apocalypticism held a central place in the early Lutheran movement. Robin Barnes has shown that astrology was not only ubiquitous in Lutheran Germany, but that it also played a key role in the formation of a distinctly Lutheran confessional culture.[5] Barnes argues that the proliferation of astrological pamphlets in the cities of Germany both prepared the ground for Luther's challenge to the Catholic Church, often presented as an apocalyptic event, and helped to shape the evangelical movement in its first century.[6] Thus, the burgeoning popularity of pious almanacs and horoscopes in Lutheran areas cannot be viewed as an aberration from their theological vision, but rather as an essential element of early evangelical culture.

Whereas many of their Catholic and Calvinist rivals proved hostile to horoscopes, leading Lutheran theologians embraced pious forms of astrology during the early decades of the Reformation. Likewise, printers in Lutheran cities kept up a steady stream of astrological pamphlets meant for a popular audience. Astrological almanacs flew off the presses in Lutheran towns, including Wittenberg.[7] These works, products of the heady apocalypticism that marked the early evangelical movement, purported to show signs of God's providence and the impending Last Judgment in the movements of the stars and the appearance of comets.[8]

Most early Lutherans eagerly accepted astrological predictions as long as they conformed to evangelical theology and eschatology. A key proponent of astrology within the evangelical community was Philip Melanchthon, who had studied both astronomy and astrology at the University of Tübingen under the noted mathematician and astrologer Johannes Stöffler. Melanchthon sought to integrate the natural philosophy of the Renaissance with the Protestant theology of the Reformation and deemed astrology to be a useful tool for both religion and politics.[9] Thus, the reformer exchanged letters with the noted Nuremberg astrologer Joachim Camerarius about the appearance of Halley's Comet in the summer of 1531. The following year, he helped Camerarius publish an astrological treatise on the comet, presenting it as an ominous portent.[10] Under Melanchthon's guidance and amid an atmosphere of apocalyptic expectation, a generation of Lutheran scholars emerged from Wittenberg who shared his view that "in the heavens, humans could behold the clearest evidence of divine Providence."[11]

Astrology and other forms of learned occultism formed an essential part of elite culture throughout the 1500s. Divination and other forms of erudite magic had flourished among educated humanists during the Renaissance, buoyed by a renewed interest in hermeticism and Neoplatonic thought. A number of famous mages operated in Germany in the sixteenth century, notorious figures who sometimes aroused opposition from clerical and secular authorities. Just as often, however, these magicians and astrologers enjoyed the support of prominent patrons. The divergent reactions these magicians' occult activities elicited within elite circles illustrate the ambiguous space that learned magic occupied in sixteenth-century Germany.

Heinrich Cornelius Agrippa von Nettesheim, among the most prominent of these figures, studied astrology under the famous Renaissance mage Trithemius, abbot of Sponheim.[12] A gifted scholar, soldier, and physician, Agrippa was also an accomplished magician. As a student at the University of Cologne, he studied Albertus Magnus's *Speculum*, a thirteenth-century defense of astrology, inspiring a lifelong pursuit of esoteric knowledge. He studied under Trithemius in Würzburg in the winter of 1509, dedicating his most important work, the three-volume *De occulta philosophia* (*Three Books of Occult Philosophy*), to the abbot-astrologer the following year. Agrippa's career shows the ambiguous position learned magical practitioners held in sixteenth-century Europe. At various times in his turbulent life he enjoyed the patronage of powerful princes and churchmen, including Emperors Maximilian and Charles V, Archduchess Margaret of Austria, and the archbishop of Cologne, and even lectured at a number of prominent universities, including Pavia. At the same time, he often ran afoul of ecclesiastical authorities for his reputation as a magician, losing many positions and leading a peripatetic life until his death in 1535. In the decades after his death, fantastic stories about his magical feats circulated, and his sinister reputation as a demonic sorcerer grew.[13]

Another student of Trithemius, Philippus Aureolus Theophrastus Bombastus von Hohenheim, known as Paracelsus, also gained notoriety and associated with some of the leading figures of the day. A Renaissance humanist, Paracelsus was born in 1493 and studied medicine at the University of Basel before earning a doctorate at Ferrara around 1516. Paracelsus was famous as a traveling physician and as a firebrand, one who refuted the ancient theories of Galen on the basis of observation and experience gained in his medical practice. He was also known for employing astrology and alchemy in treating his patients, a common aspect of medical practice during the period (and another form of magical activity sanctioned by elites). After successfully treating the famous humanist publisher Johann Froben in Basel in 1526, Paracelsus began a correspondence with Erasmus of Rotterdam, the leading humanist intellectual of his day. An irascible figure, Paracelsus aroused opposition throughout his turbulent life, but his occult activities did not prevent him from associating with famous humanists like Froben and Erasmus.[14]

Learned astrologers were also prominent at court during the early Reformation, enjoying the patronage of the greatest princes of the age. Johann Carion, for example, served as court astrologer for Joachim I Nestor, the elector of Brandenburg. Born in 1499, Carion studied under Johannes Stöffler at Tübingen (like Melanchthon) before taking up his position in Berlin. Renowned for supposedly predicting the Reformation, he was an associate of Melanchthon and an important voice in Lutheran millenarian thought. After the publication of his *Chronica,* a universal history informed by biblical prophecy and astrological principles, his fame spread. Yet despite his privileged position at court, his academic credentials, and his prominent friends in Wittenberg, Carion could not escape suspicion. In 1531, for example, a rival astrologer, Andreas Perlach, who served at the court of Emperor Ferdinand I and lectured in astrology and mathematics at the University of Vienna, charged that Carion's predictions were rooted in demonic magic.[15]

The most infamous of the period's learned magicians, one whose notoriety fostered fantastical folktales and helped shape clerical attitudes about divination, was Georg or Johann Faust, better known as Doctor Faustus. With the publication of Johann Spies's fanciful *Historia von D. Johann Fausten* in 1587, the facts about Faustus's life became intertwined with myth, but contemporary references show that a real man, renowned as a magus, stood behind the legends. We know little of Faustus's early years, but matriculation records from the University of Heidelberg suggest that he may have been enrolled there in the 1480s. By 1506, he was in Gelnhausen, working as a magician and astrologer. In the following year, Trithemius mentioned Faustus in a letter to the Heidelberg court astrologer, Johannes Virdung. The abbot reported that the man called himself "Georgius Sabellicus, Faustus junior," dismissing him as a charlatan passing himself off as a "necromancer, astrologer, and magician." He also passed along a scandalous rumor that Faustus had recently lost a teaching position owing to a predilection for pederasty.

Several years later, in October 1513, Conrad Mutianus Rufus, a humanist cleric from Gotha, encountered Faustus in an Erfurt inn and was equally unimpressed. He reported in a letter to Trithemius that "eight days ago there came to Erfurt a certain soothsayer by the name of Georgius Faustus Helmitheus of Heidelberg." He dismissed Faustus as "a mere braggart and fool," writing that "his claims, like those of all diviners are idle, and this character has not more weight than a water spider." With evident disgust, the canon sneered that "the ignorant marvel at him."[16] However, in Bamberg in the winter of 1520 the infamous astrologer and magician cast a horoscope for the local bishop, Georg Schenk von Limburg, who paid him the princely sum of ten gulden, suggesting that not everyone doubted his talents.[17]

The ambiguous position of learned magicians and astrologers like Faustus is quite apparent in the few glimpses that survive of how his contemporaries viewed him later in his career. Expelled from Ingolstadt as a disreputable "soothsayer" in 1528, a "Doctor Faustus" was denied entry into Nuremberg a few years later, owing to his reputation as a "great sodomite and necromancer."[18] Nonetheless, the noted astrologer Joachim Camerarius, friend of Melanchthon, considered Faustus a serious rival throughout the 1530s.

Although learned magicians like Agrippa, Paracelsus, Carion, and Faustus were controversial figures, their careers also illuminate the prominence of learned forms of divination in the intellectual life of sixteenth-century Germany. As hermetic occultism and Neoplatonic mysticism spread north of the Alps, famous mages like Trithemius, Agrippa, and Carion could rely on the support of powerful princes—even prince-bishops—to pursue their occult interests, including astrological ones. Meanwhile, astrological almanacs and apocalyptic broadsheets found an eager audience in the heady days of the early Reformation. As the examples of Carion and Faustus show, however, these sorts of magical activities might also arouse suspicion, owing to their association with the demonic pact. Given the ambiguous reputation of such famous occult practitioners, it is perhaps not surprising that Martin Luther proved suspicious of astrology.

Ever wary of the devil's snares, Martin Luther did not share his followers' enthusiasm for astrology. From the earliest days of his ministry he was skeptical of horoscopes. In a lecture on Deuteronomy delivered in 1523, for instance, he presented astrologers as fraudulent quacks, calling them "godless teachers who divine out of their own heads." Linking them with magicians, he charged that they "toy with consciences by means of false and specious notions and empty words, just as sorcerers and wizards deceive the eyes with sleight of hand."[19] Deriding the deceptive nature of astrologers, Luther criticized the way they led believers astray, distracting them from the only guidance that mattered—the gospel.

Luther denigrated astrology time and again by questioning its status as a science, often at Philip Melanchthon's expense. In a conversation from December 1532, for example, he denied astrology's scientific validity, asserting that astrologers "base their judgment on the results that suit them and prudently don't talk about those that don't suit." Sounding like a disappointed parent, he added, "my Philip has devoted much attention to this business, but he has never been able to persuade me to accept it."[20] Luther's disdain for astrology did little to dampen the enthusiasm for stargazing among learned Lutherans, with almanacs and horoscopes remaining exceedingly popular among the faithful during his lifetime.

While he never persuaded his followers to abandon astrology, Luther used his sermons to try to get them to look elsewhere for signs of God's will. Throughout his life, he proclaimed faith in divine providence to be superior to horoscopes. He asserted that it was pure folly to try to predict the future, arguing that even if horoscopes could reliably do so, it would be "stupidity" to dwell on these predictions. Quoting Cicero, Luther taught that ignorance is bliss, pointing out that knowing doom lies ahead is worse than uncertainty about the future. According to Luther, "an abiding fear of God and prayer are preferable to the fear of future events."[21] Given the futility of astrological prediction, he urged his followers to put their trust in God instead of looking to the stars.

Martin Luther and Popular Divination

Despite his skepticism about erudite astrology, Martin Luther always tolerated its use. He did not prove so accepting of more humble forms of divination, however, preaching that unlearned forms of fortune-telling were an unmitigated evil. Perhaps not surprisingly, learned astrologers agreed. While Luther and Melanchthon disagreed about the efficacy of learned astrology, they were united in their strident opposition to the popular forms of fortune-telling that common villagers and townsfolk practiced.

Throughout his career, Luther was clear in denouncing these everyday divinatory practices as demonic. In his 1523 lecture on Deuteronomy, for example, he urged the faithful to remember God's prohibition of divination, warning that it "conflicted with the true and pure worship of God instituted through His Word." Luther condemned "seers or soothsayers," preaching that these "wise men and women," like the possessed slave girl in Acts 16:16, reveal "things that are secret and concealed" through the aid of demonic spirits. Given its supposedly diabolical nature, the reformer insisted that even seemingly benign forms of divination must be "condemned among the people of God."[22]

Instead of relying on sinful soothsaying, Christians should remain patient in the face of divine providence, and Luther urged his readers to "accept both evil and good as coming from God alone" and to react to both "with gratitude and willing submission."[23] In Luther's view, it was placing portents before providence that rendered divination sinful. This left room for the pious astrology practiced at Wittenberg, a form of prognostication that subordinated planetary influence to God's omnipotence, but explicitly prohibited the popular divinatory practices that the unlearned employed. Thus, despite the acceptance of pious forms of astrology among many early Lutherans, the ancient notion that less erudite means of divination were based upon a demonic pact remained prominent during the Reformation.

In preaching that unlearned soothsayers gained their occult insights with demonic assistance, the first generation of Lutheran reformers were breathing new life into a notion that stemmed from the very origins of Christianity. As chapter 1 showed, the idea that soothsaying was an inherently diabolical activity had a long pedigree. In late antiquity, Christian authorities like Augustine of Hippo already condemned forms of divination popular among the Romans as pagan idolatry, preaching that these rites were performed with the aid of the devil.[24] Throughout the Middle Ages, the clergy continued this tradition, with Thomas Aquinas condemning popular fortune-telling as a diabolical activity and attacking it as antithetical to faith in divine providence.[25] This Augustinian perspective, one that linked all popular magical activity with diabolism, remained prominent at the start of the sixteenth century.

On the eve of the Reformation, Christian humanists had joined with the Catholic clergy in denouncing popular forms of soothsaying, their attitudes influencing the early Lutheran reformers. Desiderius Erasmus, for example, who was not above corresponding with erudite occultists like Paracelsus, nevertheless voiced his opposition to the everyday divination practiced by the unlearned. The famous Christian humanist reiterated the traditional Christian view that linked fortune-telling with malevolent forms of magic, citing historical examples. Erasmus pointed out that Mosaic law called for the death penalty for necromancers, who communed with "departed spirits," and that Roman law condemned soothsayers as "strangers to nature and enemies of the human race, worthy of punishment by the retributive sword, or burning, or being thrown to wild beasts." Reminding his readers that Roman law also threatened fortune-tellers' clients with banishment, Erasmus sought to dissuade them from dealing with soothsayers.[26] A decade before the Reformation, Erasmus advocated reviving the ancient Roman penalty that threatened not only diviners, but those who consulted them, with heavy punishment.

Once the Reformation began, Lutheran reformers echoed Erasmus's concerns about fortune-telling in their preaching and pastoral efforts.

Accentuating soothsaying's demonic associations, they picked up the famous humanist's call for harsher punishment for diviners and those who consulted with them, relying like Erasmus on biblical punishments as precedents. Despite these threats, delivered from the pulpit and in private admonitions, soothsayers continued their work and commoners eagerly sought their predictions, ignoring the dire warnings of their pastors.

Divination in Lutheran Theology and Pastoral Literature

In their writings on folk magic, Protestant reformers built upon longstanding clerical opposition to divination, but proved to be even more concerned about demonic temptation than medieval scholastic theologians or Christian humanists like Erasmus.[27] Evangelical authorities were deeply troubled that popular forms of divination remained so prevalent in their own day, despite their "evident" demonic origins and God's manifest condemnation of sorcery and prognostication in Deuteronomy.[28] Thus, they sought to persuade their congregants that even seemingly harmless forms of fortune-telling were sinful and to link popular divinatory practices to demonic sorcery.

The impulse to dissuade parishioners from fortune-telling began in the early years of Luther's career as a reformer, and his ardent opposition to popular fortune-telling is apparent in his most important pastoral efforts. Seeking to discourage his followers from consulting diviners, he condemned soothsayers, lumping crystal gazers and fortune-tellers together with evil sorcerers and witches, asserting that all of these magical practitioners drew their power from a demonic pact. Thus, Luther sought to persuade his flock that the village cunning folk they consulted for help in times of trouble were just as sinister as witches and seeking out soothsayers just as sinful as performing diabolical rites.

Martin Luther had condemned divination in these terms from the earliest days of his ministry, in an attempt to undermine the popularity of soothsaying in the evangelical community. In a 1518 sermon, for example, he railed against fortune-telling, which he called "a hellish trap," one that drew wavering Christians into the devil's clutches.[29] Two years later, in a

1520 exegesis that influenced his famous catechisms that appeared at the end of the decade, he characterized a range of popular magical practices as sinful, including "crystal-gazing" and "ordering one's life and work in accordance with lucky days, astrological signs, and the views of fortune-tellers."[30] Echoing centuries of Christian condemnations, the reformer preached that divination was idolatrous and a grave violation of the First Commandment.[31]

Luther was particularly concerned about professional soothsayers, who told fortunes for eager clients, warning that they were in league with the devil and sought to lead good Christians into damnation. In an Epiphany sermon from 1522, he complained about "soothsayers, who tell of future things, like the stargazers and false prophets," warning that their insights all came from the devil. He aimed his wrath at cunning folk who conversed with spirits they glimpsed in mirrors, images, glass, or crystals. Condemning these soothsayers, Luther asserted that they had the devil at their ear, helping them locate lost goods and tell fortunes.[32] The timing of the sermon is perhaps telling. Luther's attack on cunning folk was delivered on Epiphany, the feast day celebrating the visit of the Three Magi to the Christ child. Perhaps the feast day's association with the Magi (or *magoi*), Persian priests famous as sorcerers and astrologers, who followed a star to Bethlehem, seemed to him a good time to warn his parishioners about the perils of visiting their own village "wise men" for more profane ends.

Martin Luther was not alone in excoriating cunning folk and their customers, and the first generation of Protestant ministers proved tireless in their condemnations. Using the pulpit and the pen, they sought to convince congregants that divine providence governed all earthly events and soothsaying was thus fruitless. Espousing a view that often clashed with popular notions of fate and fortune, notions that supported belief in the efficacy of divination, Lutheran pastoral writings and sermons included harsh condemnations of soothsayers and their clients. For example, in 1540 the Württemberg pastor Johann Spreter asserted that: "It is certain and true that no one can say what the future holds, except the one God and those he commands through the Holy Spirit. If a warlock, witch, or sorcerer babbles on about the future it is a sham. If they happen to guess correctly, then it all comes from the devil, who in the end never tells the truth, except when it pleases him."[33]

This confusing passage exposes the contradiction inherent in early Lutheran efforts to suppress divination. Early Protestant ministers like Spreter were eager not only to associate divination with the demonic, but also to assert the cosmological incompatibility of a belief in the efficacy of divination and faith in divine providence. In presenting divination as both a dangerous, demonic threat and as a ridiculous, fraudulent activity, Spreter and his fellow reformers were reviving an ambiguity prominent in Christian condemnations since the 1350s. In their writings, Lutheran reformers appeared as unsure about whether divination was real or ridiculous as had medieval confessors like Jacopo Passavanti.

As Spreter was writing this condemnation of divination, Lutheran reformers had already begun a series of initiatives aimed at fostering Christian morality among their parishioners. Lutheran ordinances, catechisms, and visitation procedures sought at once to instruct the faithful in the Christian faith and to suppress a wide range of behaviors they deemed sinful. Divination was prominent among the sins that Lutheran authorities hoped to suppress.

The early Reformation prompted apocalyptic zeal and millenarian expectation among evangelicals, expressed in both a burgeoning enthusiasm for pious astrology and in heightened opposition to supposedly diabolical forms of popular fortune-telling. Leading reformers and humble pastors alike turned to astrological texts in an effort to discern the workings of divine providence. Despite his skepticism, Martin Luther himself displayed a grudging acceptance of these pursuits. So long as astrologers left room in their cosmology for divine providence and human free will and spoke in terms of planetary influences (rather than determination), he generally tolerated their activities.[34] Popular forms of divination, however, long linked with the demonic, invariably drew the ire of ecclesiastical authorities in the early days of the Reformation.

Lutheran reformers preached sermons and launched pastoral initiatives intended to convince the faithful that even seemingly harmless forms of divination, like crystal gazing and palm reading, were dangerous tools of the devil meant to entrap wavering Christians as the Last Judgment drew near. By midcentury, the Lutheran clergy had begun catechizing their congregants and compiling detailed visitation reports intended to bolster Protestant religiosity and morality. Both of these pastoral initiatives, in the tradition of similar efforts by medieval confessors and inquisitors, included measures meant to discover and correct parishioners who had engaged in fortune-telling.

The intensification of the clerical campaign against divination after midcentury is illustrated by the legend of Faustus. Controversial in his day as an astrologer and magician, he was infamous after his death for his purported pact with the devil. In the decades after his death, Faustus became a legendary figure, and folktales about his exploits and his damnation proliferated. During his lifetime, Faustus had been a controversial figure, often branded a disreputable charlatan. But he also enjoyed the esteem of a number of important associates, including the Bamberg bishop Georg Schenk von Limburg, who considered him a learned astrologer and paid him handsomely for his predictions. By the 1580s, however, the demonic associations surrounding Faustus had come to the fore as the clerical discourse on divination began to change.

Johann Spies's 1587 publication about the famed magician, the first printed *Faustbuch,* was a collection of folktales laden with heavy-handed references to Lutheran morality. It informed elite attitudes toward soothsaying, helping to solidify the association between divination and diabolism. According to the author, Faustus "set about making almanacs and became a good *astronomus* and *astrologus*." Faustus's skill as an astrologer, and the fame it brought him, supposedly came from his demonic companion, Mephistopheles, called a "spirit" in the text: "His horoscopes, which he sent to great lords and princes, always were correct, for he contrived them according to the advice of the spirit as to what would come to pass in the future, all such matters falling duly out even as he had presaged them."[35] A tool of the devil, even Faustus did not understand how his familiar spirit could so accurately predict the future. The author used the wicked man's discussions with Mephistopheles to elucidate the demonic origin of divination.

When Faustus asked Mephistopheles about how he predicted the future, the demon replied that "ancient haruspices and modern stargazers" alike could not accurately predict the future, because "these are deep mysteries of God, which mortals cannot plumb as we spirits can, who hover in the air beneath Heaven where we can see and mark what God hath predestined."[36] Thus, the demonic spirit not only revealed to Faustus how he was able to predict the future, but also suggested that such illicit knowledge of God's providence was impossible without diabolical aid. This passage also shows how diviners, ancient and contemporary alike, had come to be viewed by the 1580s: as evil magicians who, like Faustus, drew their insights from the devil.

The heavy-handed Lutheran moralism of the tale is most apparent in Faustus's final warning to his friends. On the eve of his damnation, when the devil was due to collect his soul at the conclusion of their infernal bargain, Faustus hosted a sumptuous farewell feast for his friends, former students, and colleagues from his days as a professor of theology. As the fateful hour drew nigh, he begged them to take his piteous fate to heart.

Sounding like a Lutheran preacher, Faust pleaded with his old friends. He beseeched them to "go earnestly and often to church, war and strive constantly against the devil with a steadfast faith in Christ, always walking a godly path."[37] Faustus's advice to his old friends, delivered shortly before he was dragged to Hell in fulfillment of his demonic pact, echoes the course that the Lutheran clergy advocated. As Lutheran authorities ramped up their efforts to eradicate divination, the tragic story of Faustus served as a vivid reminder of the terrible wages of sin and as a chilling illustration of how the idolatrous vanity inherent in divination could bring wavering Christians to damnation.

3

"UNCHRISTIAN AND DEVILISH CRIMES"

Soothsaying and Early Lutheran Disciplinary Efforts

The Wise Woman of Sundhausen (1560)

In 1560, the local authorities at Schloss Tenneberg, a ducal fortress near Waltershausen on the edge of the Thuringian Forest, wrote to their superiors in Gotha. They reported the arrest of several troublemakers in nearby Sundhausen, whose neighbors had denounced them for their unruly behavior. The suspects included a woman named Osanna Hergottin, an unnamed cooper from Bollstedt, a wandering student from Döllstädt, and a mysterious figure they called "the wise woman of Sundhausen." Under torture, the suspects confessed to many illicit activities, including fornication. However, once the authorities began to question the wise woman, they lost interest in the other suspects.

In a subsequent missive to their Gotha superiors, they reported that the wise woman of Sundhausen had long been rumored to be engaged in "sorcery" (*Zauberey*). Putting her to torture, they sought to uncover her occult crimes. The woman denied that she was a soothsayer, but in an attempt to throw the magistrates off her trail, she implicated another woman from Sundhausen. Called "Gilgin," the woman she denounced was apparently a popular soothsayer. She testified that Gilgin had plied her trade in Ohrdruf for eight years before being banished and moving on to the area near Sundhausen. The ducal officials in Gotha requested more information about her from the local authorities at Schloss Tenneberg, who reported that she had managed to find refuge in their district after promising the local pastor that she would "henceforth never again use or perform magic." The Tenneberg officials also assured their superiors that they had ordered her to attend confession, where her pastor had spoken sternly with her about her past indiscretions.

After collecting this information, the authorities at Schloss Tenneberg released their informant. They chose not to punish her for her alleged activities as a wise woman, remanding her instead to the ecclesiastical authorities for punishment. They ordered her to appear before her pastor back in her home village of Sundhausen to confess her sins and to receive a stern admonition. Furthermore, she was to take the sacrament, thereby placing her eternal soul in jeopardy if her inner conversion proved insincere.[1]

The story of the wise woman of Sundhausen reveals several salient features of popular divination, and the official reaction to it, in the Reformation era. Once informed of the allegations of soothsaying among their subjects in Sundhausen, the central authorities in Gotha quickly dropped the issue of fornication, a serious crime in sixteenth-century Thuringia, or at least left it for the local authorities to handle. Instead, they directed the local officials to focus their investigation on the wise woman's activities. The central authorities, in distant Gotha, were completely reliant on their local agents at Schloss Tenneberg to uncover and report on illicit activities in their district. In turn, the local officials, separated from the villagers they administered by status and education if not by distance, proved equally reliant on denunciations and informants to uncover crimes like soothsaying, which were performed behind closed doors. They also relied on torture. Eager to draw out the required information for their superiors, the local authorities were quick to employ torture, and coerced the wise woman of Sundhausen into confessing her own illicit magical activities (despite her earlier denials). It also compelled her to tell the magistrates about a more prominent soothsayer operating in the region, known as Gilgin. The most telling aspect of the case, however, was the Gotha authorities' willingness to leave the correction of these fortune-tellers to the local pastorate.

A decade later, official statutes appeared that threatened soothsayers with imprisonment or banishment, but as late as the 1560s secular authorities in Thuringia were content to have them punished by their pastors. Thus, like Gilgin, the wise woman of Sundhausen was simply sent to her home parish to confess her sins and repent. She does not show up again in existing court records, though this should not simply be read as evidence that she listened to her pastor. Given the weak official response and the enduring popularity of divination, it is unlikely that the wise woman of Sundhausen halted her practice or that local people stopped seeking her out for glimpses of their future.

The campaign to stamp out popular forms of divination, prompted by the sermons and treatises of Luther and the other early reformers, got off to a slow start. In the early decades of the Reformation, Thuringian soothsayers proved exceedingly popular and usually managed to avoid punishment. As in the case of these female fortune-tellers operating in Sundhausen in 1560, secular authorities usually proved content to monitor the activities of soothsayers, compiling reports and remanding them to ecclesiastical authorities for pastoral correction. In the 1560s, new demonological treatises had begun to appear, which encouraged a stronger official response. Ardent in the belief that divination was a diabolical form of sorcery just as dangerous as witchcraft, their authors called upon secular authorities to use harsh punishment to root out soothsaying once and for all.

Divination in Early Lutheran Demonology

In the mid-sixteenth century, amid rising confessional tensions and growing anxieties about demonic agency, a new generation of demonological texts and witch-hunters' manuals appeared. These influential texts reinforced long-standing theological opposition to divination and gradually supplanted late medieval texts like the *Malleus maleficarum*. Departing from the works of the early reformers, who treated divination as a matter of individual sinfulness to be handled through pastoral efforts, these works urged a new activist disciplinary agenda. Part of a broader campaign to inculcate confessional conformity and instill strict morality through harsh discipline, they called upon the ruling authorities of church and state to unite in stamping out these devilish rites.

First published in 1563, Ludwig Milichius's *Der Zauber-Teuffel (The Sorcery-Devil)* provides a striking example of this shift in the demonological literature regarding fortune-telling. In his treatise, Milichius, a lecturer at the Lutheran Gymnasium at Marburg, linked popular divination with diabolism and urged ecclesiastical and secular authorities alike to punish soothsayers and their clients. Milichius's treatise was part of a popular Lutheran genre known as the *Teufelsbücher,* which associated a range of human sins, including drinking, vanity, luxury, and sorcery, with the devil. Accordingly, he argued that all forms of magic and divination were just as sinful as witchcraft, owing to their common demonic basis.[2] Accentuating soothsaying's supposedly diabolical nature, he defined it as "answers and replies which questioners are given by the devil through various means."[3] Citing a dizzying array of sources, ranging from biblical verses to classical authorities to the writings of Augustine and Martin Luther, Milichius bombarded his readers with exhaustive treatment of every conceivable form of divination. Tracing each of these occult practices back to their supposed origins in ancient Persia, his analysis always drew the same conclusion: diviners gleaned all of their insights from Satan and deserved punishment in this world and the next.

Convinced of divination's demonic nature, Milichius ended his weighty tome with a plea for clerical and secular authorities to work diligently to eradicate it from Christian society. Like the early reformers, he called for the clergy to use the pulpit to combat the spread of superstition. He cautioned, however, that if pastors only preached in general terms about "sorcery" (*Zauberey*), their parishioners would just think about witchcraft and go on practicing other forms of folk magic like fortune-telling. Soothsaying was deeply rooted in popular culture, and had been for centuries, and many villagers saw it as benign or even beneficial. Thus, in order to stamp out all manner of folk magic and divination, the prudent pastor must teach his flock to avoid all occult practitioners, "not only witches . . . but also the other magic-users, like fortune-tellers, magicians, soothsayers, augurers, omen-readers, and dream-interpreters."[4]

Milichius made a noteworthy departure from his predecessors in acknowledging that these pastoral efforts alone would not be enough to eradicate superstition among the faithful. He also recognized that secular rulers were not doing enough to stamp out magical activity. Consequently, he also reminded rulers of their duty to punish all magical activities harshly. Citing Exodus 22 and Leviticus 20, he demanded capital punishment for "anyone who has a pact with the devil, man or woman, and becomes a sorcerer, witch, magician, fortune-teller, [or] necromancer."[5] Given his conviction that divination was inherently diabolical, Milichius argued that seemingly harmless village soothsayers deserved to die at the stake along with more obviously sinister malefactors who invoked demons or practiced witchcraft. The stern Lutheran schoolmaster also advocated punishment for the clients of fortune-tellers, advising magistrates to arrest "anyone who runs to fortune-tellers and soothsayers" and to punish them with fines, imprisonment, or banishment.[6]

Ardent demonologists like Milichius were not the only Lutherans concerned about divination, and even voices skeptical about the excessive violence of the witch hunts condemned fortune-telling. Even Johann Weyer, perhaps the most famous critic of the excesses of the early modern witch-hunts, considered divination to be a form of demonic magic and leveled his ire at professional soothsayers. Writing in the same year as Milichius, Weyer criticized the vanity of diviners, dismissing them as pompous swindlers. He asserted that "seduced by the fumes of self-esteem, and seeking prestige," ignorant fortune-tellers claim to perform "an occult art and a science of which they are actually ignorant."[7]

Later in the same passage, however, Weyer suggested that their forecasts, although usually false, are nevertheless accomplished through the aid of the devil. He warned that "in their greedy desire for fraudulent gains," soothsayers "still boast of a knowledge of divination even when they sometimes learn little or nothing through Satan's cooperation." For Weyer, diviners were either puffed up charlatans or greedy swindlers, and if they acquired even a murky glimpse of hidden knowledge, it was only through Satan's assistance.

Although famously eager to defend pathetic old women falsely accused as witches, Weyer showed no sympathy for soothsayers. Like Milichius he called for the authorities to be more diligent in punishing diviners, although he stopped short of calling for the death penalty. Urging magistrates to punish fortune-tellers, Weyer argued that "these magicians should not be tolerated, and they should not be allowed to go unpunished (as they are now), because they trust in and rely upon lies and upon the Father of Lies, as though upon a most assured witness."[8]

Twenty years later, in 1585, another witchcraft skeptic, Hermann Witekind, published his own critique of the witch hunts, *Christlich bedenken und erinnerung von Zauberey* (*Christian Reflections and Recollections on Sorcery*), under the pseudonym Augustin Lercheimer. Witekind, professor of Greek at the University of Heidelberg and former pupil of Philip Melanchthon, echoed Weyer in calling for an end to witchcraft prosecution, which was gaining steam at the close of the sixteenth century. He also mirrored Weyer in his explicit condemnations of divination and in urging secular rulers to punish soothsayers.

Although he doubted the efficacy of demonic sorcery in the face of divine omnipotence, Witekind believed that the devil could tempt wavering Christians into apostasy and saw fortune-telling as a powerful temptation. He maintained that the devil deceived fortune-tellers and their benighted clients in order to cause mayhem and to draw them farther from God and into damnation. Thus, again like Weyer, Witekind presented divination primarily as a sham, writing that its misguided practitioners should not rightly be called "*Warsager*," because they "tell many more lies than they do truths (*Warheit*)."[9]

Although Witekind discounted the veracity of fortune-tellers' predictions, he was adamant that they deserved punishment, punishment that only secular authorities could provide. He buttressed this opinion with a wealth of evidence, biblical and contemporary. Throughout the work, he returned time and again to scriptural prohibitions of divination and to the efforts of pious Hebrew rulers to drive soothsayers from their kingdom. He also related stories that brought home the dangers of divination in his own day.

Witekind reminded his readers of the tragic story of an imperial knight, Wilhelm von Grumbach, who attempted to use a peasant boy's divining skills in the service of a fallen duke and came to ruin. In 1563, Grumbach had approached Duke Johann Friedrich II in Gotha, offering to help return the electoral dignity his father had lost in the Schmalkaldic War in 1547. Grumbach persuaded the disgruntled and ambitious duke to support an uprising of the imperial knights on his behalf, promising that it would prevail without bloodshed. As proof, he produced a peasant boy regarded as a prophet who had supposedly seen a vision of the knights' triumphant victory.[10]

The wily Grumbach immediately captured and plundered Würzburg, using the plot to settle an old score, and even sought to assassinate Elector Augustus of Saxony to clear the way for Johann Friedrich II. These outrageous actions earned Grumbach an imperial ban and prompted the German princes to mobilize against him. At the imperial diet at Augsburg in March 1566, Johann Friedrich II failed to gain the support of the other German princes; even his own brother, Johann Wilhelm, duke of Saxe-Weimar, declined to assist him. In May, Johann Friedrich II joined Grumbach under an imperial ban, and Elector Augustus besieged Schloss Grimmenstein, where the conspirators were holed up. The fortress quickly fell, and the elector's forces captured the conspirators. After a hasty trial, Witekind records, Grumbach was dismembered in the town square in Gotha. Grimmenstein was pulled down, so it could never again serve as a breeding ground of rebellion, and Johann Friedrich II was deposed in favor of his brother, Johann Wilhelm. He spent the rest of his life in custody, dying in 1595.

Witekind passed over most of the political intrigue involved in the episode and focused his attention on the boy-prophet, blaming him for instigating the entire affair. He was a peasant lad from Sundhausen, as we have seen a hotbed of soothsaying in the 1560s. Called Hans Tausendschön, the boy was reputed to be an "Engelseher," who was said to receive angelic messages that afforded him glimpses of the future. For Witekind, the boy's false visions were from the devil. He presented them as the catalyst for the terrible events of 1567, the font of war, rebellion, and bloodshed. The Lutheran professor wrote with satisfaction that the evil boy-prophet was hanged in Gotha for his misdeeds.[11]

Highlighting the terrible threat that divination posed to the Christian community, Witekind complained that "the authorities in many places remained negligent" in enforcing God's prohibition of divination. He urged Lutheran pastors to preach about the evils of soothsaying, "so that the common man learns what an abominable and dangerous thing it is" for both soothsayers and their clients. He also told them to be diligent in reminding rulers of their duty to eradicate this evil. Although Witekind suggests that banishment of these "servants of the devil" might suffice, he allows that in some cases capital punishment might be required.[12] In linking divination and diabolism and in urging rulers to root it out without mercy Witekind joined a chorus of Lutheran demonologists calling for rulers to be more active in punishing soothsaying.

Protestant demonologists were not alone in condemning divination and encouraging the authorities to punish diviners; their Catholic rivals also called for harsh measures in the late sixteenth century. In 1581, the famous French political philosopher Jean Bodin published an important witchcraft treatise. Translated into German a decade later, it proved particularly influential among theologians and jurists across the confessional divide.[13] Like the medieval and Reformation-era demonologists who preceded him, Bodin did not focus solely on witches; he also excoriated fortune-tellers. The jurist and advisor to the French crown, famous for his treatise on royal absolutism, *Six livres de la République* (1576), took a hard line in suggesting suitable punishments for diviners. Presenting soothsaying as "diabolical" and as an "invention of the devil," Bodin advocated a fine for first-time offenders, the lash for those caught using it a second time, and the gallows for anyone who dared a third offense.[14]

The 1560s marked a turning point in how demonologists—Milichius, Witekind, Bodin, and the others—thought and wrote about divination. Prominent demonologists and skeptics alike, both Protestant and Catholic, agreed that fortune-telling was inherently diabolical and posed a dire threat to Christian society. In a number of influential treatises on witchcraft and sorcery, these authorities agreed across the confessional divide that soothsayers deserved harsh punishment for forging pacts with the devil, even if they disagreed about the veracity of their occult predictions. Alarmed at what they saw as a rising tide of sorcery and superstition in an atmosphere of apocalyptic anxiety, they called upon rulers to use their penal powers to stamp out popular divination.

Soothsayers and the State in Sixteenth-Century Thuringia

Efforts to suppress divination were part of a larger disciplinary agenda that began in the early years of the Reformation. As reformers worked to instill new standards of moral behavior within the Lutheran community, they turned their attention to a wide range of rowdy and sinful behaviors. These included not only adultery and fornication, and drinking and gambling, but also forms of folk magic like divination. Early Lutheran efforts to suppress fortune-telling, amplified by the Protestant and Catholic demonologies that appeared after midcentury, were part of the ambitious moral reform initiatives that swept Lutheran areas in the heady days of the early Reformation.

In Thuringia, a region marked by a complicated patchwork of tiny principalities, the new disciplinary efforts that accompanied the early Reformation occurred amid continual political fragmentation. The region's remarkable political decentralization can be traced to the late fifteenth century. In 1485, the two sons of Saxon Elector Friedrich II, Ernst and Albert, partitioned the Wettin lands between them. Ernst retained the title of Elector of Saxony and possession of northern Meissen, southern Thuringia, and the family seat at Wittenberg, while his younger brother ruled over northern Thuringia and southern Meissen. Henceforth, the fortunes of the Ernestine branch of the Wettin dynasty would be closely tied with those of Thuringia. This tradition of partition continued, increasingly fractionalizing the region.[15] When Elector Ernst died in a riding accident the following year, his son, Friedrich III, known as Friedrich the Wise, succeeded him. Friedrich established a university in Wittenberg in 1502, hiring a fiery theology professor, an Augustinian monk named Martin Luther, a decade later. In 1517, Luther's attack on indulgences became a sensation throughout the empire, and the Wettin lands became the birthplace of the Reformation.

The turbulent events of the early Reformation destabilized the region, as religious radicals threatened the existing social and political order. Using his famous professor as a pawn in the high-stakes negotiations over the imperial succession, Friedrich the Wise, an ardent Catholic, protected Luther. After Luther's defiance at the Diet of Worms in 1521, the reformer became an outlaw, and Elector Friedrich sheltered him in the Wartburg castle in Eisenach. By the time Luther finally emerged and returned to Wittenberg, he confronted the spread of a radical faction of his reform movement. Using the pulpit to denounce his rivals, he expelled his former associate Andreas Karlstadt and a group of visionaries known as the Zwickau prophets, who were preaching a violently apocalyptic message in the city. The radical implications of his movement proved difficult to stifle outside Wittenberg, however, and soon Thuringia was a hotbed of religious radicalism. Spurred on by the preaching of firebrands like Thomas Müntzer, in 1524 peasants took up arms throughout Thuringia, Franconia, and Swabia, uniting with poor townsfolk to demand the preaching of the gospel and worldly concessions from their lords. Initially supportive of the peasants' grievances against their lordly oppressors, Luther eventually sided with the princes after unruly peasant bands began burning monasteries and palaces. The Peasants' War ended in 1525 with the slaughter of thousands of the hapless rebels, and the Lutheran Reformation took a decidedly magisterial turn.

Amid the turbulent events of the early Reformation and the chaos unleashed by the Peasants' War, Lutheran authorities in Thuringia worked to impose order and inculcate evangelical norms. In the late 1520s, the region's Wettin rulers established Protestant territorial churches, entrusting them to maintain confessional orthodoxy and to enforce moral discipline. These efforts entailed both prohibiting behaviors that did not conform to Lutheran moral standards and instructing adherents in the theology of the new faith. Education was crucial to these endeavors, and throughout Thuringia, Lutheran ecclesiastical authorities sought to inculcate new doctrinal, liturgical, and behavioral standards. Catechetical instruction was at the heart of these efforts, beginning in 1529 with Martin Luther's *Small Catechism,* for the instruction of children, and his *Large Catechism,* for training congregations in the rudiments of the Lutheran faith.[16] The Lutheran clergy distributed these catechisms widely in Thuringia, using them to teach parishioners about both theology and morality.

Lutheran authorities mandated that every individual should study the catechism, entrusting pious housefathers with instructing their wives, children, and servants in its contents. Luther required "every father of a family to question and examine his children and servants at least once a week." If a housefather found his charges' knowledge of the catechism to be lacking, he urged him to "keep them faithfully at it."[17] The reformer was aware of the daunting task of remaking Christians, however, and proclaimed that for the present it would be enough if every Lutheran came to know and understand at least the Decalogue, the Creed, and the Lord's Prayer. Luther advised that "these are the most necessary parts which one should first learn to repeat word for word." To facilitate their memorization, he recommended that "children should be accustomed to recite daily when they arise in the morning, when they sit down to their meals, and when they retire at night," warning that they shouldn't be fed until they could recite these verses. He also instructed the good Lutheran housefather to ensure that his household servants knew the rudiments of the faith, urging him "not to keep them in his house if they do not know these things and are unwilling to learn them."[18]

At the parish level, Lutheran clergy had a variety of means to instruct and to correct the laity. Schools established in Protestant territories served to inculcate the new faith among the young. The pulpit also proved a potentially powerful weapon in the pastor's arsenal, although Luther often complained that congregants skipped the Sunday sermon or even profaned the Sabbath by spending it carousing in taverns. The pulpit was only effective if villagers appeared in church, a reality reformers faced in imposing their notions of acceptable behavior.[19] In addition, pastors relied on confession and communion in their efforts to reform morality in their parishes, using them as carrot and stick to entice disobedient congregants into curtailing sinful activities.[20] Finally, Lutheran pastors, like their Catholic rivals, retained daunting disciplinary powers to bring wayward parishioners to heel. They could shame sinners by mentioning their misdeeds during sermons, force them to appear in church for a humiliating public confession of their sins, or ban them from the sacrament altogether.[21]

These pastoral and disciplinary efforts represented a two-pronged attack on traditional Catholic religiosity, which the reformers regarded as a misguided faith steeped in diabolical evil and superstitious error. On the one hand, reformers sought to instruct their parishioners in the evangelical notions of true religious belief, rooted in the word of God and transmitted through catechisms, sermons, and Bible reading. On the other hand, they attempted to root out traditional Catholic rites and remedies and popular elements of folk culture, which of course included divination.

The reformers' opposition to popular forms of divination and their desire to rid the Lutheran community of such practices are readily apparent in the era's pastoral literature. In his *Large Catechism,* for example, Luther included a warning of how the idolatrous practice of fortune-telling was a sinful violation of God's First Commandment, one rooted in diabolism. The reformer counted soothsayers among the most heinous idolaters, contending that they "make a covenant with the devil," in exchange for his help in recovering lost goods through divination. For Luther, such divining was idolatrous because its practitioners, turning to the devil for help, "place their heart and trust elsewhere than in the true God."[22] Following Luther's lead, Lutheran authorities throughout Thuringia included admonitions against divination in their sermons and church ordinances and instructed pastors, consistories, and visitors to be diligent in stamping it out.

Concerned that their parishioners were engaging fortune-telling, the Lutheran clergy faced the daunting prospect of suppressing a secretive activity performed behind closed doors in rural towns and villages. Thus, the clerical campaign to eradicate it relied on official surveillance. Lutheran religious authorities proved particularly diligent in their efforts to uncover and eradicate sin at the parish level through visitations organized by the territorial church. The ill-fated Elector Johann Friedrich I established a Lutheran consistory in 1542, and he also supported Luther's program of visitations within his realm. By the 1550s, visitations had begun in earnest in the rural parishes of Thuringia, as clerical authorities worked to inculcate new evangelical norms among the populace. The visitors sent to question rural pastors and their parishioners about their religiosity and morality also sought to uncover traces of forbidden folk magic. The instructions issued to the officials charged with undertaking visitations in Ernestine Saxony in the mid-1550s, for instance, called for them to question local pastors about what sorts of sins they preached against in their sermons. Along with adultery, fornication, usury, murder, theft, swearing, and sorcery, the visitors were to verify that pastors had also warned their parishioners against dabbling with magic, including fortune-telling. They also evaluated the effectiveness of these pastors' disciplinary efforts, recording the moral lapses of their parishioners. In the village of Rastenberg, near Weimar, for example, the visitors reported that although the local pastor had adequate theological knowledge, members of his flock were still committing adultery, engaging in usury, and using magic.[23] As visitors uncovered vestiges of such sinful superstition, Lutheran authorities turned their attention to rooting it out.

The Lutheran clergy was not alone in seeking to remake moral life in their parishes, and Thuringian rulers supported the disciplinary agenda of the early Reformation. However, the punishment of soothsayers and their clients got off to a very slow start in the region. A handful of cases involving divination in the region around Gotha survive from the reign of Duke Johann Friedrich II and show the local authorities' halting early efforts to suppress the practice. In 1556, for example, an official at Schloss Tenneberg informed his superiors in Gotha that he had learned that villagers in Wahlwinkel had consulted a mysterious female soothsayer about a pair of stolen horses. Reporting that the farmers had done so "in contempt of our holy religion and in mockery of the clear preaching of the Word of God," he wrote for advice on what sort of punishment to levy. He also delivered a more troubling report. Apparently, a ducal official stationed in Aspach, a settlement near Gotha, had consulted the same wise woman for help in locating a misplaced ledger. The official, who was supposed to be reporting on the villagers' divinatory practices, was himself seeking the soothsayer's help. Like the rest of the populace, agents charged with policing divination also believed in its efficacy, demonstrating the complications and setbacks reformers faced in their attempts to root out soothsaying. The official at Schloss Tenneberg informed his superiors that he had sentenced the two villagers to eight days' confinement in the tower and reported that he would remain vigilant in case the fortune-teller entered their jurisdiction again so he could apprehend her.[24]

The case of the wise woman operating in Wahlwinkel in 1556 is typical of official efforts to suppress divination in the early decades of the Reformation. Punishment of this supposedly demonic crime remained relatively light and unevenly applied. The guilty villagers, who had sought occult help in finding their stolen horses, faced only a short stint in the tower. The wise woman operating in Wahlwinkel, meanwhile, escaped arrest altogether, despite the fact that Lutheran authorities preached that her activities were certainly diabolical. Even the hapless ducal official in Aspach, who had consulted with her about his lost ledger, thereby setting a poor example for the local villagers, seems to have avoided anything more than an official reprimand.

Another case that entered the official record six years later shows a similar reluctance from secular authorities to punish soothsaying. In 1561, ducal authorities in Gotha, the capital of the duchy, began investigating "a sorceress called 'the wise woman,'" who had been active in the region around Schmalkalden. Compiling a report of her activities, they failed to apprehend her even though she had apparently been running a thriving business as a soothsayer.[25] Like her counterpart working in Wahlwinkel six years earlier, the authorities seemed content to keep tabs on her without bringing her in for questioning.

As these cases from the 1550s and 1560s suggest, the central authorities usually failed to arrest soothsayers in the mid-sixteenth century. While officials proved capable of compiling secondhand reports about their activities and sometimes punished their clients, in practice their efforts appear halfhearted. Most diviners managed to elude arrest, and even those unlucky few whom the authorities apprehended avoided harsh penalties like banishment or flogging. In the early decades of the Reformation, official efforts to curtail fortune-telling remained largely in the hands of parish clergy.

By the 1570s, however, new official ordinances began to appear in Thuringia that promised to treat divination with a new severity. Departing from earlier practice, these ordinances took up Lutheran demonologists' calls for capital punishment for soothsayers who formed a pact with the devil. According to the 1572 *Kursächsiche Kriminalordnung* of Augustus, the elector of Saxony, for example, those who practiced "sorcery or divination . . . absolutely forbidden in both imperial law and Holy Scripture" faced a variety of serious punishments. Magicians who, "forgetting their Christian teaching," formed a pact with the devil were to be burned at the stake or beheaded. Diviners, "who through the devil's art told fortunes or spoke with the devil using crystals or in other ways," acquiring information about hidden or future things, faced beheading.[26] Likewise, a 1589 *Landesordnung* issued by Friedrich Wilhelm of Saxe-Weimar provided an exhaustive list of crimes that merited capital punishment, including heresy, robbery, murder, incest, and adultery. The ordinance also called for executing those "who prayed to the devil or practiced occult divination," showing that by the late sixteenth century the Wettin dukes had come to consider divination a demonic activity, one that merited the death penalty.[27] These laws were certainly severe, meant to deter the practice of divination, but like many of the harsh edicts of the early modern period they were not enforced. The region's criminal archives show that the authorities that issued these laws, content to threaten soothsayers, never carried out the harsh penalties they mandated for divining—with one possible exception.

On the heels of this new draconian legislation against soothsaying, amid a spate of witch-hunting in the region, a deadly case of divination occurred in Erfurt in 1587. The case, which cost a local wise woman her life, shows an intensification in official efforts to investigate and punish popular divination as confessional tensions and witchcraft fears increased in the region. In December 1587, the city council in Erfurt investigated a city watchman for consulting a "wise woman" and employing counter-magic after a dispute with one of his companions. The municipal watchman, Jost Vogt, had accused the city piper, Nickell Steffens, of stealing a Martinmas goose that had been roasting in the oven in the watchtower. Vogt hurled insults at the suspected thief and demanded that he pay for the goose, but proclaiming his innocence, Steffens refused. A few days later, while Steffens was in Jena playing at a wedding, he experienced a sudden and terrible pain in his eye. Once he returned home, "overcome by fear and melancholy," he called for the hangman to diagnose the cause of his pain. While this might seem a strange request to modern readers, folk belief had long ascribed medical knowledge and magical perception to executioners. Reviled and feared in early modern society, they nevertheless often served as magical healers and witch-finders.[28] By the time the hangman arrived, Steffens's shirt was soaked with the fluid running from his afflicted eye.

Examining his patient, the executioner immediately asked the watchman "what sort of worthless people he had been associating with," suggesting that he had fallen prey to evil black magic. A day later, a doctor removed the piper's afflicted eye.

Seeking information about who was responsible for the loss of his eye, Steffens went to visit a "wise woman" whom he found by consulting several women in his neighborhood.[29] Asked to identify his assailant, she told the piper to gaze into her crystal, where he would see the culprit. Steffens refused, or at least, hoping to distance himself from her occult activities, he testified that he had refused. Consulting the crystal herself, and no doubt astutely discerning Steffens's own suspicions, she named the true thief and the one who had bewitched him. She told the piper that it had been Vogt's own son who had stolen the goose, but that the watchman, convinced that Steffens was the culprit, had asked a witch to strike out the innocent man's eye. After confronting Vogt, Steffens denounced him to the authorities, apparently willing to divulge his own dealings with a cunning woman to get justice. The city magistrates questioned the alleged malefactor about the incident a month later, uncovering surprising details about the relationship between divination, folk magic, and witchcraft.

Put to torture, Vogt admitted that he had indeed consulted a mysterious "wise woman" to find who had stolen the purloined goose. According to Vogt, he had run into the soothsayer on the road by chance, and he had asked her on the spot to help him find the thief. She merely laughed, telling him that the day was dark and that she couldn't discern who the culprit was. She told him to come back the next day. Perhaps she was reluctant to deal with a stranger before she could ask around about him; perhaps she really believed that she had the power of divination and the stars were not aligned right.

In his desperation to find the criminal, he continued his search for a soothsayer who would help him that night. He testified that on his way home he had stopped to see a woman named Otilia. She recommended another wise woman and agreed to bring her to the watchtower on the following Sunday. When the appointed day came, and the wise woman arrived, she immediately demanded payment for her services. After settling on a price—two groschen—the wise woman asked Vogt to tell her about the crime. She produced a crystal, and peering into its depths, she informed the watchman that she could identify the thief. Just as he suspected, the wise woman named Steffens the piper. For three more groschen, she offered to help him get his revenge. She promised that she would strike out one of the piper's eyes—a common curse used in countermagic. The magistrates had heard enough. Denouncing Vogt's "unchristian and devilish crimes," they passed sentence: he was to be beaten through the streets of Erfurt by the hangman and banished from the city for life.

Vogt's criminal file provides evidence of how victims of theft in early modern Germany turned to soothsayers to name thieves and even to seek vengeance through black magic. When the authorities questioned the wise woman he had employed, the testimony she delivered also affords us an exceedingly rare glimpse into the world of the era's professional fortunetellers. Eager to expose the diabolical nature of the woman's magical activities, the authorities questioned her about how she had managed to identify the thief. She admitted that she had used a crystal, explaining that when she gazed into it she saw a small black figure who answered all her questions. She reported that the figure appeared whenever she called upon him "in the name of the Father, the Son, and the Holy Ghost." Cunning folk often incorporated Christian phrases and iconography into their magical operations, reflecting the syncretic nature of folk religion. Accordingly, soothsayers and their clients did not consider fortune-telling to be a demonic or unchristian activity. Theologians, however, were unequivocal. Despite the Christian trappings, theologians preached that all divination drew its power from the devil, and the wise woman's invocation of the Trinity did not help her.

Pushing on, the magistrates compelled her to admit that she had actually called upon the devil to work her witchcraft. Under torture, the soothsayer confessed to having used black magic against the suspected thief, Nickell Steffens, and even revealed her method. She testified that after she collected her fee from Vogt, she had pounded a nail into a bench, uttering a curse: "Strike out Nickell's eye in the name of the devil." She specified that for the hex to work, the nail had to be found on a Friday, explaining that she had learned the method from "the wise woman of Daferstedt, called Martha."

As the questioning continued, the confessions that the authorities elicited grew darker—and conformed more closely to demonological expectations about witchcraft. Relying on torture and leading questions to elicit and shape her confession, they drew forth tales of demonic seduction and evil hexes. She admitted to having used a hex to kill Gertrude, a woman who had had an affair with the wise woman's husband, by hammering one of her cursed nails into the woman's front door. She also testified that she had met the devil several times: first in the guise of a charcoal burner in Ilvershofen, a village outside Erfurt. He asked her to cut her finger and sign herself over to him with her blood, telling her that he would be "her Pfarrherr" (pastor) and that she would benefit from his counsel. Likely in a last-ditch effort to save her life, she told the magistrates that she had "refused to make a pact with him, much less commit fornication with him."

The wise woman testified that the devil had come to her several more times in an attempt to get her to give herself over to him, including one occasion on a bridge before the city gate, when he appeared with one foot like that of a goat and the other like a goose. The scribe noted that at this point she paused in her testimony, begging the magistrates for mercy. They didn't grant it. Her official sentence does not survive, but a terse note appended to her file reveals her fate. The wise woman of Erfurt died at the stake.[30]

The 1587 case of the wise woman of Erfurt demonstrates how seriously the municipal officials began to take soothsaying as witchcraft fears swept through the region. It is also an exception. While the case initially centered on soothsaying, the wise woman of Erfurt revealed that she did not restrict her occult activities to divination. Under interrogation, she confessed that she had formed a pact with the devil and had used black magic to maim and to kill. This turned a soothsaying case into much more and eventually led to her execution. In fact, it is the only case I uncovered in the Thuringian archives where the authorities enforced the statutory penalties for divination, executing a soothsayer and banishing her client. However, it is not an example of the harsh punishment demanded by the authorities for divination. Rather, it appears that in this case the officials of Erfurt arrested a soothsayer only to find a witch.

* * *

Martin Luther and his fellow evangelical reformers urged parishioners to abandon soothsaying, condemned as diabolical since the earliest days of the Reformation. In the first generation of the Protestant Reformation, the Lutheran clergy included the suppression of popular forms of divination in its efforts to remake the Christian community through preaching, catechizing, and confession. Early visitation efforts in Thuringia sought to uncover fortune-telling and to ensure that Lutheran pastors remained diligent in preaching against the supposedly demonic practice.

Despite the reformers' high hopes, these ambitious pastoral efforts met with indifference in the region's parishes. Visitation records from midcentury reveal the clergy's frustration that many sinful behaviors, including soothsaying, remained widespread in the countryside. As Gerald Strauss pointed out long ago, the early reformers' lofty goals often ended in failure and frustration.[31] Their early efforts to root out fortune-telling tell a similar story.

In the face of these difficulties, the Lutheran clergy could not rely on much help from the region's secular authorities, as prosecution for soothsaying proved haphazard into the 1560s. A strident new demonological literature appeared after midcentury, however, supplanting earlier works on witchcraft and sorcery. Without exception, these influential works, whether written by Protestants or Catholics, witch-hunters or skeptics, advocated harsh punishment for diviners and their clients. Calling for enhanced discipline amid rising confessional tensions, they called upon secular authorities to aid the clergy by bringing capital punishment to bear against soothsayers.

As apocalyptic anxieties, confessional hostilities, and witchcraft fears mounted at the close of the sixteenth century, harsh new laws against divination show a growing concern with it among Thuringia's secular authorities. Meanwhile, the execution of the wise woman of Erfurt in 1587 demonstrate that at least some authorities in the region were willing to execute soothsayers—at least those who became implicated in witchcraft allegations. Of course, this 1587 case was unique, and the region's rulers usually proved reluctant to execute or even punish fortune-tellers. It would be another six decades, after the trauma of the Thirty Years' War before demonologists began calling upon secular authorities to execute diviners and their clients alike.

4

"HEATHENISH AND FORBIDDEN ABOMINATIONS"

Condemnations of Fortune-Telling during the Wars of Religion

Ernst the Pious (1653)

Duke Ernst I of Saxe-Gotha took the throne in 1640, amid the chaos and destruction of the Thirty Years' War. Having come of age in a time of war, Ernst had fought for the Protestant cause in Swedish service and knew well the horrors of battle. As soon as he began his reign, the new ruler set about trying to restore order in his realm. For Duke Ernst, dubbed "Ernst the Pious," the way to bring peace and prosperity to his shattered duchy was to foster an intense Lutheran piety among his subjects. Accordingly, Ernst quickly introduced regular visitations, mandatory catechism instruction, and compulsory education. Within two years of taking the throne, with war still raging in Germany, Ernst also began construction of a new palace, one he would eventually name Schloss Friedenstein (Stone of Peace) in celebration of the Peace of Westphalia.

When the last foreign troops finally left the devastated region in 1650, Ernst set about surveying the damage wrought by decades of war, which had brought violence, pestilence, and hunger to his beleaguered subjects. Having lost his father as a boy, Ernst had been raised at his uncle's court in Weimar, where devout court preachers and tutors instructed him and instilled in him the rigorous regimen of prayer, catechism study, and Bible reading that would shape his intense piety. They also taught the young prince that calamities like the Thirty Years' War were God's punishment for sin left unpunished, and Ernst's wartime decrees invariably present true repentance as the only way of averting God's wrath and restoring peace and prosperity. In a fiery 1647 proclamation, for example, Duke Ernst declared that the ongoing miseries of war were "God's whip and rod of anger," which would continue until the populace repented of their sins.[1]

Given his ardent belief that the horrors of the war had been caused by unpunished sin, Ernst the Pious sought to restore order by instructing his subjects in the Christian faith and through the imposition of rigid discipline. In 1653, he issued his *Landesordnung,* a draconian new territorial law code aimed at promoting Lutheran piety and punishing sin. His determination to stamp out sin—including soothsaying—as a means of averting divine wrath stemmed from his staunch religiosity, prompted by the preaching of the Lutheran clergy and the tracts of prominent theologians and demonologists, works housed in his impressive ducal library in Schloss Friedenstein.

This chapter explores the harsh condemnation of popular divination penned by theologians and demonologists in the wake of the Thirty Years' War, which prompted Thuringian rulers like Ernst to take a harder stance against soothsaying. The bitter memory of the war years inspired Lutheran clerics to redouble their efforts against divination, which they blamed for its horrors. Meanwhile, territorial rulers, seeking to stem the tide of disorder, renewed their determination to enforce confessional conformity and police moral behavior. Seeking to harness these disciplinary energies, demonologists and theologians attacked homespun forms of divination with increasing vigor after the war. Amid the disorder, anxiety, and trauma that followed the conflict, clerics who had survived it urged rulers to take violent action against diviners. By the 1650s, the Lutheran clergy's strident condemnations prompted secular authorities to intensify their efforts to prohibit popular forms of divination.

Demonology and Divination on the Eve of War

In the decades before the outbreak of the Thirty Years' War, tensions between Protestants and Catholics, and between adherents of Luther and Calvin, were rising in Germany. The threat of war loomed as confessional animosities mounted and witch-hunting began in earnest. In these

Contemporaries hailed Duke Ernst the Pious as the model Protestant prince, as in this hagiographic account of his reign published several years after his death. From *Wolverdiente Ehren-Seule / Dem weyland Durchläuchtigsten Fürsten und Herrn / Herrn Ernst Hertzogen zu Sachsen . . . Aufgerichtet zum Friedenstein* (1678). (Thüringer Universitäts- und Landesbibliothek UrMEL Digitization Database)

anxious times, ardent demonologists, Lutheran, Catholic, and Calvinist alike, reiterated the centuries-old notion that soothsaying was inherently diabolical. Likewise, they chastised rulers in increasingly strident terms for neglecting their duty to punish the grave sin of divination and began urging them to use capital punishment to deal with soothsayers and their clients. Lutheran pastors, working to instruct the laity in proper piety and stamp out sin and superstition, proved especially concerned with the practice of folk magic.[2] As Lutheran clerics redoubled their efforts to suppress occult activities, divination became an increasingly prominent target of their pastoral and disciplinary writings.

The Lutheran superintendent of Mecklenburg, Andreas Celichius, for example, condemned soothsaying unequivocally in a 1593 work. Citing the well-worn biblical stories of the so-called witch of Endor and the soothsaying slave girl from Acts, he hammered home God's prohibition of fortune-telling. Warning against the occult practice in starkly apocalyptic terms, Celichius accentuated soothsaying's diabolical nature and the threat posed by the devil's lies. Like other Lutheran authorities, he also called for stricter punishment of diviners, presenting them as agents of Satan's wrath amid the looming end-times.[3]

At the start of the seventeenth century, a Lutheran pastor from Nebra named David Meder published a series of sermons on witchcraft and sorcery that also pushed for harsher punishment of soothsayers. More importantly, his homilies boiled down the learned theological opposition to divination in an effort to disseminate it to the laity. Published in 1605, Meder's book of sermons condemned fortune-telling in conventional terms by asserting that "all magicians, sorcerers, soothsayers, and spellcasters" were united by a shared pact with the devil.[4] Building his case that popular forms of divination were inherently demonic, Meder related the story of the "Erfurt soothsayer" from Luther's *Table Talk*, repeating the reformer's account word-for-word for his audience.[5] Having asserted the diabolical threat posed by divination, Meder called upon secular authorities to remember their God-given responsibility to wield the sword against these "baneful people and to extirpate their sins and deeds with utmost seriousness."[6] Citing the book of Jeremiah, Meder warned rulers that the failure to punish not only witches but also soothsayers would bring down the Lord's wrath as it did upon the inhabitants of ancient Moab.[7]

While Lutherans like Celichius and Meder were particularly concerned with popular magical practices, they were not alone in excoriating soothsayers. Catholic authorities proved equally committed to their destruction. Writing in 1590, the notorious Catholic bishop of Trier, Peter Binsfeld, for example, proved eager to see diviners executed. Having presided over a savage witch-hunt in Trier that claimed hundreds of lives, Binsfeld published an account of the prosecutions, meant to justify the affair. Like his Lutheran rivals, Binsfeld did not restrict his condemnation to witchcraft. Rather, he wrote scathingly about common forms of divination as well.

Citing Catholic authorities reaching back to Augustine, Binsfeld reinforced the ancient assertion that soothsaying, a form of heresy like sorcery and witchcraft, was accomplished only through "the power and help of the devil." Citing Thomas Aquinas, he listed various forbidden means of acquiring this occult knowledge such as interpreting dreams, consulting the dead, reading palms, interpreting omens, and casting lots, presenting them as all equally worthy of harsh punishment.[8]

Arguing that divination had fundamental affinities with witchcraft and heresy, heinous crimes punished by burning at the stake, he asserted that diviners deserved the same judgment.[9] Binsfeld called upon magistrates to use sword and fire to deal with "fortune-tellers and sorcerers, [who were] not only the children of Belial, but also the servants of Beelzebub, Behemoth, Astaroth, and similar vermin," since they "lead many from the towns, villages, and other places to the devil and into his unfortunate servitude."[10] Writing in an era of frenzied witchcraft prosecution, the Catholic bishop viewed divination as a demonic threat akin to witchcraft, one that demanded a strong response from secular authorities. For Binsfeld, this meant capital punishment.

The Reformed theologians of the era matched the revulsion at divination exhibited by their Lutheran and Catholic rivals. In 1608, for example, the Calvinist theologian Abraham Scultetus, court preacher for the "winter king," Elector Frederick V of the Palatinate, delivered another scathing condemnation of divination. In a pair of sermons printed under the title *Warning against the Fortune-telling of Sorcerers and Astrologers* (*Warnung für der Warsagerey der Zauberer und Sterngucker*), Scultetus divided all magical practitioners into two "guilds," identifying the first of these as the fortune-tellers (*Warsager*), including "those who mark auspicious days, those who pay attention to the cries of birds, those who seek omens, those who have prophetic dreams, and those who ask questions of the dead."[11] The second guild was composed of maleficent sorcerers and witches.

Like centuries of Christian moralists before him, Scultetus asserted that witches and fortune-tellers alike drew their power from Satan.[12] Decrying the popularity of divination even among his own reformed parishioners, Scultetus made contempt for magical practitioners a sign of true Christian devotion. He declared that "whoever hates the devil in his heart, he also hates the devil's companions: all fortune-tellers, conjurers, and spell-casters."[13] Scultetus, like other theologians writing on the eve of the war, used the language of sin and morality in their attempts to persuade common people to turn their backs on folk magic.

Warning his flock that "God punishes sorcery with everlasting death," he instructed them to abandon divination in favor of faith in God's eternal plan.[14] Rather than rely on divination, which he derided as "entirely false and godless," Scultetus encouraged his parishioners to avoid this sinful temptation and turn toward Christian faith instead. Appealing directly to his audience (and echoing Isaiah 8:19), Scultetus urged them to turn to God for help, rather than some "gypsy" who turns up by the city gates when "they want to learn something or know something." He even sought to enlist their aid in his campaign against divination, advising them, when "people on the market or at home say to you that you must consult the fortune-teller (*Warsager*), spell-caster (*Segnerin*), and soothsayer (*Zeichendeuter*) to seek their help," ask them "should not a people turn to their God instead?"[15]

Scultetus hoped to convince his parishioners that prayer and faith in divine providence provided their best bulwark against misfortune and that turning to divination instead meant choosing the devil over God. He also did not shrink from advocating punishment for those who ignored God's commandments. Citing biblical injunctions against divination, he urged rulers to execute anyone who sealed a pact with the devil in an attempt to perform prognostication. According to Scultetus, even those who performed these forbidden rites without an explicit demonic pact deserved banishment.[16] Thus, at the dawn of the seventeenth century the Calvinist court preacher echoed other demonologists of the day, Lutheran, Catholic, and his fellow Calvinists, in calling for pious rulers to order the death penalty for soothsayers and harsh punishment for their clients. Meanwhile, war edged ever closer, and the terrible conflict that finally erupted in 1618 prompted Thuringia's Lutheran authorities to confront soothsaying with a renewed ferocity.

Soothsaying in Wartime Thuringia

The Thirty Years' War was an unparalleled disaster for the Holy Roman Empire, and few areas suffered as badly as Thuringia. The devastation wrought by the conflict and the enduring legacy of anxiety and hardship left in its wake brought a new urgency to the efforts of the region's Lutheran authorities—both clerical and secular—to eradicate popular forms of fortune-telling. As in the early days of the Reformation, however, Thuringian authorities confronted a burgeoning divinatory culture as they pursued this disciplinary agenda.

Ignoring their pastors, seventeenth-century villagers and townsfolk used popular forms of divination in an attempt to uncover hidden knowledge and to foretell the future—as they had always done. One prevalent type of divination, scrying, was used to reveal hidden identities, with clients consulting soothsayers to uncover thieves and witches or even in hopes of identifying future spouses. A dairymaid wondering about whom she would someday marry, a parent seeking to confirm suspicions about who had bewitched an ailing child, or a miller hoping to recover stolen grain all might turn to scryers for answers.

Scrying, an elaborate procedure where soothsayers conjured a visual image of a subject in a glass or a crystal, was on one end of a continuum of divinatory activities. Occult means of answering simple yes/no questions by manipulating a sieve and shears or a Bible and key lay on the other end of the continuum, with variants on casting lots, such as reading signs in droplets of lead or wax dripped into a container of water, or a handful of beans cast on the floor, somewhere in the middle. Whereas laypeople might make use of common forms of divination like casting beans or turning the sieve, more sophisticated forms like scrying, which relied upon keen perception of human relationships among clients and suspects, were generally the domain of professional cunning folk.[17]

Traditional forms of divination like casting lots, reading palms, and gazing into crystal balls or mirrors had been an important part of popular culture for centuries and remained so during the Thirty Years' War. Amid the chaotic conditions of the war years, official efforts to suppress magic and to prosecute witchcraft faltered in most areas of Germany, so quotidian magical activity does not appear in the archival record as often as it does before or after the conflict. Local officials were no doubt more concerned with marauding soldiers, epidemic disease, and widespread famine than in pursuing village witch-doctors and fortune-tellers, but it is also safe to assume that folk divination remained at least as prevalent as it had been before the war. After all, people's desire to use divination to deal with uncertainty and misfortune likely grew more intense amid the chaos and hardship of the war years.

The traumatic experience of the Thirty Years' War also affected elite attitudes toward learned astrology, causing enthusiasm for horoscopes and almanacs to wane. The ambiguous status of erudite forms of divination within Lutheran culture, a hallmark of early Reformation thought, endured into the 1600s, and astrological texts remained extremely popular in the decades prior to 1618. Before the war, educated Lutherans still eagerly sought astrological predictions that conformed to evangelical theological and eschatological understandings: between 1550 and 1620, more than thirteen hundred editions of popular astrological pamphlets appeared in Lutheran Germany.[18] Astrology also remained popular at court in the early seventeenth century. Johannes Kepler, the Lutheran astronomer famous for his discovery of the laws of planetary motion, for example, was employed at the court of Emperor Rudolph II at Prague between 1600 and 1612 primarily as an astrologer, casting horoscopes for courtiers and dignitaries.[19] Protestant communities also sought to discern

God's providence in marvels and portents, and broadsheets proclaiming such wonders proved exceedingly popular.[20] As long as these activities did not clash with Protestant theological conceptions regarding the primacy of divine providence and human free will, most Lutheran clerics tolerated them in the decades leading up to the war.[21]

Amid the chaos of the Thirty Years' War, the Lutheran clergy's enthusiasm for these pious forms of divination waned. As Robin Barnes has argued, the traumatic events and chronic uncertainty of the war years put an end to many Lutherans' faith in astrology as a way to discern God's will. As the conflict dragged on, and the fortunes of the Protestant camp waxed and waned, pious elites began looking to newsletters and broadsheets for information rather than the stars.[22] By the 1620s, leading Lutheran theologians had turned their backs on astrology, and humble pastors soon followed suit. In 1624, for example, a pastor named Henning Friedrich published a treatise in Erfurt condemning astrological almanacs as idolatrous and unsuitable for the Christian home.[23] After the war ended, theologians and demonologists, increasingly disillusioned with astrology, also proved more determined than ever to stamp out the popular forms of fortune-telling that had proliferated during the conflict, occult activities they had long opposed.

The Thirty Years' War came to Thuringia in 1620. The region was among the hardest hit by the war's terrible devastation, as troops burned villages, spread disease, and displaced streams of refugees. Thuringia experienced a full generation of violence and hardship at the hands of rampaging mercenary armies, who did not end their brutal occupation until 1650.[24] The destruction was particularly acute between 1630 and 1635, as Swedish and imperial forces clashed in the region, their troops supporting themselves through plunder and extortion. Thuringian villagers, caught between these rapacious armies, were left starving, made refugees, or murdered.

Thuringia suffered at the hands of marauding armies, Catholic and Protestant, as hungry soldiers requisitioned supplies and ruthless generals burned villages to deny sustenance to their enemies. In 1631, Tilly's Catholic forces ravaged Thuringia after their infamous sack of Magdeburg. The following year, imperial troops under Pappenheim plundered the region again on the eve of the battle of Lützen, burning a dozen villages and slaughtering many of the inhabitants.[25] The Swedes also rampaged through Thuringia. In October 1634, Swedish forces retreated into Thuringia after their defeat at Nördlingen, occupying Erfurt and quartering troops throughout the devastated region.

By 1635, Thuringia had become a battleground as Swedish troops fought pitched skirmishes with imperial forces stationed in the region. Amid the chaos, Protestant and Catholic troops both put settlements to the torch: imperial troops burned parts of Großbrüchter and Mühlhausen in 1635, and Swedish forces burned the village of Waltershausen the following year.[26] The winter of 1634–5 was a particularly bitter time of hunger and misery for the inhabitants of the beleaguered region. In the later 1630s, repeated outbreaks of plague ravaged Thuringia, and then at the end of the decade the survivors experienced the worst famine in living memory.[27]

Thuringia was shattered by the war, having lost almost half of its population to famine, disease, or displacement before the last foreign troops finally left the area in 1650.[28] In the decade after the occupying troops finally left the region, Lutheran pastors who had lived through the trauma of the war years preached sermons that presented the conflict as part of a diabolical attack on the Protestant community. For these preachers, amid the chaos of war the devil had used witchcraft and magic as a way to lure devout Christians into damnation. At the same time, they preached that order and decency could be restored after the horrors of the war years only if Christian piety was rejuvenated and Lutheran religiosity stringently enforced. Thus, they cast divination as a grave sin and called on rulers to punish it accordingly.

During the postwar period a number of Lutheran pastors published sermons in an effort to disseminate the learned theological condemnation of soothsaying. These sermon collections called upon pastors to use the pulpit to help eradicate divination by transmitting the learned clerical discourse on its evils to their congregants in their own homilies. Clergy also hoped their sermons would prompt rulers to punish diviners and their clients with renewed severity. In one such work, published in 1660, a Lutheran pastor in Frankfurt am Main named Bernhard Waldschmidt offered a series of sermons based on the Old Testament story of the so-called witch of Endor.[29] As chapter 1 showed, the Endor story had fascinated theologians and demonologists since the fifteenth century. Interestingly, in his title Waldschmidt identified the woman as the "Pythonissa Endorea," that is, as an oracle, rather than as a "witch." His conflation of witchcraft and divination reflects his fierce determination to root out soothsaying in the wake of wartime devastation. Striking an apocalyptic tone, in his first sermon he preached that in these miserable "last days" his parishioners were suffering under the devil's increasing rage (*Zorn*), and with it the terrible sin of divination was becoming evermore prevalent.[30]

Violently opposed to soothsaying, Waldschmidt explained that there were permissible ways of foretelling the future. He included divine prophecies like those described in the Old Testament, which were accomplished through the Holy Spirit, and "natural" forms of divination like medical prognoses and astrology, which he claimed are based upon natural laws. Likewise, a theologian or pastor could predict that the prayers of the faithful would bring divine mercy or that the impenitence of the sinful would bring God's wrath. Conversely, he asserted that popular forms of fortune-telling, which he termed "*Divinatione infernali,*" could only be accomplished with a demonic pact, whether through speech alone (as described in Acts 16:16) or in the use of instruments like a crystal ball or sieve and shears.[31]

Preaching that foreknowledge was God's privilege alone, he asserted that anyone who "predicted future things with the aid of the devil or his instruments, the sorcerers, wise men, mirror- and crystal-seers," robbed God of the honor of his omniscience.[32] Warning his parishioners that soothsayers often made use of Christian sayings or invoked the Lord in their magical operations, he went on to charge nevertheless that those who consulted diviners might as well throw God from his throne and replace him with the devil, "the great dragon, the old serpent, Satan."[33] In his sermons, Waldschmidt preached against diviners *and* their clients. Thus, he went on to condemn not only these professional diviners, including "gypsies, wise men, crystal- and mirror-seers, and sieve-drivers," but also "the people among us who when something is lost, run to such wise men and wise women, to old witches and hags, hoping to find the thief."[34]

It is notoriously difficult for modern historians to assess how parishioners took such injunctions from their pastors, but Waldschmidt gives us a clear indication of how he thought the campaign against divination was going. He ended his work by lamenting that his parishioners were ignoring his sermons about the dangers of soothsaying. While this might have been included merely for dramatic effect, or simply represents the typical complaint of an underappreciated pastor, it also speaks to the continued popularity of divination in the late seventeenth century. According to Waldschmidt, despite the clear command of God and warnings of pastors, Christian communities still teemed with "those who run after the soothsayers, in order to do nothing else but seek the help and counsel of the devil."[35]

For Waldschmidt, as for many of his clerical colleagues, the solution was harsher punishment for diviners, and he called on secular rulers to provide it. Casting soothsayers as "Satan's children," he pointed to Old Testament prohibitions of divination to justify capital punishment for their evil deeds. The Lutheran pastor preached that all "Christian authorities" were bound by "God's word and their office" to punish soothsayers, denounced as "instruments of the devil," with fire and sword.[36]

Waldschmidt was not alone in his attempts to fight against divination from the pulpit in the decades after the Thirty Years' War. In 1667 another influential book of sermons appeared that sought to persuade the Lutheran faithful to abandon popular magical practices and rulers to punish soothsayers. The author, a Lutheran pastor in Esslingen named Johann Jacob Faber, also railed against divination in strident terms, equating it even more closely with witchcraft than Waldschmidt.

In 1639, Faber had fled his hometown of Giengen amid the horrors of the Thirty Years' War and settled in Esslingen. Before taking the pulpit in Esslingen, he had experienced the horrors of war firsthand: rampaging soldiers had repeatedly sacked his hometown, with imperial forces putting it to the torch after their victory at Nördlingen in September 1632. Long after the war, the trauma it produced seems to have haunted the refugee pastor, and a decade after the end of the conflict he helped ignite a vicious witch-hunt in his new parish. Between 1662 and 1665, thirty-three suspected witches went to the flames in the city.[37] Defending the witch hunt, Faber published a book of sermons on witchcraft and sorcery in 1667, preaching that punishing the grave sin of witchcraft was necessary to avert God's wrath.[38]

Faber did not restrict himself to condemning witchcraft, however. He also warned of the dangers of divination. According to the Esslingen pastor, divination stood as one of the greatest challenges facing the postwar Christian community. In his book of sermons, sprinkled with advice for his fellow Lutheran pastors, he excoriated practitioners of divination, including soothsayers and fortune-tellers, "who foretold the future or found lost things." He condemned the activities of these diviners, whether they gained their occult insights through "inspiration from the devil, or through crystals, mirrors, the cry of birds, viscera, or animals, or through the spirits, which men call '*Spiritus familiares*.'" Accentuating these soothsayers' supposed diabolical associations—and using martial language that evoked the horrors of the war years—he presented them as members of the "hellish host, the sinful guild and great armada of the demonic war-captain," Satan.[39]

Johann Faber's abhorrence of divination was shaped by his traumatic experiences during the Thirty Years' War. Blaming "old papist superstition" for demonic sorcery and divination, he proclaimed that the "hellish sorcerers-guild and witch-vermin in Germany" had caused the catastrophic war, as well as the pestilence and starvation it brought in its wake.[40] He offered his sermons as a defense against the devil's machinations. Urging secular authorities to punish cunning folk and their clients, he prayed for the day when divination, along with the evil folk who practiced it, would be eradicated.[41] The devastation wrought by the war evoked a desperate plea for action from the Esslingen pastor.

Faber's sermons are a good example of the dialectic between the print culture of theologians and demonologists and the oral culture of villagers and townsfolk, with the sermon bridging the gap between the two. The pastor referred to the works of influential demonologists from both sides of the confessional divide, citing the *Malleus maleficarum* and the works of Catholic authorities like Peter Binsfeld and Martin del Rio alongside the sermons of his Lutheran colleague Waldschmidt. Despite three decades of religious war, Faber reached across the confessional divide to support his warnings about the threat of diabolical magic, using his fiery sermons to boil down these ponderous demonological tomes for his parishioners.

Faber also marshalled his biblical knowledge to warn of God's wrath and to link divination and witchcraft. He reminded his flock of God's punishment of the Hebrew king Manasseh, who had restored pagan practices including "all manner of sorcery, witchcraft, divination, and soothsaying." He recalled for them how the Lord had brought the Assyrians to destroy Manasseh's kingdom as punishment for his sins, a potent warning with the horrors of the Thirty Years' War still so fresh.[42] Returning to the sins of his own flock, Faber warned that people in the thrall of the devil could be found on any German street, just as in ancient Canaan. Thus, he drew a striking parallel between the idolatry of ancient paganism and modern folk magic and between the divine punishment God had visited upon the ancient Israelites and the more recent devastation Germany had suffered during the Thirty Years' War.

The Esslingen pastor conflated witchcraft and more benign forms of magic, and he warned that these diabolical activities risked bringing God's wrath down upon the community. He preached that "damned sorcery, spell casting, witchcraft, soothsaying, fortune-telling, and similar superstition are abominable and repulsive sins" that were all equally worthy of God's punishment.[43] The theological notion of earthly calamities as punishment from God for sins within the Christian community had long been a prominent feature of Protestant theological discourse, and it was given a powerful impetus by the catastrophe of the Thirty Years' War. In 1605, the Lutheran pastor David Meder had warned his parishioners that God would punish them for their soothsaying as he had the ancient Moabites. The horrors of the Thirty Years' War had seemingly brought such warnings to pass. Seeking to restore order in the wake of the calamity, pastors like Faber who had survived the war used the threat of divine wrath to dissuade the faithful from resorting to divination and to persuade secular authorities to punish it more stringently.[44]

Throughout his fiery sermons, Faber portrayed divination as an inherently sinful pursuit based upon a satanic pact. Condemning those who "conjure the devil, or other occult images, in a glass, or show something stolen in a sieve or in water, or predict and reveal future things in peculiar ways," Faber left no doubt about how these soothsayers worked their wonders. He preached that these evil soothsayers derived their sinister powers through a "*Spiritus familiares,*" a demonic spirit in the form of a spider, a fly, a dog, or a cat.[45] Warning his audience to avoid these magical practitioners, he argued that even if diviners clothed their wicked art in Christian trappings like "biblical words, psalms, sayings, Pater nosters, or Ave marias," their activities were nevertheless superstitious and forbidden by God's commandments.[46]

Faber was horrified that divination remained so prominent within the Lutheran community and preached that Satan used it to ensnare unwary Christians. The Esslingen pastor complained that "there are people, who in sickness, in missing this or that stolen item, or in other types of misfortune, consult all kinds of suspicious people, spell casters, crystal seers, sieve drivers, and use their services." Cautioning his parishioners, he warned that these misguided fools thereby allowed "the devil to bind their hands and feet with his magical fetters (*Zauberstricken*)."[47] Thus, Faber preached that even seemingly benign magical pursuits represented a grave threat to the embattled Lutheran faith, and to Christian salvation, one that needed to be eradicated.

Faber viewed the prevalence of divination in light of the violence and devastation wrought by the war, and he presented the disorder it spawned in apocalyptic terms.[48] Citing Revelation 12:12, he asserted that the devil's rage in his own day showed that he and his parishioners were living in the prophesied end-times and explained the proliferation of sin throughout the land. Faber warned that the devil, hoping to carry the souls of wayward Christians into his hellish kingdom before the imminent Last Judgment, stood behind the rising tide of "sorcery, divination, witchcraft, incest, and bestiality" that had appeared in the wake of the conflict.[49] He saw his sermons as a defense against the devil's schemes and admonished his audience to remain vigilant against the wiles of Satan and his minions and to struggle against demonic temptation.

For Faber, the clergy formed an essential bulwark against these hellish superstitions, and he advised that pastors "should with all possible diligence eradicate the shameful, blasphemous art of divination completely from their churches." Anyone found to be dependent on this craft "should be made red-faced with shame and entirely excluded from the community."[50] He advised pastors to deal in three stages with members of their congregation denounced by their neighbors for dabbling in the occult. First, the pastor should preach in "living color" about the evils of magic and sorcery, in an attempt to dissuade them from taking part. If his wayward parishioners did not turn from divination, the pastor should follow up with private exhortations. As a last resort, Faber advised pastors to ban recalcitrant "sorcerers and soothsayers" from confession and communion, especially if the secular authorities proved slow to punish this "great and grotesque vice."[51] Recognizing the need for the clergy to enlist rulers to help in eradicating divination, the Esslingen pastor seems to have understood that the secular authorities often failed to perform this duty.

Like other Protestant theologians, Faber counseled Lutheran pastors to exhort rulers to punish diviners and their customers alike. He urged secular authorities to do their duty by punishing "all magical and superstitious people" who dabbled in "sorcery, soothsaying, fortune-telling, spell-casting, and other devilish arts."[52] In addition, the Esslingen pastor charged secular authorities with chastising all those who "kept company with such people and relied upon their guidance and help" and prayed for the day when these "heathenish and forbidden abominations," along with the evil sorcerers and soothsayers who committed them, would be rooted out of the Christian community.[53] Faber's call for official action against soothsayers did not fall on deaf ears, and at least one Thuringian ruler took up the preacher's challenge.

Divination Prohibitions in Seventeenth-Century Thuringia

The trauma of the Thirty Years' War, and the impassioned clerical condemnations it spawned, also affected official disciplinary initiatives in postwar Germany. The ardent opposition to divination so apparent in the theological discourse of the confessional era was reflected in the laws of seventeenth-century Thuringia. Duke Ernst I, the Thuringian prince encountered at the beginning of this chapter, appeared particularly hell-bent on enforcing godly discipline in his realm. Seeking to restore order in the wake of the Thirty Years' War, he launched a comprehensive campaign to instill piety and reform morality among his subjects in the tiny Thuringian principality of Saxe-Gotha, a territory he had carved out while fighting for the Swedes.

Taking the throne in 1640, Duke Ernst sought to enforce strict Lutheran religiosity within the duchy. Known as Ernst the Pious, he was hailed in his day as the model Protestant prince, his reforms immortalized and idealized in Veit Ludwig von Seckendorf's *Teutscher Fürsten-Staat*. This influential 1656 work, which went through twelve editions by 1754, sought to instruct princes on how best to administer their realms and was informed by Seckendorf's service at Ernst's court.[54] As he sought to restore order and stability, Ernst worked to establish compulsory education, to reinforce catechetical instruction, and to build an impressive ducal library filled with classic literary, philosophical, and legal works, along with theological treatises and books of Lutheran sermons. He also issued stringent territorial ordinances and sought to police the behavior of his subjects.

As part of these disciplinary efforts, Ernst issued a number of ordinances and mandates intended to compel his subjects to abandon divination, efforts that were part of a broad program of moral reform aimed at maintaining Lutheran orthodoxy within the duchy. Stamping out demonic "superstitions"—including divination—was prominent in these efforts.[55] In an attempt to inculcate his staunchly Lutheran aversion to divination among his subjects, Ernst authorized a series of sermon instructions for the duchy's clergy, instructions that charged them with preaching against occult prognostication. These directives echoed the published sermons of clerical authorities like Faber and Waldschmidt, whose works had a place in Ernst's ducal library at Schloss Friedenstein in Gotha. In Faber's 1667 book of sermons, for example, he had advocated sermons as the cornerstone of Lutheran efforts to stamp out sorcery and divination. The Esslingen pastor instructed the clergy that it was their responsibility to remind their congregants that "all Christians and children of God" risked divine wrath if the godly magistrate failed to punish "soothsayers, spell-casters, and devil-worshippers." Grouping these sinners together with "the incestuous, sodomites, and other unclean dogs," he warned rulers that if they failed to act, God's anger would fall on the entire community.[56] In his own directions to his pastors, Ernst took up this charge, proving equally forceful in his condemnation of divination.

Duke Ernst's sermon instructions demonstrate how central the campaign against divination was to his efforts to reinvigorate Lutheran devotion in his realm. They informed the duchy's pastors about what to include in their sermons on "superstitious practices," which the frustrated authorities complained "are very prevalent in our times."[57] Citing the writings of Martin Luther and the Acts of the Apostles, the instructions required pastors to preach about the spiritual perils of divination, warning their congregants to avoid popular folk customs relating to auspicious days, astrological horoscopes, or portentous omens lest they suffer eternal damnation. They also directed pastors to instill fear in the hearts of their parishioners by teaching them that divination was nothing but "devilish idolatry" and as such a damnable violation of God's first commandment. Finally, they required the local pastorate to remind the duke's subjects that God orders the magistrate to punish such superstition severely, in an effort to deter them from dabbling in the occult.

Duke Ernst buttressed these pastoral initiatives with a series of legal prohibitions that treated divination as a serious criminal offense. The legal mandates he issued built upon foundations laid by his Wettin ancestors, who had long prohibited divination. In the comprehensive territorial ordinance that was the cornerstone of his disciplinary campaign, Duke Ernst dealt harshly with divination. First issued in 1653, the ordinance was reissued in an expanded version in 1667 and drove reform efforts in the duchy until the end of Ernst's reign. Decrying the prevalence of fortune-tellers among his subjects, he complained that "many endeavor to perform divination, and others attempt to get advice from soothsayers," declaring his intention to rid his domain of these evil sinners. Accordingly, Ernst decreed that those who consorted with the devil in order to divine hidden or future things, that is, itinerant fortune-tellers and village cunning folk, were to be beheaded. Concerned with maintaining Christian piety within the duchy, Ernst also prohibited his subjects from consulting these professional soothsayers and ordered that anyone who visited such "crystal-gazers and fortune-tellers" risked imprisonment, fines, or even banishment from the territory.[58] The draconian nature of the duke's proscription of divination demonstrates his determination to deter his subjects from seeking occult knowledge, but apprehending soothsayers or those who consulted them proved challenging.

Divination was a clandestine activity, performed far from the prying eyes of the ducal authorities. Consequently, Ernst relied upon the pious laymen who staffed the local circuit courts (*Rügegerichten*) to uncover forbidden occult activities and punish their wayward neighbors. The circuit courts met four times a year in every town, village, and rural district in the duchy, judging offenders rumored to have engaged in immoral behaviors. Divination figured prominently among the list of offenses these courts were to investigate, and Ernst ordered the circuit court judges to find out whether "anyone had invoked the devil or practiced divination . . . or sought counsel from a devil-conjurer," meaning a professional fortune-teller.[59] He authorized them to punish anyone found to have engaged in these activities with imprisonment, fines, or hard labor. They were to report particularly serious cases to the consistory for further punishment. As in Faber's Esslingen, the anxieties spawned by the Thirty Years' War and the survivors' frantic efforts to restore order fostered an atmosphere conducive not only to hunting witches, but also to suppressing popular magical activities like fortune-telling.

At the dawn of the seventeenth century, as confessional tensions mounted in Europe, demonologists attacked divination with renewed vigor. As deadly witch-hunts gripped Germany, theologians and demonologists, Lutheran, Catholic, and Calvinist alike, railed against the danger of soothsaying, working to link it with witchcraft. In a flurry of new demonological treatises that supplanted earlier works from the fifteenth and early sixteenth centuries, these moralists called on secular authorities to punish fortune-tellers and those who consulted them.

In the wake of the Thirty Years' War, a conflict that gripped Thuringia with particular ferocity, the region's pastors preached fiery sermons in hopes of persuading their parishioners to eschew fortune-telling. Viewing the war and the horrors it unleashed as part of Satan's attempts to destroy the evangelical community, these pastors also urged the region's rulers to stamp out sinful divination. It was amid the chaos and anxiety spawned by the war that the campaign against divination became part of a larger effort to restore order and instill discipline in postwar Thuringia. Calling for capital punishment, the region's pastors, haunted by their wartime experiences, urged Protestant princes to eradicate divination in the name of instilling godly discipline among their beleaguered subjects.

Thuringia's Ernestine princes responded to these calls by issuing draconian legal prohibitions against divination, part of a campaign of enhanced disciplinary initiatives in the decade after the Thirty Years' War. One of these rulers, Duke Ernst I of Saxe-Gotha, took his responsibility to punish these sinners to heart. The next chapter explores the efforts of Thuringian princes like Ernst to rid their territories of divination through official punishment. As we will see, in postwar Thuringia these efforts proved far more daunting than pastors like Waldschmidt or Faber had imagined.

5

"BORN UNDER AN UNLUCKY SIGN"

Cunning Folk and Their Clients in an Age of Witch-Hunting

The Old Man of Streufdorf (1679)

In the summer of 1679, an aged villager named Caspar Nußmann appeared in the village church in Streufdorf to confess his sins before his neighbors. The ducal officials in Gotha had just released the poor linen weaver from custody after having charged him with consulting a soothsayer. The authorities decided to release the old man after he petitioned them for leniency, but they ordered him to confess before his congregation about dabbling with divination. In the parish church, before his fellow parishioners, Nußmann apologized for having consulted a pair of soothsayers, one in faraway Bavaria and another in nearby Westhausen, in hopes of recovering a measure of stolen linen. Recounting these sinful activities, he warned his fellows to eschew such forbidden activities. Satisfied with his public show of contrition, which no doubt gave the local pastor ample opportunity to rail against divination from the pulpit, the authorities allowed him to return home to his infirm wife.[1]

Nußmann's occult activities were quite familiar to the Thuringian villagers hearing his confession. As in all the towns and villages of early modern Germany, divination was an everyday activity. The most common goals of divination were to avoid personal misfortune or deal with its effects. Thus, individuals performed simple divinatory rites for themselves or consulted professional soothsayers to identify thieves who had stolen their property or unmask witches who posed mortal danger to their family and livestock.

Divination had been practiced for centuries with common people's use of folk magic continually condemned and prohibited by clerical and secular authorities. While learned elites, secular and clerical alike, often practiced their own learned natural magic with impunity, they assumed the unlettered could only accomplish magical feats with the assistance of the devil. Anxiety about folk magic intensified in the fifteenth century, and late medieval demonologists penned fiery condemnations of popular divination. The Reformation bred renewed opposition to soothsaying, and as confessional tensions mounted at the end of the sixteenth century, Lutheran clerics redoubled their efforts to suppress it. In the wake of the Thirty Years' War, Lutheran theologians preached that earthly calamities were a manifestation of God's wrath at sin left unpunished, and folk magic figured prominently in their catalog of vices.[2] Amid the lingering hardship and anxiety in the decades after the war, rulers answered the clerical call to wield the sword of justice and intensified their disciplinary efforts by issuing new statutes and sought to restore order by punishing a wide range of moral infractions.

Witch-hunting also intensified in the region after the Thirty Years' War. As witchcraft suspicions were often mediated through divination that cunning folk and witch-doctors performed, officials began to show more interest in uncovering instances of soothsaying. Thus, the archival records from seventeenth-century Thuringia examined in this chapter shed light on divination's role in popular culture and the tenacious hold of these occult practices. The region's secular authorities redoubled their efforts to prohibit and punish witchcraft and divination after the war, encouraged by the clerical establishment. Meanwhile, many commoners continued to rely upon one form of banned magic, divination, to deal with the other, witchcraft. Although postwar legislation prohibited soothsaying and prescribed heavy penalties for diviners and their clients, villagers' suspicions that they or their families had been bewitched prompted them to seek occult assistance. Soothsayers could confirm witchcraft suspicions and offer powerful means of resolution and sometimes retribution. Recourse to these age-old responses to bewitchment, though, put them at odds with the local authorities. As we will see, in the age of the witch hunts, secular authorities in Thuringia were determined to impose godly discipline among their subjects by issuing laws, ordering sermons, and levying punishments aimed at rooting out divination.

Despite the harsh laws and surveillance measures rulers enacted in the wake of the Thirty Years' War, divination was usually performed in secret. Consequently, it rarely came to light in Thuringia. While it was a commonplace activity in the region's villages, very few cases came before the local courts and punishment of fortune-tellers and their clients always remained haphazard. The cases that survive in the region's archives show that the hard-line stance of the era's legislation, which called for the death penalty for soothsayers and banishment, imprisonment, or heavy fines for their clients, was not reflected in actual verdicts. When soothsaying came to the local authorities' attention, they generally treated it as a nuisance crime, not only ignoring their own ordinances, but also the advice of Lutheran theologians and demonologists. Therefore, while laws against soothsaying in postwar Thuringia suggest a fierce resolve to prohibit the practice, in practice rulers still proved reluctant to bring the full force of their penal authority to bear against diviners.

Soothsaying and Witch-Hunting in Seventeenth-Century Thuringia

As Thuringia's authorities scoured the villages of the region hunting witches after 1650, they also encountered cunning folk. Although some divination cases came to their attention after diviners or their clients were denounced by their neighbors, soothsaying remained a shadowy, closed-door affair and usually only came to light as officials collected testimony during the course of witchcraft investigations. Many of these witchcraft cases involved the activities of cunning folk, who confirmed villagers' suspicions and emboldened the bewitched to take countermeasures. These diviners' involvement in substantiating witchcraft suspicions increasingly brought them to the attention of the authorities in the era of the witch hunts.

Intense witch-hunting came late to Thuringia and lasted in the region long after it had ceased in other areas of Germany. A recent study of witch-hunting in Thuringia identifies 1,565 witch trials in the region between

1526 and 1731. Witchcraft prosecution in Thuringia was rare until an enforcement wave hit that lasted from 1598 until 1631, peaking in 1629—a year with more than forty cases. Prosecutions dropped off sharply after 1631, as the Thirty Years' War raged in the region, until another significant period of witch-hunting began in 1656. The ravaged region, having lost half its population during the war, endured another witchcraft panic from 1656 to 1700, although isolated cases continued during the early eighteenth century. Seventy-five percent of these cases ended in the execution of the suspected witch, placing Thuringia statistically in line with the rest of German-speaking Europe, the so-called heartland of the witchcraze.[3]

As in the rest of Europe, witchcraft prosecution in Thuringia invariably began at the village level, after rumors of bewitchment reached the ducal officials or victims of witchcraft denounced a suspected witch to the secular authorities. As in other areas of Europe, denunciation usually stemmed from long-standing suspicions of *maleficium,* harmful magic that caused illness or death in children or animals, lameness in adults, or hampered milk production.[4] In Thuringia, villagers often took lice infestation within a household to be a sign of a witch's hex. When they suspected bewitchment, people generally brought charges against their neighbors only as a last resort. Testimony often revealed that the supposed witch had been under suspicion for decades before her frightened neighbors, who had sought to deal with her through various countermeasures, finally turned to the authorities. Countermeasures against witchcraft ranged from passive ones like avoiding the witch, using protective amulets, or praying to more active means like appeasing or threatening the witch, afflicting her through counter-magic, or resorting to mob violence. Before any of these measures could be employed, however, the witch needed to be identified, often with the aid of cunning folk.[5] For villagers, divination was a necessary first defense against the horrors of bewitchment. Bringing formal witchcraft accusations could be costly and even dangerous, as individuals often feared the revenge of suspected witches, magical or otherwise. Therefore, before approaching the authorities, villagers sought out diviners to confirm their suspicions and provide enough evidence to ensure a conviction. Once the authorities initiated an investigation into witchcraft charges, traces of these divinatory practices, usually obscured, sometimes entered the official record. Thus, in the seventeenth century it was ultimately the official obsession with hunting witches that revealed the clandestine divinatory practices carried out in Thuringian villages.

Soothsaying had long been illegal in Thuringia. Evidence suggests, however, that in the face of misfortune all sorts of people—ranging from the impoverished linen weaver in Streufdorf trying to recover stolen cloth to the ducal official in Aspach trying to find his missing ledger—turned to it anyway. In the wake of the Thirty Years' War, Lutheran pastors decried divination's ubiquity and blamed it for the war's devastation, and secular authorities intensified their efforts to root it out. As witch-hunting returned to the troubled region after 1650, however, local authorities encountered the shadowy occult activities of diviners and their customers more frequently than they had before the war. Pursuing witches in small towns and villages, they often collected testimony not only about witchcraft, but also about magical witch-finding. Witch-finding was an important form of folk divination, and people fearing bewitchment relied on a variety of means to find out who had placed a hex on them. Professional witch-finders sought to diagnose witchcraft and identify witches by gazing into the victim's eyes, scrutinizing drops of molten lead that had been dripped into basins of water, or examining the urine of the bewitched. With the surge in witch-hunting in seventeenth-century Thuringia, these forms of magical witch-finding became more prominent in the official record. As magistrates collected testimony about suspected bewitchment, they often included witnesses' consultations with witch-finders among the evidence against the accused. This indicates that while they deemed these activities illicit, they also trusted the occult insights of cunning folk.

Diviners before the Court in Postwar Thuringia

When witch-hunting returned to Thuringia after a lull during the chaos of the Thirty Years' War, the region's secular authorities began to take an increasing interest in the occult activities of soothsayers. While eager to burn witches, they proved less interested in executing diviners. Despite the draconian statutes against divination that rulers issued after the war, officials often failed to prosecute soothsayers or even to mount a serious investigation of their activities. Encouraged by the Lutheran clergy, secular authorities like Ernst the Pious had, in fact, issued new statutes that demanded harsh punishment, even death, for diviners. Yet, as the witch hunts raged, and diviners emerged as figures in these cases, secular authorities' determination to implement harsh punishment for soothsayers and their clients evaporated. Firebrand Lutheran preachers like Waldschmidt and Faber, who called upon rulers to put an end to soothsaying, must have watched with grave disappointment.

By the 1660s witch-hunting had returned to Thuringia, and officials began collecting testimony about the activities of soothsayers working as witch-finders. Duke Johann Ernst II of Saxe-Weimar, for example, eager to destroy the covens of witches he feared were festering in the dark corners of his realm, launched an intense witch-hunt that uncovered evidence of soothsaying. In the winter of 1663, in the course of a witchcraft investigation against a poor villager named Martha Keller, the duke's officials in Eisenach uncovered magical witch-finding activities performed by a hangman.[6] Early in the investigation, a villager named Hans Schneff testified against Keller, informing the authorities that the villagers had brought a bewitched boy to the executioner in Schweinfurt, about eighty miles to the south in Franconia. They hoped he could divine who had placed the hex on the afflicted boy, who had fallen lame.

Schneff testified that by scrutinizing the shapes made by drops of molten lead when dripped into a basin of water, the executioner had confirmed the villagers' fears of witchcraft. Furthermore, the witch-finder had predicted that as soon as the boy returned home and crossed the threshold of his father's house, the next person to enter would be the witch. He foretold that when the witch entered, the boy would feel lice crawling on his neck and that the witch would ask a trivial question. When Martha Keller, long suspected to be a witch, entered the boy's home after his return, the villagers had found their witch. In her subsequent interrogation, the old woman testified that she had heard from a neighbor that the afflicted boy's father had traveled to Schweinfurt to consult the executioner. She admitted that she had visited the boy's home after his return, asking to buy some wool (in reality, she may have been anxious about the hangman's diagnosis and hoped to show that she bore no ill will to the boy). Her intentions aside, Keller vehemently denied that she came immediately after his return. The authorities must not have been convinced. On 25 February 1663 Martha Keller was sent to the flames.[7]

It is particularly noteworthy that the authorities took the hangman's magical identification of the witch seriously. While they deemed divination to be a sinful form of idolatry, echoing Lutheran demonologists, they agreed with their subjects about its efficacy. Princes and peasants were not only united in their aim to rid Thuringia's villages of witches, but also in their faith in the power of diviners to reveal them. The authorities decided to execute Keller, at the urging of her fearful neighbors, but they chose not to punish the villagers for consulting a soothsayer. Focused on exterminating witches, the ducal officials ignored the villagers' magical activities, likewise ignoring the Lutheran clergy's call for them to execute fortune-tellers and banish their clients.

This book began with the story of a soothsayer who appeared in the village of Ohrdruf in 1671. It is worth taking a more detailed look at the case of the wise man of Ohrdruf here, since it affords a rare glimpse into the mysterious activities of the soothsayers who wandered the villages of Saxe-Gotha in the seventeenth century. Like the hangman from Schweinfurt, the wise man of Ohrdruf preformed the role of witch-finder. While the case came to the attention of the ducal authorities after a dispute between quarreling neighbors, it was the wise man's use of divination for witch-finding that prompted an official investigation.

The case occurred late in the reign of Duke Ernst the Pious, as his officials scoured the duchy in an attempt to uncover magical activity and witchcraft.[8] On 16 July 1671 the ducal officials in Gotha received a letter from a villager, Hanns Mertz. Mertz complained about his neighbor, Hans Karst, who Mertz said "never went to Church and instead of listening to the Sunday sermon, got completely drunk on liquor and beer and profaned the holy day by playing his bagpipes."[9] In addition to Karst's excessive love of bagpipes and booze, Mertz also complained that "just about every day, Karst hangs around in front of his house and insults me, calling me a rogue, a murderer, a thief, and even worse things."[10] Finally, Mertz got to the root of the matter, reporting that "Karst has called my wife a witch and my daughter a little witch at least ten times."[11] Mertz then implored the authorities to put a stop to his neighbor's slander.[12]

Three days later, the authorities questioned Hans Karst, the troublesome neighbor, and divination quickly became the focus of their investigation. During Karst's interrogation, ducal officials discovered that the villagers, Karst among them, had been engaging in a variety of forbidden "superstitious activities," meaning divination. Having also heard allegations of witchcraft, the authorities promptly abandoned the issue of slander for the more pressing issues that were emerging. Brushing the neighbors' quarrels aside, the duke's officials asked Karst instead about his dealings with a mysterious fortune-teller. The ducal officials had not restricted their questioning to Karst, but had also been busy collecting testimony from the other villagers, where they learned of his commerce with a cunning man. Letting Karst know that they were on to him, the magistrates asked him if "he was willing to confess that he had recently bought bagpipes from a so-called 'wise man,' who had warned him that his neighbor's wife intended to bewitch him."[13] Once Karst admitted that he had in fact consulted with the fortune-teller, the authorities compelled him to divulge as much information about his mysterious associate and his occult activities as he could.

Karst testified that the man was a tanner from Holstein, who carried a "planet book" (an astrological treatise used to cast horoscopes), and he confirmed that the stranger had indeed warned him that his neighbor's wife planned to harm him with witchcraft.[14] He added that everyone in the village had long suspected that Mertz's wife was a witch, which suggests that like most professional witch-finders, the wise man had ascertained and confirmed suspicions the villagers already harbored.[15]

After they were through with Karst, the authorities called their next witness, Ursula, Hanns Mertz's daughter. Ursula, the daughter Karst had called "a little witch," had been in the Karst house when the "wise man" began telling people's fortunes. She described the methods used by the soothsayer for the authorities, testifying that he offered to tell her fortune in exchange for a mug of beer. According to Ursula, in order to ascertain her fate, the stranger had gazed deeply into her eyes, telling her that she was "born under an unlucky sign and that she was in great danger of dying in a fire."[16] He specified that the threat would be most acute "right after her first marriage and warned her that she should never entrust the fire to her servants, but rather should always tend to it herself."[17] This sort of warning, about a credible, specific threat that was also avoidable (and therefore would not necessarily come to pass), was a stock-in-trade of the fortune-tellers' art in the early modern period. Given the suspicions the villagers harbored about Ursula and her mother, the soothsayer's warning was perhaps also a reference to burning at the stake, that is, a veiled accusation of witchcraft made in reference to her fearful neighbors' suspicions about her.

The last witness, a villager named Martin Aschenbach, was questioned on 7 August, and his testimony sheds light on the fortune-teller's more sinister activities. Aschenbach testified that he stopped by the Karst house and was surprised to find a crowd of people there clustered around a stranger, whom his neighbors identified as a "wise man, who could tell fortunes."[18] According to Aschenbach, the soothsayer looked at him intently and asked "if he had not once been bitten by a dog in this very house?" Amazed, Aschenbach had responded that he had indeed, six years before (although he testified that he was disappointed that the wise man could not tell him which leg had been bitten!).

Aschenbach testified that Hanns Mertz's wife, the suspected witch, was among the villagers eager to have their fortunes told by the wise man. He described Frau Mertz holding out both of her palms for the soothsayer to read, asking him to divine whether she was a witch or not. With the region in the midst of an intense witch-hunt, her neighbors' suspicions could prove deadly, and she was likely attempting to convince them of her innocence. Thus, divination not only served villagers looking to prove that their neighbors were witches, but also might help a suspected witch clear her name. The wise man proved reluctant to grant Frau Mertz's request, perhaps nervous about confronting a suspected witch to her face. Consequently, Aschenbach reported that the wise man "didn't want to have anything to do with her."[19] An hour later, however, as Mertz's wife was leaving, the soothsayer had warned his host, Karst, that she was indeed a witch, and she wanted to "make him crippled and lame with her hexes."[20] This revelation, probably based upon an astute reading of the suspicion and animosity the villagers exhibited toward the suspected witch, brought the simmering feud between the neighbors to a head, sparking the official investigation.

A few weeks after collecting all these depositions, the authorities quietly let the matter drop, most likely because the quarreling neighbors had reached an out-of-court settlement. Not every witchcraft accusation ended at the stake, and suspected witches and their supposed victims sometimes settled their differences outside of the courtroom. Facilitating just such a reconciliation was one possible outcome of the magical detection of witchcraft, although the activities of witch-finders could also elicit formal witchcraft charges, recourse to counter-magic, or threats of violence aimed at the suspected witch. In each of these cases, the witch-finder served a vital role in dealing with the social tensions engendered by (or expressed through) witchcraft fears.[21] Official witchcraft prosecution was driven by popular cooperation, as scholars have long recognized, but as the Ohrdruf case shows, it was also often facilitated by divination. Pastors might rail against these practices from the pulpit, but villagers considered magical witch-finding an indispensable defense against bewitchment. Likewise, the ducal authorities deemed it a useful tool in proving witchcraft allegations, despite prohibiting divination in their own statutes. Ohrdruf's pastor no doubt would have considered the wise man's witch-finding activities to be diabolical. For the ducal authorities, though, these kinds of occult activities were an essential component of investigation and evidence collection in witchcraft cases. There was little incentive, therefore, for officials to actively enforce divination statutes when their subjects feared bewitchment.

Two years later, another witch-finder emerged in the course of a witchcraft investigation in the neighboring duchy of Saxe-Weimar. The episode reveals how the activities of cunning folk came to light during witchcraft investigations—and how the authorities, occupied with hunting witches, used it to their advantage. The 1673 case, which took place during a witch hunt launched by Duke Johann Ernst II, also illustrates how villagers used cunning folk not only to detect, but also to remedy suspected witchcraft.

In March 1673, the authorities in Kaltennordheim summoned a tavern keeper from the village of Unterweid named Johann Strauss to testify in a witchcraft case. One of Strauss's neighbors, a woman named Anna Reich, long suspected of witchcraft, stood accused of bewitching cattle as well as several children. In a terse deposition, Strauss testified that on the urging of his godmother he had consulted a wise woman to confirm the villagers' suspicions, and the diviner had discerned an image of Anna Reich in a crystal. She had also predicted that someday the witch "would be punished by the religious and secular authorities."[22] A month later, Strauss was called back by the authorities for further questioning. During his testimony, Strauss revealed interesting details about the role of magical witch-finding in early modern folk culture.

In his second interview, the forty-year-old tavern keeper not only revealed more about his visit to the mysterious wise woman but also revealed that he had not gone alone. The episode had begun, according to Strauss, when he had accompanied Mattheus Reich to see the diviner. Mattheus Reich was a kinsman of the suspected witch, Anna Reich, and the two men went to the wise woman after Mattheus's wife and children had fallen ill. Strauss testified that the wise woman had used a crystal to determine that it was Anna, Mattheus's cousin's wife, who had bewitched his loved ones. The men asked if she could break the hex and restore his ailing family, but the wise woman informed her clients that they had come to see her eight days too late, and now he would certainly lose his wife and children. (In practice, cunning folk often proved reluctant to attempt to heal seriously ill patients, fearing witchcraft allegations if the patient worsened under their care). However, the wise woman gave him six nails she had blessed, instructing him to hammer three into his sick wife's bedpost and the rest into the bedroom door. She assured him that the nails would draw the suspected witch to his house so he could confirm that she was the culprit. Strauss went on to testify that Mattheus Reich's wife had died at the very hour the wise woman had predicted and that the magic nails had indeed drawn the suspected witch, Anna, to his door. He concluded his testimony by reporting that Mattheus Reich had denounced Anna to "the Lutheran authorities," probably meaning her pastor or the local consistory. According to Strauss, the clerical authorities had punished Mattheus

Reich for consulting the "wise woman" by ordering him to confess his sin in church and barred him from communion for a year. The verdict in Anna Reich's case before the court does not survive. However, the record ends with an ominous report that a convicted witch who had already gone to the flames had seen Anna at the witches' dance.[23] Given the pace of executions in the region in the 1670s, such damning "proof" likely doomed her.

The Anna Reich case shows that at the height of the witch hunts in seventeenth-century Thuringia, secular authorities took divination seriously—not as a dangerous crime that demanded harsh punishment, but rather as a valuable form of evidence that substantiated witchcraft accusations. They may have believed the Lutheran clergy's assertion that it was diabolical, but they still deemed witchcraft a far more serious threat than soothsaying. Thus, they were content to remand Mattheus Reich to his pastor, who levied a minor penalty, using him as an example of sinful behavior for the local parish, but likely executed his kinswoman, the suspected witch. Given his grief at the loss of his wife and children, and his confidence that Anna Reich's witchcraft was responsible, it's not improbable that he thought vengeance was worth confessing his sin and missing communion. Recourse to divination afforded Mattheus Reich a means of confirming his suspicions and seeking retribution, offering a more direct means of dealing with his misfortunes than the prayers and patience advocated by his pastor. As usual, the ducal authorities in Weimar did not even bother to pursue the wise woman Mattheus Reich had consulted.

While witchcraft investigations uncovered most of the divination that entered the official record in seventeenth-century Thuringia, not every villager who appeared before the authorities after consulting cunning folk feared bewitchment. Many sought help from soothsayers in hopes of recovering stolen property. The 1679 case that opened this chapter offers a useful example. The authorities in Saxe-Gotha punished the old linen weaver, Caspar Nußmann, for practicing divination in August 1679. The case took place during the reign of Ernst the Pious's son, Duke Friedrich I. Although a devoted alchemist, who built an impressive occult library and assembled an alchemical laboratory at Schloss Friedenstein, Friedrich was also a committed witch-hunter who drew the typical elite distinction between learned and popular magic. Nußmann came to the attention of the ducal authorities after he consulted two wise men regarding a theft. When a measure of his linen went missing, Nußmann had gone across the border into Bavaria to consult a wise man in Gückelhirn in an attempt to find out who had stolen his property. Dissatisfied with the Bavarian's services, he subsequently met with a second soothsayer in Westhausen (near Gotha), who used a crystal to find the thieves.[24]

Thief-finding was among the most common services that professional seers performed. In a subsistence society where rural people often had trouble safeguarding their property, there was plenty of demand for diviners' thief-finding services. Cunning folk relied upon a dizzying variety of arcane means to locate lost or stolen goods. Some practiced scrying, which entailed gazing into a crystal or a mirror in an attempt to discern an image of the thief. Others turned to the sieve and shears, holding the sieve suspended from the shears as the names of suspects were recited and looking for the implement to move as the culprit was named. Often the mere threat of consulting a soothsayer prompted thieves to return the purloined property secretly in order to avoid magical identification.[25] Such preemptive return of stolen goods shows that thieves feared this occult system of investigation, which could bring criminal charges or a violent confrontation with their neighbors. In the close-knit rural communities of seventeenth-century Thuringia, reputation was paramount, and being labeled a thief or a witch was a serious matter. Soothsaying offered victims of theft or bewitchment a way of substantiating their suspicions about their neighbors, but it also afforded suspects an opportunity to make redress in an attempt to repair the tear in the local social fabric and restore their good name.

For the authorities in Saxe-Gotha, these occult activities, so integral to village society, were sinful and, more importantly, sowed discord among neighbors. Thus, the high court sentenced Nußmann, who had admitted to his crimes in a written appeal for leniency, to several days' imprisonment. Upon his release, they ordered him to confess his sins publicly in church, no doubt an edifying (or perhaps enjoyable) experience for his fellow parishioners, and to pay all the court expenses associated with his case. Once again, the local authorities chose to disregard the harsh penalties listed in their own criminal code and applied only petty punishments. As usual, they settled on ecclesiastical penalties, leaving pastors to deal with divination as a moral issue, rather than as a crime.

These cases from seventeenth-century Thuringia demonstrate the local authorities' halfhearted efforts to prohibit occult activities in the region and reveal some of the most prominent functions of divination within the adumbral world of early modern folk culture. They also show the appeal of fortune-tellers during the period and how eagerly villagers consulted these magical practitioners, despite clerical admonishments and the risk of punishment. Like Nußmann and Karst, the villagers and townsfolk of the duchy consulted professional diviners in order to deal with the uncertainties of life and for help when confronted with misfortune. Gazing upon their clients or relying upon occult aids like crystals or astrological charts, early modern cunning folk, foreign and native, itinerant and local, used divination in an attempt to foretell the future, find stolen goods, and identify witches. As these cases illustrate, early modern Germans, occupying a mental universe animated by supernatural forces both malevolent and benign, and living in an era of uncertainty and want, consulted soothsayers in difficult times, seers who sometimes confirmed their darkest fears about their neighbors.

Popular forms of divination—witch-finding, thief-finding, and fortune-telling—served a variety of functions within early modern society. Sometimes soothsaying helped limit social conflict within tight-knit communities, offering villagers and townsfolk means of settling conflicts within the community and of dealing with personal misfortune. Divination, or the threat of resorting to it, was frequently the first step in dealing with theft or witchcraft suspicions and offered the added benefit of not involving local officials. A generation of studies of early modern witch-hunting has demonstrated that reporting suspected witches to the authorities was usually the last resort when allegations surfaced, since villagers were reluctant to invite the expense and scrutiny involved with official witchcraft investigations. Given this reluctance, suspected witches often lived among their suspicious neighbors for decades before being arrested. Early modern villagers lived alongside suspected witches by relying on established internal systems of redress against witchcraft: cajoling or threatening the suspected witch to get her to lift a malicious hex or working counter-magic in an attempt to break her curse.[26]

Divination served as a means of confirming witchcraft fears so the victim could seek remedy, and thus it helped to keep most witchcraft accusations within the village and out of the courts. Often the mere threat of consulting a known witch-doctor was enough to facilitate the reconciliation necessary to defuse the social tensions at the heart of witchcraft fears. Similarly, the announcement by victims of theft that they were going to consult a well-known soothsayer to uncover the culprit often prompted the thief to return the stolen goods. In both of these cases, witch-finding and thief-finding, divination served to defuse serious discord in the community in ways that could be managed at the village level without resorting to the law. When victims of bewitchment denounced their neighbors to the authorities, however, their suspicions verified by cunning folk or hangmen, divination could have deadly consequences.

Divination could have destabilizing effects, confirming accusations of witchcraft or theft and prompting violent reactions or denunciations of suspects to the authorities. As the Reich case suggests, once bewitchment was suspected and a respected witch-finder confirmed long-standing suspicions about a putative witch, the afflicted might turn to the authorities for justice, often with fatal results. In the era of the European witch-hunts, the arrest of a single suspected witch could even spark a full-blown outbreak of witch-hunting, as suspects under torture revealed the names of other members of their supposed coven, as happened to Anna Reich. Divination played a prominent role in early modern folk culture, but one that was highly ambiguous. It could promote social stability and provide psychological remedy in the face of misfortune, but could just as easily stoke violent responses to simmering ill will or even spark deadly witchcraft panics. Despite these unpredictable outcomes, divination remained a key element of early modern folk culture, as villagers and townsfolk attempted to comprehend and manipulate their daily experiences.

In seventeenth-century Germany, Protestant reformers urged rulers to stamp out divination in an effort to purify the true church. Battling soothsaying, which they viewed as a vestige of Catholic and pagan superstition, pastors sought to save wavering Christians from the machinations of the devil. Facing the daunting tasks of reforming morals, educating the populace, and confronting witches and heretics, Thuringian rulers issued harsh prohibitions of divination, likely in a bid to appease the Lutheran clergy. But the region's secular authorities failed to enforce these statutes effectively. Most Thuringian rulers' efforts to prohibit divination appear tepid when compared with the deadly intensity of their witch-hunting activities. Even particularly activist rulers like Ernst the Pious, dedicated to rooting out sorcery and divination, soon found that the disciplinary tools at their disposal proved inadequate for the task. Early modern law enforcement was hampered by a crippling lack of resources and rudimentary surveillance capabilities. When dealing with secret crimes like witchcraft or sorcery, official disciplinary efforts relied almost entirely on the cooperation of the populace, who were required to provide denunciations and witness statements from their neighbors in order to identify suspects and initiate official investigations. In the case of divination, villagers proved reluctant to bring information about these activities to the courts, since it proved so useful in dealing with their misfortunes. When rulers managed to uncover traces of soothsaying, they usually contented themselves with handing down petty punishments to the few unlucky offenders who came before the court and relied instead upon fiery sermons and draconian laws in hopes of deterring the rest of their subjects from dabbling in the occult.

Amid vehement clerical disapproval and lax enforcement of official prohibitions, divination flourished in seventeenth-century Thuringia. As Robin Briggs argues, regarding the prevalence of cunning folk in early modern Europe, "their sheer numbers and ubiquitous presence at once sustained the world view they represented and clogged any official attempt at repression."[27] Thus, like villagers and townsfolk throughout Europe, Thuringians used a wide array of customary forms of divination, simple means of fortune-telling passed down orally from generation to generation, in their attempts to uncover hidden knowledge and predict the future. They also employed professional fortune-tellers and witch-doctors, itinerant seers and local cunning folk who made their living by identifying thieves and witches, diagnosing bewitchment, and telling fortunes. Despite widespread use, though, their illicit nature often drove these practices underground, away from authorities who would disapprove, so that few of those who consulted soothsayers ever appeared in court.

Deeply rooted in early modern culture and serving an array of important functions within village society, divination proved remarkably resistant to official repression. Promising a means to recover stolen property, confirm witchcraft suspicions, and reveal future threats and opportunities, but also capable of prompting deadly reactions to suspected *maleficia,* it remained a valued means of dealing with misfortune and social conflict. Consequently, owing to the feebleness of official efforts to police divination and its enduring popularity, Lutheran authorities' attempts to dissuade the rural population from engaging in these magical practices proved futile. The sporadic efforts of the era's Protestant authorities to root out these occult practices mark the limits of Lutheran reform efforts and demonstrate the tenacity of a vibrant folk culture that proved unyielding in the face of official efforts to suppress it.

At the height of the seventeenth-century witch-hunts, the Lutheran clergy failed to convince the populace to abandon divination, largely because the rulers themselves ignored their calls to treat it as harshly as witchcraft. Lutheran reformers' attempts to root out popular forms of divination after the Reformation foundered because of tensions between clergy, rulers, and populace, each with their own distinctive attitudes toward magical activity. Villagers needed divination to identify witches, and secular authorities implicitly condoned its use when they relied on the testimony of witch-finders to support their witch-hunting activities. Ultimately, Lutheran demonologists and theologians failed to persuade parishioners to abandon traditional forms of divination or rulers to treat divination with the same severity as they did witchcraft.

6

"SUPERSTITIOUS ACTIVITIES"

Elite Skepticism and Folk Magic in Enlightenment-Era Germany

A Daughter in Waltershausen (1718)

In the spring of 1718, a family in the Thuringian village of Waltershausen came to the attention of the ducal officials in Gotha after engaging in disturbing "superstitious practices." On 17 June 1718, Waltershausen's fire marshal, Balthazar Stegmöller, had discovered a mysterious sack hanging in the fireplace of the Schröter family. He promptly reported his sinister discovery to the local authorities, who summoned the various members of the household for questioning.

The ducal officials began their investigation aggressively, trying to catch Hermann Schröter's widow, Martha, off guard by confronting her with allegations from unnamed informants. After a long series of seemingly innocuous questions, they sprang the trap, asking her whether her daughter had recently had some of her property stolen from a market stall on the village bridge and had then "hung a sack in the chimney, so she could reveal the thief." When the widow proved evasive, they halted the interrogation and had one of their officials retrieve the sack that had been found in the fireplace. Inspecting it, they found it to be filled with dark earth and bits of wood. On 29 June, they questioned the family maid, Catharina Thomin, from the nearby village of Schwarzhausen. Catharina initially proved tight-lipped, but she ultimately revealed that she had heard her mistresses speaking about the sack. The magistrates pounced, summoning Martha again, demanding to know why she had denied knowing about her daughter's suspicious activities.

Two weeks later, they finally questioned their primary suspect, the daughter, Barbara Elisabetha, asking her straightaway why she had hung the suspicious bag in her mother's chimney. Faced with the evidence they had already collected, she did not dare deny the charges against her. Rather, she shrewdly sought to downplay her involvement in magic. Prevaricating, she testified that she had done it merely "in jest and as a silly game, and because she had heard of it from other people," trivializing her magical activities. She also assured them that she had had no evil intentions and added that in any case the operation had not worked. In an attempt to persuade the authorities that she had already been convinced of the error of her ways, she also mentioned that her brother-in-law, the schoolmaster in nearby Hörselgau, had already chided her for dabbling in such matters.[1]

The young woman's response shows an important change in the way suspects spoke about magic before the ducal officials. In the sixteenth and seventeenth centuries, when learned elites and humble villagers alike accepted the reality of magic and witchcraft, suspects never asserted that they had employed divination on a lark. Instead, once cornered by the authorities they threw themselves upon the mercy of the court, meekly begging forgiveness and accepting the jail stints, fines, and shaming penalties they received. By the early eighteenth century, however, as the witch hunts were drawing to a close and the local authorities appeared more skeptical of witchcraft and magic, defendants like Barbara Elisabetha responded to official charges by portraying their occult activities as nothing more than silly games, testifying that in hindsight they had come to share the magistrates' growing doubts about the efficacy of magic.[2] Her strategy before the court seems to have worked: satisfied that her dabbling in the occult was merely a youthful indiscretion, the authorities let the matter drop.

At the dawn of the eighteenth century, as the Enlightenment began to make inroads among European elites, official disciplinary efforts and the rural population's use of magic both shifted in subtle ways. The enlightened skepticism about magic that was spreading in the urban salons and universities of Europe was slow to reach Thuringia. As witchcraft prosecution finally ceased in the region in the 1700s, however, local officials came to treat magical belief as an annoying superstition, a vestige of rural backwardness. The region's secular authorities remained hesitant to convict soothsayers and their clients, just as they had been in the preceding centuries. The reasons for their reluctance shifted dramatically, however. Enlightenment-era officials gradually came to view soothsaying as an example of ignorant superstition, rather than evidence of a demonic pact. In fact, the very definition of superstition shifted during this period. For centuries, the authorities had traditionally viewed "superstitious activities" like Barbara Elisabetha's in religious terms—as signs of misguided or misdirected religious faith. Now, with the spread of the Enlightenment, this traditional definition of superstition began to give way to its modern meaning, based on rational thought—an irrational or unverifiable belief.[3]

As elites gradually abandoned the belief in magic they once shared with commoners, villagers retained their fear of bewitchment and continued to rely upon divination to deal with adversity. This divergence in supernatural beliefs prompted commoners to change the ways in which they talked about witchcraft and magic in court. Faced with elite skepticism, they proved increasingly evasive about their magical activities. As the cases presented in this chapter will show, villagers in eighteenth-century Thuringia carefully crafted their testimony to downplay their steadfast belief in witchcraft and their stubborn recourse to divination.

Divination, Elite Skepticism, and Cultural Change

The horrors of mass witch-hunting persisted longer in Thuringia than in most other areas in Europe. While witch-hunting declined precipitously in most German regions after the 1630s, in Thuringia intensive witchcraft prosecution continued into the early 1700s.[4] Witch-hunting tapered off in the region during the Thirty Years' War, only to be followed by a major witchcraft panic in its chaotic aftermath, lasting from 1656 to 1700. Sporadic witchcraft prosecution continued in Thuringia during the early eighteenth century, with the last recorded execution occurring in 1731.[5] During these deadly witch-hunts, demonologists and theologians equated witchcraft with divination in their treatises, and diviners sometimes played a role in witchcraft investigations. The new ideas of the early Enlightenment eventually eroded elite belief in witchcraft and magic, but a creeping judicial skepticism preceded these intellectual changes.[6] Undermining elite fears of witchcraft, these momentous intellectual and legal innovations also changed official attitudes toward divination, affecting how it was treated in court.

In the late seventeenth century, judges and jurists in Europe's urban centers and university towns began to cast doubt on the methods of witchcraft prosecution, fearing that innocent victims were being sent to the flames. Many of these critics of the brutal methods of witch-hunting retained a staunch belief in the reality of witchcraft and diabolism but doubted magistrates' ability to prosecute the mysterious crime of witchcraft fairly. Thus, driven by these jurists' procedural concerns, the decline in European witchcraft prosecution began before European intellectuals mounted a serious challenge to the belief in witchcraft or the demonic pact.[7] Gradually, however, the rationalist and empiricist impulses that propelled the early Enlightenment began to affect elite attitudes toward magic. By the end of the seventeenth century, a radical new "mechanical philosophy," based on the Cartesian notion that the universe operates as a machine according to natural laws, slowly began to make inroads among European elites. This rationalist cosmology eventually began to undermine belief in witchcraft and magic, as well as miracles and demonic possession.[8]

Although witch-hunting lingered on in Thuringia until the 1730s, by the mid-eighteenth century the ducal courts and universities of the fragmented region were emerging as centers of the German Enlightenment. Given its political fragmentation, Thuringia was no longer at the forefront of imperial politics, and increasingly the region's rulers sought to make a name for themselves as great patrons of the arts. Accordingly, in the eighteenth century, Thuringia became a leading center of the German Enlightenment with the emergence of Weimar Classicism. In 1741, Duke Ernst August I ended the cycle of dynastic partition. He adopted primogeniture, beginning Saxe-Weimar's rise to becoming a grand duchy. When his son died after a reign of just ten years, his son's widow, Anna Amelia, became regent of Saxe-Weimar and guardian of their nine-year-old son,

Carl August. She soon set Weimar on the path to becoming a crucial cultural center.

Educated by the noted poet and author Christoph Martin Wieland, Duke Karl August was deeply interested in literature, art, and scientific investigation. In 1775, having reached his majority, he invited the great poet and writer Johann Wolfgang Goethe to Weimar and placed him on his privy council. The famous scholar soon made Weimar a leading center of intellectual activity, drawing other giants of the German Enlightenment to the new "Athens on the Ilm." With Johann Gottfried Herder and Friedrich Schiller, Goethe launched a neoclassical philosophic and literary movement that lasted until Schiller's death in 1805 and had an enormous influence on German culture, including its attitudes toward the occult. Goethe's *Faust,* which he began working on in the 1770s, helped transform the way that his elite audience viewed witchcraft and diabolism by making these once-feared crimes into subjects of literary entertainment.

At the same time that Goethe and Schiller were making Weimar one of Germany's cultural capitals, Thuringia was also becoming associated with early Romanticism, a movement that focused on human emotion and the irrational in response to the excessive rationalism of Enlightenment thought. Like the Enlightenment, Romanticism would come to affect the way that learned elites viewed popular magic like divination. In the late 1790s, a circle of influential Romantic authors and playwrights emerged at Jena, powered by the literary journal *Athenaeum,* edited by the brothers August and Friedrich Schlegel. At Jena, the brothers collaborated with leading Romantic writers and intellectuals, including Novalis, Ludwig Tieck, Johann Gottlieb Fichte, and Caroline Schelling. The works of these Jena Romantics explored human passions and the supernatural, often drawing on the medieval past and German folktales for inspiration. Some of these Romantic fairy tales even involved divination. In Ludwig Tieck's *Der Hexen-Sabbat* (1832), for example, an alleged witch is imprisoned after a witch-finder discerns the signs of her diabolical pact by gazing into her eyes, a technique commonly employed by rural cunning folk.[9] By making witchcraft and magic into literary tropes, Romantic authors followed Goethe in transforming witches, once frightening figures, into objects of popular entertainment.[10] As we will see, these sorts of Romantic tales would eventually help foster a reevaluation of traditional magical beliefs among German intellectuals.

While intellectual skepticism based upon the tenets of the Enlightenment and the transformation of magic into a literary trope by Romantic authors both affected elite attitudes toward witchcraft and divination, theological shifts ultimately proved more significant in the rise of skepticism about magic among elites. By the late seventeenth century, the intense biblicism that had been a staple of witchcraft skepticism since the days of Johann Weyer finally began to undermine the supposed scriptural basis of witch-hunting among educated elites. For example, through biblical philology, the Hebrew text of Exodus 22:18, the famous injunction "Thou shalt not suffer a witch to live," long understood as a mandate to execute witches, was retranslated to refer only to poisoners.[11] In the absence of this mandate, many Protestant elites came to think of suspected witches, sorcerers, and soothsayers as wayward sinners rather than the devil's minions, worthy of pastoral correction instead of capital punishment.

A few skeptics offered a more radical challenge to traditional demonological beliefs. The Calvinist theologian and pastor Balthasar Bekker, writing in Amsterdam in the early 1690s, argued on the basis of Cartesian philosophy and scriptural exegesis that witchcraft and magic were impossible. Thus, he denied the existence of *all* magic, including fortune-telling, declaring that "there is no magic, except in the minds of men, no ghosts, no divination, nor any demonic possession."[12] For Bekker, learned demonology and popular belief alike represented vestiges of pagan error and refuted the true sovereignty of God. Bekker's writings were soon translated from Dutch into German (as well as French and English) and gradually helped to undermine confidence in the reality of witchcraft and folk magic among educated elites. As Euan Cameron argues, Bekker's simultaneous critique of elite and popular magical beliefs, with its assertion that giving credence to any spiritual forces aside from God was sinful error, proved a radical departure from established demonological traditions, one that ultimately led to a wholesale redefinition of the concept of superstition.[13]

In Germany, the work of Christian Thomasius was crucial to this process of reappraisal, although the famous Halle jurist stopped short of

Bekker's wholesale denial of the reality of magic. In 1701, he published *Dissertatio de Crimine magiae (Dissertation on the Crime of Magic)*, a scholarly work that called witchcraft prosecution into question by attacking the overzealous use of torture. A moving indictment of coerced confessions, the work was translated into German two years later and circulated widely, arousing substantial controversy. Although he had given a legal opinion that favored the torture of a suspected witch in 1694, upon reflection Thomasius eventually came to doubt many of the central beliefs of early modern demonology, perhaps owing to the growing influence of Pietism in Halle.[14] Ultimately, he came to deny the earthly power of the devil and hence the reality of the Witches' Sabbath, night flight, and the satanic pact.[15]

Despite his rejection of these key demonological tenets, Thomasius's skepticism was highly qualified. His views expose an important blind spot in Enlightenment-era thought about popular magical belief. Although he doubted demonological fantasies about flying witches and diabolical sabbaths, he did not refute the occult abilities of soothsayers. Nor did he doubt that these diviners derived their insights from the devil, writing that "I allow that by these people certain things are done which are not illusions or fraudulent and cannot be ascribed to the natural powers of bodies and natural elements, but must come from the devil."[16] In an apparently contradictory fashion, Thomasius's rational religiosity at once denied the devil's power to affect the physical world and allowed for the diabolical inspiration of diviners.

Furthermore, Thomasius did not shrink from calling for the punishment of soothsayers. He asserted that these evil magic users should be banished from Christian polities, asserting that "no-one should permit crystal-gazers, exorcists, and conjurors to live in a well-ordered republic, but should expel them from it or when the opportunity arises to punish them in more severe ways."[17] The ambivalence at the heart of Thomasius's skepticism is striking: his growing doubts about witchcraft did not undermine his belief in the existence of soothsaying or dampen his enthusiasm for punishing it.

The intellectual changes of the early Enlightenment were long credited with bringing an end to the witch hunts, with reason overcoming ignorance and superstition. Whig historians of the late nineteenth and early twentieth centuries argued that educated elites' abandonment of supposedly "superstitious" magical beliefs after 1650 was a key development in the eventual triumph of Western rationalism. Since the 1970s, however, scholars have demolished this positivist modernization narrative.[18] They have demonstrated that the spread of the materialist "mechanical philosophy" among learned elites was much more gradual and far less complete than once supposed. They have shown that skeptics struggled to convince jurists and magistrates, most of whom remained fervent believers in witchcraft and magic until well into the eighteenth century.[19]

In the early 1700s even the qualified reevaluation of traditional demonological beliefs by skeptics like Bekker and Thomasius met with furious opposition from many of their contemporaries. Balthasar Bekker's Cartesian skepticism was so unwelcome among his peers that it cost him his position as a reformed minister in Amsterdam. In Germany, Thomasius's work proved instrumental in spreading the new skepticism, but it also aroused heated opposition. In 1722, Johann Weidner, a Rostock theologian, contradicted Thomasius, asserting that witches could indeed fly with the aid of the devil. Likewise, the famous Halle medical professor Friedrich Hoffmann asserted in 1725 that witches could work *maleficium* through demonic agency. Finally, as late as 1738, another professor at the University of Halle, Ernst Johann Friedrich Mantzel, defended traditional witchcraft beliefs on the basis of biblical evidence. Given such ardent defense of traditional demonology, there is an emerging realization among modern scholars that in the area of magical beliefs, the early Enlightenment was somewhat less "enlightened" than has often been supposed.[20]

Some learned commentators not only vigorously defended traditional notions of witchcraft, but also urged the continued hunting of witches and diviners alike. Michael Berns, a Lutheran pastor from Hamburg, wrote a scathing rebuttal to Bekker in 1708, which accused the skeptic of denying the very existence of the devil and associated him with the "arch-atheist" Spinoza.[21] For ardent defenders of traditional demonology like Berns, continued belief in witchcraft and magic were a valuable bulwark against the materialism of radical thinkers like Hobbes, Spinoza, and Descartes.

They viewed such "Sadducism" as a creeping form of atheism lurking in the shadow of the new mechanical philosophy. In response, they sought to maintain traditional beliefs in the "invisible world" in order to shore up Christian theology in the face of early Enlightenment materialism. The debate in Germany intensified as influential English works defending the belief in witchcraft and sorcery were translated into German. The most important among them was Joseph Glanvill's *Saducismus Triumphatus,* which first appeared in a German edition in 1701.[22]

In the 1700s, as skeptics and believers debated the reality of magic and witchcraft, the polemical culture of the early Enlightenment spawned new ways to attack magical beliefs, including popular forms of divination. Enlightened thinkers' attacks on credulity shifted from dry learned treatises that parsed Hebrew syntax in the Old Testament to satire and ridicule intended to discredit traditional magical belief and demonology alike.[23] In 1705, for example, Johann Georg Schmidt, an apothecary and naturalist from Reinsfeld in Thuringia, published a work entitled *Die gestriegelte Rockenphilosophie* (*The Dressed-Up Distaff Philosophy*) that subjected hundreds of popular magical beliefs to such derision. Presenting traditional magical practices in misogynistic terms, literally as "Old Wives' Tales," Schmidt sought to discredit them as ignorant and foolish.

The work proved exceedingly popular among enlightened thinkers, going through five editions, with the last appearing in 1759. While Schmidt's introduction makes clear his disdain for these practices, and for the women supposedly prone to believing in their efficacy, his book is little more than a compendium of popular superstitions. He includes an exhaustive list of divinatory practices in his account, detailing, for example, how young maidens would strip naked and pray to St. Andrew on 30 November, asking him to bring them a vision of their future husbands in their dreams.[24] While Schmidt scoffed at what he deemed to be silly superstitions, he also asserted that they were inherently demonic, an age-old contradiction in elite critiques of popular magic. After complaining that "a ravenous wolf is not so hungry for his prey as a maid is for a man," he warned that the superstitious "Andreas prayers" of these "whores" were nothing more than appeals to Satan, "because all superstition stems from the devil."[25]

If Schmidt is to be believed, Christmas Eve must have been a particularly busy time for superstitious women. He described how maids supposedly divined if they would remain in the employ of their masters by throwing a shoe and interpreting the future from the way it landed and how young girls could venture into a chicken coop at midnight to listen for the sounds made by the hens and roosters to determine if they would find a husband in the coming year. Another entry detailed how women sought to divine whether their men had been true, again on Christmas Eve. Schmidt complained bitterly about how such credulous women profaned such a holy night through their superstitious activities.[26] An early Enlightenment rationalist, Schmidt sought to portray these magical beliefs as ignorant and foolish, but he also relied on Christian morality to undermine them.

While Schmidt lampooned popular magical beliefs for a learned audience, another enlightened author, Christian Ludwig Hahnzog, wrote sermons for the edification of his rural flock. A Lutheran pastor in Welschleben, near Magdeburg, Hahnzog sought to acquaint his parishioners, whom he described as mired in backwardness and superstition, with enlightened principles and rational religion. He published a book of pro-Prussian patriotic sermons for the peasantry in 1785 and collections of sermons advocating popular education informed by Enlightenment principles in 1788 and 1803.[27] Before publishing these patriotic and educational works, Hahnzog challenged the superstitions that he encountered in the course of his pastoral duties. In 1784 he published *Predigten wider den Aberglauben der Landleute* (*Sermons against the Superstitions of the Peasantry*), a book of sermons aimed at convincing his flock to embrace enlightened reason and abandon their superstitious beliefs, which he excoriated as "a poison that infects and often kills religion, reason, composure, and the noblest gift of God, human happiness."[28] Hahnzog based his sermons on his experience as a young pastor assigned to a rural parish, and he relates that in the early years of his ministry his tone was too harsh as he railed against superstition, alienating his flock. He asserted that after gaining more experience, he adopted the somewhat gentler attitude of this sermon collection.[29] Like the demonologists of the fifteenth century and the reformers of the sixteenth, Hahnzog was not only concerned with witchcraft, but also with folk magic, and so divination featured prominently in his sermons.

While Hahnzog still couched his objections in religious terms and argued that belief in witchcraft, magical charms, and divination was sinful, as a proponent of Enlightenment rationalism he also sought to explain them away using reason and science. He explained, for example, that comets were not portents of looming calamities, but rather predictable, natural phenomena. Using a historical example, he pointed out that the appearance of a great comet in 1759 had come too late to predict the start of the Seven Years' War, "a gruesome conflict that had already been raging in Europe, America, and Asia for three years."[30] Thus, Hahnzog's work marks the shifting definition of superstition from the premodern one, an erroneous or misdirected religious faith, to the modern one, an irrational or unverifiable belief.

Hahnzog's sermons also reflected an emerging, intensely rational form of Protestant religiosity, with little space for wonders and miracles. He acknowledged the existence of the devil but asserted throughout his sermons that only God could foretell the future. A proponent of an austere, reasoned Protestantism, Hahnzog preached that the days of prophets and divine revelations were over, stating that "God no longer gives the gift of prophecy nowadays."[31] Departing from earlier skeptics like Christian Thomasius, he also denied that the devil could offer soothsayers any glimpses of the future. Hahnzog urged his parishioners not to run to consult wise women (he asserted that in his day the common people thought only women still had the "gift" of soothsaying) when someone has stolen something from them, asking them instead to trust in God. Speaking directly to his parishioners, he counseled them not to give their money to soothsayers. Instead, he urged them to "pray and work hard, and trust in the blessed and soothing hands of God."[32] For Hahnzog, divination was impossible, and anyone who consulted a fortune-teller was not only wasting his or her hard-earned money, but also failing to place adequate faith in divine providence. In other words, he demoted divination from a dire demonic threat to a silly peasant belief and a minor moral failure. While practicing popular magic signaled a sinful lack of faith on the part of villagers, it did not mark them as minions of the devil.

Heinrich Ludwig Fischer, a Lutheran pastor and schoolmaster writing several years after Hahnzog, also tried to disabuse the rural population of their superstitious delusions. Fischer, however, toned down the moral aspect of his pastoral duties, approaching rural superstitions in a manner that foreshadowed the folklorist approach of later Romantic scholars who sought to uncover the customs and traditions of the German *Volk*. Fischer published his popular compendium of folk beliefs under the title *Das Buch vom Aberglauben* (*The Book of Superstitions*) in 1790. In this work, which eventually grew to comprise three volumes, each of which went through several editions, Fischer displayed an interesting historical awareness. He presented the witch hunts as an unfortunate vestige of a benighted age, expressing gratitude that they had drawn to a close and writing that "we are lucky that we no longer live in a time when we are in danger of being forced to confess under torture that we are witches." He lamented

An impoverished female fortune-teller reading the palm of a well-dressed client. From Heinrich Ludwig Fischer, *Das Buch vom Aberglauben* (1790). (Harold Jantz Collection of German Baroque Literature and German Americana, David M. Rubenstein Rare Book & Manuscript Library, Duke University)

the many "good women" and "old people" wrongly accused during the era of the witch hunts, contrasting those dark days with his own enlightened present.[33]

Fischer's works were intended to serve as aids in the education of Germany's rural populace by exposing the absurdity of superstitious beliefs. Like Hahnzog, he employed the modern conception of superstition, defining it as "an unfounded opinion" and declared his intention to show how "laughable" and "stupid" such beliefs were.[34] Accordingly, he directed much of his ire against divination, ridiculing the impoverished villagers who gave their hard-earned money to wandering gypsies who promised to tell their fortunes but really just swindled them. He went on to attack folk prophets as rabble-rousers, astrologers as false and fraudulent, and the women who told fortunes by reading palms, coffee grounds, or tarot cards as nothing more than con artists.

Folk Magic and Rural Society in Eighteenth-Century Thuringia

The creeping skepticism about magic and witchcraft that appeared in the salons of Paris and the lecture halls of Halle in the early Enlightenment was slow to affect the local authorities in rural Thuringia. As witchcraft prosecutions finally drew to a close in the region in the early 1700s, however, official attitudes toward divination gradually began to change as well. Officials continued to hand down rather petty punishments for such "superstitious activities," but their justification for punishing divination changed dramatically. Influenced by the rising tide of skepticism in elite circles, they increasingly treated the local populace's divinatory activities as instances of fraud or ignorance rather than demonic sorcery.

These shifts in official attitudes in Thuringia were subtle and were not reflected in the territorial ordinances issued in the early 1700s. Eighteenth-century law codes from Thuringia generally repeated verbatim earlier versions of prohibitions against divination. The 1705 *Landesordnung* of Saxe-Altenburg, for example, still treated fortune-telling as a serious crime. In a section of this territorial law code on "The Punishment of Magical Activities" (*zauberischer Händel*), the local authorities still proclaimed divination to be a capital offense: "Likewise, those who dare to use the devil's arts to tell fortunes or to speak with the devil or have similar contact with him, using crystals or through other means, and to acquire reports or experience of secret or future things from him, are to be punished with the sword." While they did not call for the death penalty for those who consulted soothsayers, the local magistrates threatened the clients of cunning folk with a variety of heavy punishments: imprisonment, heavy fines, and even banishment for repeat offenders.[35]

The text of this 1705 ordinance is an exact word-for-word copy of Ernst the Pious's *Landesordnung* of 1667, issued at the height of witch-hunting in the region, and thus retains the charged demonological language of the seventeenth century. By the time the 1705 ordinance was published, however, the attitudes it espoused were increasingly up for debate among Thuringia's learned elites. As we have seen, the Thuringian apothecary Johann Georg Schmidt published his scathing satirical work ridiculing popular magical beliefs that same year. A few years earlier, in 1701, Christian Thomasius had published his skeptical treatise criticizing the witch hunts. It is important to remember, however, that Joseph Glanvill's *Saducismus Triumphatus,* a work dedicated to defending traditional beliefs in witchcraft and demonic magic, also appeared in 1701. Similar stinging rebukes of the progressive skepticism of Thomasius and Bekker continued to emanate from German universities until the end of the 1730s. Thus, as educated elites across Europe debated the very existence of magic and the demonic pact, Thuringian law codes continued to portray divination as inherently diabolical and deserving of the harshest punishment.

The ardent belief in the satanic nature of divination and the official concern with punishing diviners displayed in the law code certainly was not reflected in the way that Thuringian magistrates actually handled the cases that came before them in the 1700s. Ever since the start of the Reformation, official efforts to suppress divination had been halfhearted, despite the impassioned condemnations offered by the Lutheran clergy. The hesitancy to enforce the most draconian statutes against soothsaying continued, but by the eighteenth century the justification for punishing diviners had begun to change. As official skepticism about diabolical magic increased, criminal cases began to portray divination as an ignorant superstition that undermined order, a troublesome form of fraud rather than a demonic threat.

The archival records from the region demonstrate not only an increasing skepticism about the reality of magic among local authorities, but also show how these shifting attitudes prompted villagers to change the way they testified about their magical activities in court. The 1718 case from the village of Waltershausen that opened this chapter, involving what the ducal authorities called "superstitious practices," illustrates both of these shifts. Officials in Waltershausen recorded that the village fire marshal had reported the Schröter family after he found a strange sack hanging in their chimney. When the ducal officials questioned the family, they soon discovered that it was the family's young daughter, Barbara Elisabetha, who had hung the sack in hopes of divining who has stolen some missing goods. Under intense questioning, the young woman admitted that she had attempted to practice divination, but she cleverly downplayed her activities. Careful to inform her interrogators that her soothsaying had not worked, she then sought to trivialize her actions by testifying she had done it merely "in jest and as a silly game, and because she had heard of it from other people."[36]

Barbara Elisabetha's testimony reveals a key shift in how suspected diviners spoke about magic to secular magistrates. In the sixteenth and seventeenth centuries, when learned elites shared an ardent belief in magic and witchcraft with their subjects, alleged diviners invariably admitted their occult activities, and the authorities usually responded by handing down relatively petty punishments: short jail terms, fines, and shaming penalties. By the early eighteenth century, however, officials appeared increasingly skeptical about popular magical beliefs. In response, defendants like the young woman from Waltershausen became more evasive in the face of official charges. Like Barbara Elisabetha, they sought to deflect official charges by presenting themselves as ignorant bumpkins who now understood the folly of their "superstitious activities." In her case, the strategy worked, and satisfied with her contrition, the authorities dropped the case.

The skeptical attitude that the authorities adopted in the Schröter case was a recent development. As late as the 1690s, with deadly witch-hunts raging, magistrates still defined divination in religious terms, although they rarely punished it as harshly as witchcraft (or as harshly as their own statutes demanded). Some diviners, however, faced punishment. Thus, for example, in January 1692, Heinrich Hirsch, an elderly villager from Tiefenort, found himself before the court in Eisenach facing the charge of having employed divination.[37] The authorities charged that two neighbors had paid Hirsch to perform "forbidden divination, employing various superstitious, evil means." The official record echoed the Christian abhorrence of magic so prominent in the sermons and church ordinances that fueled the witch hunts. It condemned Hirsch's "sorcery and so-called divination, which is not to be tolerated by Christians," evil deeds done "in defiance of the word of God."

Languishing in jail, Hirsch submitted a petition for clemency. The old man swore never to engage in such "evil" again, reminding the authorities that he had already been imprisoned for seven weeks and that his eighty-year-old wife desperately needed him at home. The magistrates decided to show mercy and two weeks later, "owing to his age and weakness," finally released him. Heinrich Hirsch's punishment was unusually harsh. The justification, however, was typical of the era of active witch-hunting, with the authorities treating it as a form of demonic sorcery that was an affront to God.

By the mid-eighteenth century, the official discourse on folk magic had changed dramatically. Although the divinatory practices that appeared before the court were often similar to those magistrates had encountered in the 1600s (and the penalties handed down also remained similar), the language that appears in the official record shifted. Gone were the theological references to evil and Scripture, replaced by a marked skepticism. In May 1741, a decade after the last witchcraft conviction in Thuringia, a trio of apprentice papermakers stood accused of "superstitious activities" after consulting a cunning man. One of them, Johann Stoß, was arrested in March after witnesses reported that he had gone with the paper mill's maid to consult a soothsayer operating in Waltershausen in an attempt to recover stolen property. The way the officials referred to the cunning man is awkward but revealing. Eager to distance themselves from popular magical beliefs, they called him a "wise (so-called) man [*einen Klüge (so genandten) Mann*]" to make clear that although the court had no doubts that the populace regarded the Waltershausen soothsayer as a practitioner of magic, the judges themselves were very dubious that he possessed a special sort of wisdom. In other words, the strange placement of the parentheses suggests that the issue was not whether the soothsayer was allegedly operating as a "wise man," but rather that in the court's eyes he was only allegedly "wise," that is, only *reputed* to be a soothsayer.

After questioning Stoß, the magistrates reported that the cunning man had revealed the identity of the thief only after the maid suggested the suspect's name. His suspicions confirmed, Stoß had asked the soothsayer to use witchcraft to strike out the thief's eye, a common curse levied against thieves, since it would both punish and mark the culprit. Stoß divulged that two of his companions had also accompanied him to take part in these "outrageous and superstitious activities," and the authorities ordered their immediate arrest after their initial interrogation. The three apprentices were each sentenced to fourteen days' imprisonment, with Stoß restricted to bread and water for the first eight days for asking the cunning man to enact magical revenge.[38]

The Stoß case reveals several important changes in attitudes toward magic and witchcraft among both the authorities and the populace. In the 1700s, recourse to divination to substantiate witchcraft suspicions, so prevalent during the era of the witch hunts, disappears from the official record. As the authorities proved increasingly reluctant to bring witchcraft charges against suspected witches, villagers in turn became more evasive before the court. Since the ducal authorities refused to pursue witchcraft allegations, it no longer paid to divulge the names of suspected witches detected by magical means. With the secular authorities unwilling to initiate official witchcraft investigations, villagers could no longer rely on the state for help in cases of bewitchment and had to fall back on traditional remedies, ones peddled by cunning folk.

Facing skeptical magistrates, villagers avoided mentioning witchcraft and only admitted to other more benign magical beliefs. As a result, instances of using divination to reveal thieves or locate stolen goods became more prominent in the official record. Although these victims of theft might risk punishment for soothsaying, revealing their activities to the authorities might also help them regain their property. Dropping the name of a suspected thief might draw a petty punishment for engaging in "superstitious activities," but it could also prompt the authorities to question the purported thief or scare the culprit into quietly returning the stolen goods.

After midcentury, elite skepticism became even more readily apparent in the official record. By the end of the 1750s, almost thirty years after the last witchcraft trial in Thuringia, the local authorities had become reluctant to punish "superstitious activities" per se, focusing instead on the social disruption caused by these occult practices. In a case from September 1759, Barbara Fiedler from the forest village of Tambach appeared in court on the charge of consulting a well-known cunning woman operating in Schmalkalden, "the so-called chicken-thief" (*die sogennante Hünerfängerin*).[39] Fiedler had drawn official attention in the course of a theft investigation, when a witness denounced her for visiting the soothsayer in hopes of locating a sum of stolen money. According to the official record, the fortune-teller had used "playing cards"—a tarot deck—to reveal the thief. Fiedler was sentenced to three months' labor in the workhouse spinning yarn. Rather than convicting Fiedler for engaging in "superstitious activities," however, the authorities punished her instead for defaming the innocent man the diviner had named. For the local officials, the threat posed by folk magic had shifted from engaging in demonic apostasy to fomenting social disruption.

The officials' growing skepticism about folk magic is revealed in the term they used to describe the wise woman's activities with the tarot deck: *Gaukelei,* a word that had once been used for sorcery, but by the eighteenth century had come to mean an illusion (*Blendwerk*) or even a foolish prank (*Possen*).[40] By the end of the eighteenth century, Thuringian magistrates had ceased viewing witchcraft and sorcery as serious, or even credible, threats. Accordingly, punishment began to give way to incredulity. While divination was still technically illegal, by the 1750s the local archival records show it being treated as "superstitious" in the modern sense, as a foolish delusion or fraudulent activity.

A final case, from 1774, shows how far this official skepticism had advanced by the end of the century—and how tenacious popular magical beliefs remained in the face of intellectual and official disapproval. In late November 1774 two men from Wippra appeared before the ducal authorities in Saxe-Weimar for "consulting a fortune-teller" (*Wahrsager*). According to the authorities, the men had gone to visit the soothsayer after someone had stolen a measure of grain from one of their threshing barns. Calling the magical practitioner a "fortune-teller or so-called wise man," the magistrates recorded that the village authorities in Illmenau had already handled the matter. Satisfied with the way the local officials had dealt with the errant villagers, the central authorities did not appear overly concerned about the illicit activities they had uncovered. In the end, they did not even bother to sentence the villagers themselves (or even to record the punishment they had received in Wippra).[41] By the end of the eighteenth century, Thuringian central authorities proved far less eager to punish folk magic than they had been in the period of the witch hunts and had come to treat "superstition" as a minor annoyance. A vestige of rural foolishness to be handled through educational initiatives and pastoral efforts, rather than fines and imprisonment, they only deemed divination to be a problem when it threatened to disturb the peace in the rural communities where it still flourished.

In the course of the eighteenth century, members of Europe's intellectual and ruling classes, eager to distinguish themselves from the "vulgar" populace, increasingly proclaimed belief in witchcraft and magic empty and foolish. They gradually redefined superstition itself, giving it the contemporary definition of a principle that cannot be scientifically verified, as opposed to the traditional meaning that associated it with mistaken or misdirected religiosity. By the end of the 1700s, the mechanical philosophy fostered by the Enlightenment had won out. Intellectuals discredited the basis of magical belief by radically separating the spiritual and physical worlds.

Theological changes bolstered these intellectual developments. Embracing a new rationalist theology, enlightened clergymen denied the continued existence of either the magical or the miraculous in the contemporary world. Rooting their theology in a rigorous new biblical philology, they circumscribed the earthly power of demons and refuted the reality of witchcraft. This new skepticism about the reality of magic, espoused in pamphlets and books written by forward-thinking intellectuals and enlightened ecclesiastics, gradually spread from educated elites to the urban middle classes in the course of the eighteenth century.

Despite these developments, the new intellectual and theological currents in Europe were slow to affect official law enforcement in Thuringia. As the archival record from the region shows, traditional magical beliefs endured in the countryside, and local authorities continued to punish these activities until the end of the eighteenth century. A crucial shift occurred around midcentury, however. Whereas before 1750, secular authorities still punished divination as a violation of Christian commandments as their predecessors had done a century before, after midcentury they began to treat folk magic as an ignorant superstition and punished it as a form of fraud or disorderly conduct. By the end of the century, they rarely bothered to punish the "superstitious activities" of their rural subjects at all.

That the supernatural had become a matter of controversy among many jurists and theologians in the wake of the witch hunts mattered little to the inhabitants of rural villages in Thuringia. In the region's rural communities belief in witchcraft and folk magic still flourished throughout the 1700s. Despite the changing views of intellectual elites, much of the rural populace continued to fear bewitchment and relied on magical remedies throughout the so-called Age of Reason. After the witch hunts ended and judicial authorities grew increasingly reluctant to investigate witchcraft allegations, individuals continued to think and act in a world animated by magical forces and to rely on soothsaying in the face of misfortune. Enduring the rigors of a premodern subsistence economy, villagers still sought to cope with misfortune and uncertainty in the same manner as their ancestors, and their responses often included recourse to divination. They continued to understand sudden loss and to express social strife in the language of witchcraft and magic, consulting witch-doctors and soothsayers and using traditional charms and incantations.[42]

Villagers understood, however, that the views of the central authorities had changed, so they changed how they testified in court. They kept their suspicions of bewitchment to themselves, since they could no longer rely on the courts to prosecute suspected witches. But they continued to testify in court about their interactions with diviners in cases of theft, a crime their rulers still recognized. By the close of the eighteenth century, educated elites had relegated witchcraft and soothsaying to fairy tales and stage productions, and they regarded the enduring magical beliefs of the rural populace as nothing but foolish superstitions. In the rural districts of Thuringia, however, villagers still turned to diviners for answers in an uncertain world.

CONCLUSION

This book began with the story of a mysterious wise man who had entered the Thuringian village of Ohrdruf in 1671, late in the reign of Duke Ernst the Pious. In exchange for a mug of beer, he had told the villagers' fortunes, warning one of them about the spells cast by a witch. The ensuing neighbors' squabble sparked an abortive official investigation that uncovered the fortune-teller's occult activities. He was far from the last soothsayer the officials in Gotha encountered, and almost 170 years later, they investigated another wise man plying his trade in the duchy. Dating from the mid-nineteenth century, the case took place in the reign of Ernst II of Saxe-Coburg and Gotha, a descendant of Duke Ernst the Pious, and it shows the prominent place divination retained in modern Thuringian villages.

The incident involved a recalcitrant cunning man and faith healer named Johann Michael Koch. In May 1840, he was arrested and brought before the magistrates in Ohrdruf for engaging in "superstitious activities" that included several forms of divination. Koch's divinatory practices were strikingly similar to those of soothsayers like the wise man of Ohrdruf in the 1600s. The local Thuringian authorities charged Koch, a sixty-three-year-old former linen weaver, with employing "criminal fortune-telling arts" to perform divination for three women. The women testified that they had journeyed together to see Koch owing to his fame throughout the region as a healer and fortune-teller. The authorities dismissed Koch's abilities out of hand, identifying him as a "known con man."

However, the women placed great faith in the old weaver, asking him to provide a range of occult services.

The first of the women, the wife of a teamster, testified that she had traveled to visit Koch after several horses purchased by her husband mysteriously died. The couple feared witchcraft, and suspected their neighbor, an old widow, of bewitching their horses. Acting as a witch-finder, the nineteenth-century soothsayer confirmed the woman's fears and warned her that there were indeed malevolent witches afoot, going on to reveal that her village harbored a coven of forty-three to be exact: seventeen male and twenty-six female witches. After agreeing to use counter-magic to punish the widow for her hexes, Koch then provided his occult services to the other women, poor day laborers' wives, interpreting a dream for one and healing another.[1] The women may have believed in Koch's powers, but the magistrates certainly did not. Treating him as a troublesome fraud, the authorities sentenced Koch to a two-month jail stint for his occult practices. But the matter did not end there. They would deal with the stubborn soothsayer frequently during the next decade, as he served clients from all across the duchy. Over the years, his business remained brisk, and clients traveled great distances to consult him. One even came from Stollberg, a journey of more than 120 miles, showing the great stock he placed in the diviner.

In 1844, Johann Koch attracted official attention again. Jailing him in the *Zuchthaus,* the authorities collected testimony from his former clients, building a case that centered on the disruption his occult activities caused. They alleged that his witch-finding activities had turned a daughter against her mother in Schwarzhausen, his dowsing had instigated a wild treasure hunt in Krautshausen, and his faith healing had defrauded twenty-two gulden from four patients who had traveled from Gotha to seek his occult cures. Interrogated about the nature of his occult activities, he testified that "he knew not how God conferred the power on him when he called on Him." Calling him a "swindler," and noting that his daughter had recently given birth out of wedlock (for the authorities a sure sign of his poor character), the investigating officer recommended a stiff punishment for Koch, owing to his incorrigibility.[2]

The authorities' efforts to keep Koch on the straight and narrow seemed to have failed, and two years later he was in custody again. This time, before sentencing the stubborn soothsayer, the frustrated magistrates turned to medical and psychological experts in order to investigate his occult powers. They began by looking into his activities as a faith healer. They asked the territory's chief medical official, Dr. Lecker, to examine the old healer and soothsayer in an effort to determine whether he was "a con man, a mad man, or whether he had some special power to heal." Lecker interviewed Koch for four days, reporting that the old man had learned "sympathetic medicine" as a surgical orderly in an Austrian unit during the Napoleonic Wars. Koch told the physician that he practiced his "secret" cures first on cattle and eventually on people. He practiced without incident until he was sixty, when he ran into trouble with a disgruntled patient.[3]

In his report, Lecker describes Koch's "simple" method of treating patients, detailing how the old man prayed over them, asking that the "blood of Jesus Christ wash away their sin." He also noted that Koch was evasive when asked about the "inner workings" of his craft and maintained that the old man never asked for payment from his patients, living in abject poverty. Interestingly, the medical expert did not ask Koch where he got the power to perform his other services for his clients—soothsaying, witch-finding, and magical treasure-hunting. Instead, the physician focused on Koch's medical practice, seeking a scientific explanation for his fame as a folk healer by subjecting him to a series of pseudoscientific experiments.

Koch failed to show any extraordinary abilities until Lecker tested him with a magnet. According to the physician, when he placed a discharged magnet in Koch's hand, the old weaver re-magnetized it. In his summary report, the physician testified that Koch was not a deliberate fraud and that he was "by nature magnetic." Lecker cited the work of Franz Anton Mesmer, whose esoteric theories of "animal magnetism" were stirring heated controversy among scientists and physicians in the 1840s.[4] Using Mesmer's theories to buttress his diagnosis, the physician sought to contrast his own scientific interpretation with "earlier times," when magical belief flourished, "and the devil reigned in every head."[5] For Lecker, the old man's preternatural abilities were not out of the question, but they needed to be explained using scientific reason rather than superstitious belief.

Dr. Lecker was not the only expert the authorities in Gotha consulted, however, to evaluate Koch. Another learned specialist enlisted in the case was the physician Dr. Friedrich Kirmair, whose more intense skepticism of the old man's abilities led him to seek a diagnosis of mental illness. Kirmair interviewed Koch in his cell and wrote a detailed report, which included the wise man's colored jailhouse drawings. In these strange sketches, Koch produced cluttered depictions of Jesus, the Lamb of God, crucifixion scenes, and unidentifiable mystical symbols. Contradicting Lecker, the alienist reported that there was nothing special about the old weaver. He was just a deluded old man suffering from what Kirmair called "*Mania Religiosa,* a variety expressed as *Daemoniamania.*"[6] Apparently, the local authorities were no more swayed by the alienist's diagnosis of mental illness than they were the physician's hypotheses about Koch's animal magnetism. Still convinced the old weaver was a charlatan, they kept him in custody as they pondered what to do with him. The official record trails off with Koch still in jail awaiting sentencing.

This would not be Koch's last stay in the *Zuchthaus,* however, and he was jailed repeatedly over the course of the next decade. In the spring of 1848, as the March Revolution rocked Thuringia, the ducal authorities arrested him yet again for "charlatanism and soothsaying."[7] In September 1850, he was jailed in Gotha for eight days after a gendarme in Nazza caught him performing occult services for a woman and her daughter.[8] The last time Koch appears in the archival record he was being released from jail yet again, in September 1854—by that time he was aged seventy-four—having served a six-month sentence for engaging in his usual "superstitious activities."[9]

The case of Johann Koch shows that a wide range of occult practices survived in the villages and towns of Thuringia until well into the nineteenth century. Like cunning folk operating in the region two centuries before, he provided a range of occult services for his clients, including fortune-telling, witch-finding, counter-magic, and magical healing. Like them, his magical activities were tinged with Christian devotions, and

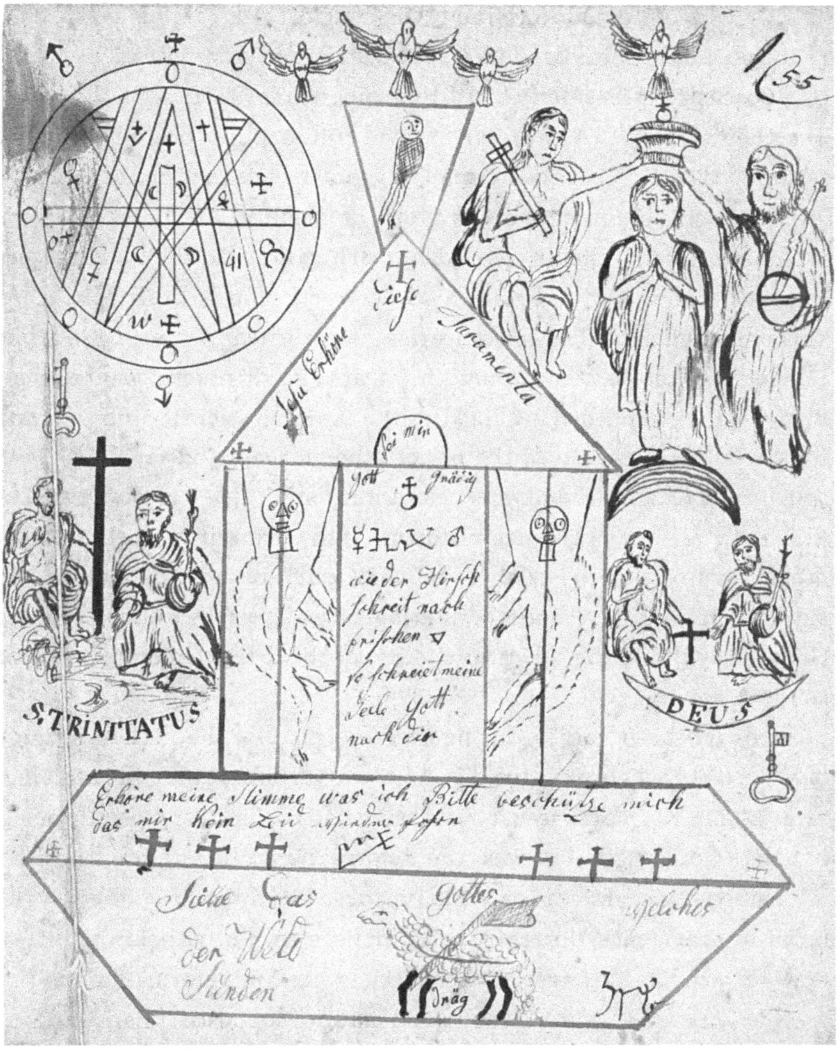

While in custody in 1846, Johann Koch produced several mystical drawings, which the authorities included in his criminal file. (Landesarchiv Thüringen, Staatsarchiv Gotha, Justizamt Nazza Nr.366, Bl.55.)

clients came from far-and-wide to consult him. His case also indicates that the educated elites of his day—government officials, physicians, alienists—retained an interest in these magical beliefs. The ducal authorities in Gotha, confronting the disruptive effects of Koch's magical activities, concerned themselves with punishing the old man. The learned experts who examined Koch, however, sought to explain his magical activities using science. Dr. Lecker, the district physician, relied upon the pseudoscience of mesmerism, still quite popular in Germany in the 1840s. The alienist, Dr. Kirmair, implemented rudimentary proto-psychiatric techniques to diagnose the old man's magical beliefs in terms of an excessive religiosity, branding them as a form of insanity.

Johann Koch's clients needed no such rationalizations, as the old weaver's widespread reputation as a diviner and a healer show. As Thuringian villagers had for centuries, they turned to cunning folk like him for magical assistance when they feared bewitchment, wanted their fortunes told, or needed healing. Despite the rapid scientific progress and industrial development of the period, the villagers and townsfolk who sought out Koch in the nineteenth century still turned to occult practitioners to deal with personal misfortune and uncertainty. In the form of dream augury, fortune-telling, and even witch-finding, divination had survived in the rural corners of Thuringia even after the railroad came to Gotha in 1847 and the constitutionalists of the Erfurt Union met in that city in 1849.

Three centuries earlier, during the Reformation, the Lutheran clergy had launched a vigorous campaign to root out the sort of popular divination Johann Koch practiced. Soothsaying had been discouraged throughout the Middle Ages, but with the Reformation, Protestant authorities intensified efforts to eradicate the practice. Given recent studies on the belief in providence, portents, and prophecy within Lutheran parishes, however, scholars now recognize that the Protestant Reformation was not as wholly "rational" and "disenchanted" as once supposed.[10] Early modern Lutherans relied on a wide range of divinatory practices, both erudite and homespun. Pious forms of astrology, sanctioned by the clergy, flourished among learned Lutherans in the early decades of the Reformation.[11] The Lutheran clergy's position on less erudite forms of divination, however, was unequivocal. Martin Luther denounced such soothsaying as demonic from the start of his career as a reformer. In a 1518 sermon, for example, he railed against fortune-telling as a spiritual danger, "a hellish trap" that drew wavering Christians into the devil's clutches.[12]

Echoing Luther, later Protestant ministers proved tireless in their efforts to convince the faithful that popular forms of divination were demonic and must be rooted out from the Christian community. The devastation of the Thirty Years' War fostered apocalyptic anxieties, and in the wake of the war new works appeared that condemned popular divination with increased severity. Departing from the works of the early reformers, who treated divination as a matter of individual sinfulness, these works introduced a new activist rhetoric and called upon secular authorities to stamp out these devilish rites.

In postwar Thuringia, Protestant princes appeared eager to answer the call. As they sought to reform popular culture and instill Protestant morality among their subjects, Lutheran rulers issued draconian laws, empowered consistories, and authorized visitations to root out such "sinful" behavior. Despite these official efforts, however, the archival record shows that in practice punishment did not match the ferocity of the statutes. While Thuringian rulers sought the appearance of being stringent in their reform efforts, and no doubt wanted to appease their court preachers, their enforcement of the laws against divination remained halfhearted.

Although particularly zealous rulers like Ernst the Pious sometimes managed to arrest soothsayers and their clients, efforts to suppress divination proved futile. Early modern law enforcement was always uneven in its application, relying on harsh prohibitions and exemplary corporal punishments in an attempt to deter lawbreakers. In practice, however, even determined secular authorities lacked the resources to police their subjects effectively and could only prosecute when they received denunciations. In applying their penal authority, rulers could not impose their will and had to rely on their subjects' cooperation at every turn. Thus, official penal procedures were only effective when they enjoyed the support of the populace and did not deviate too sharply from accepted norms.[13]

Given these halfhearted and ineffective efforts to suppress soothsaying, recourse to popular forms of divination remained widespread in Thuringia long after the Reformation. Clerical calls to curtail it faltered in the face of both official apathy and popular resistance. Official apathy sometimes concealed a passive acceptance of soothsaying. Ducal officials sometimes relied on the assistance of the very cunning folk they were supposed to be punishing, as we encountered in chapter 3 with the Aspach official who lost his register and turned to a wise woman for help. Given divination's ubiquity, Protestant princes in the region proved willing to issue legislation banning divination and to endorse the clergy's attempts to root it out through sermons, catechisms, consistories, and visitations. In practice, however, they proved more interested in hunting witches than soothsayers. Meanwhile, many of their subjects continued to practice divination and consult cunning folk, blending the teachings of the Lutheran clergy with traditional forms of folk belief when facing hardship.

While many parishioners no doubt embraced the austere providentialism of Lutheran orthodoxy, the era's visitation reports and criminal cases show that others sought out the aid of either their local clergy or cunning folk with equal enthusiasm in times of adversity. Given the continued popularity of occult soothsaying in Thuringia's villages and small towns, it is no wonder that enforcement of the official statutes against divination proved so weak. While Thuringian villagers were eager to cooperate with the authorities in eradicating witches, and willingly denounced their neighbors for moral lapses, they proved more reluctant to testify against a trusted soothsayer.[14] Many parishioners continued to draw a practical distinction between helpful and harmful forms of magic, ignoring their pastors' call to avoid supposedly diabolical diviners.

The reluctance of the populace to denounce soothsayers stemmed from the crucial role that these trusted magical practitioners played within the resilient folk culture of the era. A rich substratum of magical beliefs operated in tandem with official Christianity in the Lutheran parishes of early modern Germany.[15] In the face of official repression, many of Thuringia's rural inhabitants retained a belief in a universe animated by magical forces, both benign and malevolent, and still relied upon divination for protection and reassurance.[16] The educational and disciplinary initiatives that accompanied the Reformation did little to hamper these activities. In fact, the violence and uncertainty of the confessional age, presented in moralized and even apocalyptic terms by the Lutheran clergy, likely made soothsaying more appealing than ever to anxious villagers.

Although the Lutheran clergy preached a theological message that accentuated God's providential role and denied the power of Catholic rituals and magical rites alike, many of their parishioners clung to traditional folk beliefs that offered solace in an uncertain world. Scholars increasingly view popular magical beliefs as a crucial component of early modern culture, one that operated in tandem with orthodox religiosity. Edward Bever, for example, has argued that in early modern Europe magic "played at least as great a role as formal Christianity," pointing out that it offered practical solutions to everyday problems, instead of addressing "cosmological issues or the moral requirements of salvation" like the official religion of the pastors.[17] It is important to remember that clerics and rulers, as well as commoners, experienced the Reformation within the context of these traditional beliefs.

Early modern Europeans understood the universe to be populated with an array of supernatural forces. Everyday life was suffused with efforts to influence entities that could help or harm: God and the devil, angels and demons, fairies and witches, spirits and ghosts. While God might visit his wrath or his deliverance on the world, in the popular imagination he often remained somewhat remote. Living in great want and threatened by unpredictable misfortune, common people used magic in an attempt to placate or control other supernatural entities that could offer protection or bring disaster. In an uncertain world magic offered common people protection by supplying "a practical form of help or self-help concerned with very concrete problems of daily life."[18]

Protestant reformers repudiated the sacrality of many Catholic practices and objects, but they did not abandon belief in supernatural intervention in the world. In fact, by emphasizing how God made his displeasure manifest through portents, prophecies, and plagues, they may have increased anxiety among their parishioners, who could no longer rely upon the sacramental remedies once offered by the Catholic clergy for succor. Amid this anxious atmosphere, and no longer forced to compete with parish priests in offering their services, cunning folk continued to ply their trade in Protestant areas, and their business thrived.[19] To the consternation of their pastors, common people still turned to diviners in troubled times.

Early modern parishioners resisted efforts to repress popular divination not only because it proved so useful in dealing with adversity, but also because many refused to see it as sinful. Despite the sermons and censures of the Lutheran clergy, many ordinary Thuringians persisted in viewing magic as morally neutral, its morality determined only by the ends to which it was put. A helpful activity, one motivated by good intentions—avoiding hidden dangers, diagnosing mysterious illnesses, and uncovering malevolent witchcraft—divination did not seem evil to soothsayers or their clients, despite what their pastors told them.[20] Given soothsaying's value in dealing with practical problems, and the common view that it was morally ambiguous at worst, it is no surprise that it proved so durable in the face of official repression.[21]

While divination remained an everyday activity for many Thuringian villagers until well into the eighteenth century, members of Europe's intellectual and ruling classes gradually came to regard belief in magic as empty and foolish. In the early Reformation, clerics, rulers, and commoners had shared a magical worldview that accepted the reality of witchcraft, sorcery, and divination, although they differed on the issue of demonic agency. By the mid-1700s, elite and popular attitudes about magic began to diverge, as elites adopted an enlightened skepticism in order to differentiate themselves from the "vulgar masses." Among the learned, Cartesian materialism became more prominent, with intellectuals discrediting the basis of magical belief by radically separating the spiritual and physical worlds. Meanwhile, these new intellectual currents also affected Protestant theology as the clergy adopted a new rationalist theology with less room for the magical or the miraculous. Even though the supernatural had become a matter of controversy among jurists and theologians in the wake of the witch hunts, belief in divination and other forms of folk magic still flourished in the rural communities of eighteenth-century Thuringia.[22]

By the mid-eighteenth century, the juridical discourse on folk magic had changed dramatically from that of the era of active witch-hunting. Although the magical practices that were brought before the court were often similar to those magistrates had encountered in the 1600s, the language that appears in the official record had shifted. Gone were the theological references to evil and Scripture, replaced by a marked skepticism. By the 1740s, Thuringian magistrates had ceased regarding even witchcraft, much less divination, as a serious or credible threat. Accordingly, punishment began to give way to incredulity and mockery. While divination was still technically illegal, the local archival record shows it being treated as "superstitious" in the modern sense, as a foolish delusion or fraudulent activity, as opposed to the traditional understanding that associated it with religious error or diabolism.[23] Despite such official skepticism, however, it was practiced surreptitiously in the villages and towns of Thuringia until modern times.

While divination never died out completely, there is no doubt that its role in German society had diminished greatly by the time Johann Koch was plying his trade in the 1840s. Historians have provided a number of explanations for the decline of magical belief that supposedly accompanied modernity, but there is little consensus. Euan Cameron argues that the theological campaign against superstition that began in the Middle Ages and intensified during the Reformation reduced the fear of the devil, paving the way for Enlightenment-era skepticism and fostering the decline of magical belief among educated elites.[24] Based exclusively on learned theological treatises and demonologies, however, his study does little to explain how attitudes changed among the majority of the populace. His focus on the clerical discourse on "superstition" may also have caused him to underestimate just how much "enchantment" remained in eighteenth-century Europe, even among educated elites.

Edward Bever, on the other hand, relying on archival sources from early modern Württemberg, argues that popular magical beliefs dwindled by the eighteenth century largely in response to official repression. Bever contends that "all trials for beneficent magic appear to have fallen off during the late seventeenth century, at least in part because the practices they punished were suppressed: practiced less frequently and/or more furtively."[25] In his view, during the witch hunts, cunning folk gradually abandoned their activities due to official harassment and the fear of being accused of witchcraft.

Bever's argument that official disciplinary initiatives suppressed magical activities does not work for early modern Thuringia. Enforcement of the statutes against divination and other forms of folk magic remained tepid in the region and the penalties handed down exceedingly mild. In fact, many of the divination cases examined in this book only came to the attention of the authorities when a villager incriminated himself or herself. In hopes of initiating an official investigation of an alleged witch or thief, villagers sometimes proved willing to divulge that a soothsayer had confirmed their suspicions. Thus, villagers proved willing to risk punishment for consulting diviners in order to get the courts to punish local malefactors. This usually proved a safe bet, since the authorities rarely punished those who testified about consulting a cunning man or a wise woman, and when they did it was invariably with a trifling penalty. In any case, it is misleading to infer, as Bever does, that declining prosecution rates signal a decline in a given criminal behavior. It is just as likely that a decline in prosecutions signals a shift in official interest in a particular crime or even a decrease in the number of denunciations delivered to the authorities.

While Cameron and Bever provide a wealth of useful insights, they both work within a modernization paradigm rooted in Weber's notion of disenchantment. They echo Weber in arguing that magical belief declined as the appearance of new intellectual and theological currents and the emergence of the bureaucratic state paved the way for modernity. In light of this Weberian perspective, it may seem surprising that Johann Koch, the wise man we examined in the beginning of this conclusion, was still plying his trade with such success in the 1840s and 1850s.

The marked similarity between Koch's magical activities and those of Thuringian cunning folk operating in the region in the sixteenth and seventeenth centuries is indeed striking. The fact that clients traveled considerable distances to consult with the old wise man in the 1840s and 1850s should not be surprising, however, because a new consensus is emerging that calls the entire notion of disenchantment into question, undermining the supposed links between modernity and the abandonment of magic. Instead of magical belief gradually declining in the face of modernity, scholars have identified a cyclical alternation between periods of disenchantment and re-enchantment. Rather than focusing on the decline of magical belief, scholars have begun to acknowledge the prevalence of magical and esoteric beliefs in modern Europe.[26]

While the Reformation had a dramatic impact on how Protestants understood the sacred and affected their understanding of how believers accessed divine grace, scholars have long recognized that its effect on popular magical belief was far more limited.[27] The ambitious reform efforts that accompanied the Protestant Reformation could achieve much when clerical and secular authorities, showing a willingness to accommodate traditional beliefs, worked alongside the populace to pursue reforms. However, when the interests of rulers and subjects diverged, or when the authorities refused to negotiate with the populace, change was more difficult. When reform efforts met with resistance, as they did in the suppression of divination, they often faltered. Given the difficulty in pursuing unpopular reform initiatives, it should come as no surprise that traditional magical beliefs like those practiced by Johann Koch survived in rural areas of Europe into the nineteenth and even twentieth centuries.

Rural villagers and townsfolk were not alone in continuing to harbor magical beliefs into the modern period. A scholarly consensus has emerged, viewing elite culture during the so-called Age of Reason as more enchanted than once supposed.[28] In fact, recent studies have even suggested that the early Enlightenment actually served to *stimulate* learned interest in the supernatural with skeptics and defenders of traditional beliefs in magic and witchcraft producing ponderous tomes and pithy pamphlets on the subject that drew a wide readership.[29]

It appears that the notion of "disenchantment" itself was a cultural construct, an intellectual posture adopted by seventeenth- and eighteenth-century elites as a means of differentiating themselves from the masses on the basis of their supposed skepticism.[30] Recent studies suggest that even this superficial sort of disenchantment conceals an abiding interest in the occult among Enlightenment-era elites, who did not so much abandon magical belief as banish it from the public sphere. Afraid of inviting ridicule by professing interest in the occult, enlightened gentlemen increasingly came to treat it as matter for private reflection. Thus, the occult interests of the educated elite gradually disappeared from published works but persisted in private letters and notebooks and in literature and theater.[31]

The dramatic reemergence of supernatural belief and magical practice among educated elites in the nineteenth and twentieth centuries has further challenged the disenchantment paradigm. Increasingly, scholars view the burgeoning popularity of esotericism, occultism, and spiritualism in the late nineteenth century less as a new phenomenon than as the reappearance of supernatural beliefs that were sublimated but not eliminated by the Enlightenment.[32] Likewise, it is increasingly apparent that the ground magical belief lost to science was gained in the realm of the imagination. No longer figures of dread, the soothsayer, the sorcerer, and the witch emerged as stock characters in the fairy tales collected by early folklorists, in the literature and drama of the Romantic period, and in the popular mass media of the modern age.[33]

The prevalence of the occult in European culture after the Enlightenment has prompted some historians to question the validity of the disenchantment paradigm altogether. Instead of asking why magical belief disappeared, and explaining its continued presence as a mere vestige of traditional cosmologies, scholars increasingly question whether modernity and enchantment are truly incompatible.[34] Studies of late nineteenth-century Germany, for example, have demonstrated that magical belief began to flourish again among large segments of the German bourgeoisie. By the 1880s Germany had a number of occult journals in circulation, more than two hundred clubs dedicated to esoteric pursuits in operation, and more than six hundred mediums working in Berlin alone.[35] Examining German Theosophists in the late nineteenth and early twentieth centuries, Corinna Treitel concludes that modernity and modern occultism, which arose together, are intimately linked. She demonstrates that the occult was not a fringe activity in fin-de-siècle Germany, but rather that it informed avant-garde modern art, had short-lived but important connections to mainstream science through parapsychology, and was prominent in mass consumer culture as well.[36]

While Treitel's study undermines the disenchantment paradigm by demonstrating that the occult was an important facet of modernity, her work obscures the links between the new occultism and old magical beliefs. As Thomas Laqueur points out in a provocative essay, practitioners of nineteenth- and twentieth-century occultism consciously incorporated elements of traditional magical beliefs, harkening back to ancient occult traditions. He argues that for adepts, the occult, and especially modern esotericism, seeks to answer timeless questions about the meaning of the universe and the transcendence of the spirit. Thus, it serves as a form of religion, one suited for the eclecticism and individualism of the modern world by eschewing both church and dogma.[37]

The recent reappraisal of modernity, casting it as enchanted in a distinctively modern way, calls into question the entire notion of teleological disenchantment. In a thoughtful essay, Alexandra Walsham encouraged scholars to think of disenchantment as part of a cycle "in which opposing impulses interacted dynamically and played off each other in a reciprocal and dialectical fashion."[38] By abandoning the strictly teleological modernizing narrative, the cyclical phases of dis- and re-enchantment that occurred between the medieval and modern periods become comprehensible. Movements like the Enlightenment that accentuated rationalism faced backlash from subsequent movements like Romanticism or modern occultism that not only accentuated the irrational but also recoiled from what some regarded as the barren materialism of modern scientific and industrial progress. Thus, the proliferation of modern occultism flies in the face of a linear disenchantment paradigm, which views magical belief only in terms of its vestiges.

In early modern Thuringia, soothsaying was certainly not a mere survival of some primitive cosmology, hanging on in the face of modernization and progress. Instead, popular forms of divination like palm reading, crystal gazing, and sieve turning endured as important means of understanding and confronting misfortune and uncertainty. The campaign to eradicate popular forms of divination in the wake of the Reformation failed because Lutheran theologians and demonologists proved unable to convince either Protestant princes or common parishioners that soothsaying posed a deadly threat to the Christian community. Secular authorities resisted clerical pressure to treat divination as a diabolical crime deserving of capital punishment. Instead, they reserved the death penalty for witchcraft and, ignoring their own draconian statutes, handed down petty punishments for soothsayers and their clients. Facing only halfhearted disciplinary measures and ignoring the warnings of their pastors, villagers and townsfolk continued to rely on divination in times of hardship. Given the crucial functions soothsayers performed in early modern society, commoners proved reluctant to denounce the wise men and women who served their villages, crippling official disciplinary efforts. As a result, divination survived into modern times, marking the limits of the reform initiatives that accompanied both the Reformation and the Enlightenment and showing the resilience of early modern folk culture.

Divination persists, but its prevalence has gradually diminished in the modern world amid rapidly changing social conditions. In the end, it was not the reforming zeal of the Lutheran clergy or the penal power of the Thuringian princes that caused divination to fade to the margins of modern society. Rather, changing conditions gradually made occult prognostication seem somewhat superfluous. In the late nineteenth century, as the dearth and anxiety that had plagued the early modern period slowly receded, people had fewer reasons to consult soothsayers. With increasing urbanization, rural inhabitants left behind village animosities and the uncertainties of farming and raising livestock and fears of witchcraft subsided, making divination seem less essential. The spread of compulsory education and mass conscription, along with the appearance of mass media, transport, and new modes of consumption, broke down old forms of folk culture. Modern medicine, insurance, and social welfare programs gradually took the place of magical protections from harm.[39] Ultimately, divination moved to the realm of the imagination, still appearing in the literature and drama of mass consumer culture long after modern society had begun to offer reliable substitutes for the warnings of soothsayers. Amid the insecurities of modern life, though, divination still proves surprisingly durable. As a glance at the horoscope section of any newspaper shows, it even survives today as the only form of occult activity widely practiced in the modern West.[40] Like early modern Thuringian villagers, people continue to use divination to make sense of their lives.

NOTES

Introduction

1. Thüringisches Staatsarchiv Gotha, Justizamt Ohrdruf (vol. 89); Loc. B, Nr. 11–23: Hanns Karsten wegen Däller wegen Hexerei (1671). Please note that the Thuringian archival records include various spellings of proper names. The defendant in this case will appear as Hans Karst.
2. In recent works, Michael Bailey and P. G. Maxwell-Stuart have both identified this gap in the existing scholarship. See Bailey, *Magic and Superstition in Europe,* 7; and Maxwell-Stuart, ed., *Malleus Maleficarum,* 10–11. An exhaustive literature exists on witchcraft and witch-hunting in early modern Germany. It is impossible to survey this entire corpus here, but important examples include H. C. Erik Midelfort, *Witch Hunting in Southwestern Germany, 1562–1684: The Social and Intellectual Foundations* (Stanford, 1972); Gerhard Schormann, *Hexenprozesse in Deutschland* (Göttingen, 1981); Walter Niess, *Hexenprozesse in der Grafschaft Büdingen: Protokolle, Ursachen, Hintergründe* (Büdingen, 1982); Wolfgang Behringer, *Hexen und Hexenprozesse in Deutschland* (München, 1988); Herbert Pohl, *Hexenglaube und Hexenverfolgung im Kurfürsten Mainz: Ein Beitrag zur Hexenfrage im 16. Und beginnenden 17. Jahrhundert* (Stuttgart, 1988); Günther Jerouschek, *Die Hexen und ihr Prozeß: Die Hexenverfolgungen in der Reichsstadt Esslingen* (Esslingen, 1992); Rainer Walz, *Hexenglaube und magische Kommunikation im Dorf der frühen Neuzeit: Die Verfolgungen in der Grafschaft Lippe* (Paderborn, 1993); Gunther Franz and Franz Irsigler, *Hexenglaube und Hexenprozesse im Raum Rhein-Mosel-Saar* (Trier, 1995); Rainer Decker, *Die Hexen und ihre Henker: Ein Fallbericht* (Freiburg, 1994); Wolfgang Behringer, *Witchcraft Persecutions in Bavaria: Popular Magic, Religious Zealotry, and Reason of State in Early Modern Europe* (Cambridge, 1997); Alison Rowlands, *Witchcraft Narratives in Germany: Rothenburg, 1561–1652* (Manchester, 2003); Manfred Wilde, *Die Zauberei- und Hexenprozesse in Kursachsen* (Köln, 2003); Lyndal Roper, *Witch Craze: Terror and Fantasy in Baroque Germany* (New Haven, 2004); Rita Voltmer, *Hexenverfolgung und Herrschaftspraxis* (Trier, 2005); Johannes Dillinger, *Böse Leute: Hexenverfolgungen in Schwäbisch-Österreich und Kurtrier im Vergleich* (Trier, 1999), published in English as *"Evil People": A Comparative Study of Witch Hunts in Swabian Austria and the Electorate of Trier* (Charlottesville,

2009); and Thomas Robisheaux, *The Last Witch of Langenburg: Murder in a German Village* (New York, 2009). For a useful, concise survey of the German witch-hunts, see Thomas Robisheaux, "The German Witch Trials," in Levack, ed., *Oxford Handbook of Witchcraft*, 179–98.

3. See Wilson, *Magical Universe*, for a fascinating discussion of the ubiquity of magic, including divination, in premodern Europe. For the prevalence of divination in early modern Europe, see Edward Bever, "Popular Witch Beliefs and Magical Practices," in Levack, ed., *Oxford Handbook of Witchcraft*, 52; and Euan Cameron, *Enchanted Europe*, 63–69.
4. For a detailed study of the uses of divination in early modern Württemberg, see Bever, *Realities of Witchcraft and Popular Magic*, 216.
5. Few scholars have explored the activities of the magical practitioners known as cunning folk. Notable exceptions include Eva Labouvie, *Verbotene Künste: Volksmagie und ländlicher Aberglaube in den Dorfgemeinschaften des Saarraumes (16.–19. Jahrhunderts)* (St. Ingert, 1992); Willem de Blécourt, "Witch Doctors, Soothsayers, and Priests: On Cunning Folk in European Historiography and Tradition," *Social History* 19 (1994): 285–303; Walter Rummel, "'Weise' Frauen und 'weise' Männer im Kampf gegen Hexerei. Die Widerlegung einer modernen Fabel," in Christof Dipper, Lutz Klinkhammer, and Alexander Nützenadel, eds., *Europäische Sozialgeschichte. Festschrift für Wolfgang Schieder* (Berlin, 2000), 353–75; Owen Davies, *Popular Magic: Cunning-Folk in English History* (London, 2003); Bever, *Realities of Witchcraft and Popular Magic;* and Johannes Dillinger, *Magical Treasure Hunting in Europe and North America: A History* (Basingstoke, 2012).
6. For the history of divination in the ancient world, see Bever, *Realities of Witchcraft and Popular Magic*, 219–20.
7. See Collins, ed., *Cambridge History of Magic and Witchcraft.*
8. For medieval attitudes toward magic, see Kieckhefer, *Magic in the Middle Ages.*
9. Clark, "Protestant Demonology," in Levack, ed., *New Perspectives on Witchcraft, Magic, and Demonology*, 179–215.
10. See Clark, *Thinking with Demons*, 460–64.
11. Max Weber, *The Protestant Ethic and the Spirit of Capitalism* (New York, 2002; first English ed. 1930). First published in 1905 as *Die protestantische Ethik und der Geist des Kapitalismus*, Weber's work has had a major influence on Reformation history. For a lucid discussion of this scholarship, see Michael Saler, "Modernity and Enchantment: A Historiographical Review," *American Historical Review* 111:3 (June 2006): 692–716. See also Robert W. Scribner, "The Reformation, Popular Magic and the 'Disenchantment of the World,'" *Journal of Interdisciplinary History* 23 (1993): 475–94; Richard van Dülmen, *Religion und Gesellschaft. Beiträge zu einer Religionsgeschichte der Neuzeit* (Frankfurt am Main, 1989); Cameron, *Enchanted Europe*, 10–11; and Thomas A. Brady Jr., "Social History," in Steven Ozment, ed., *Reformation Europe: A Guide to Research* (St. Louis, 1982), 161–81.
12. Useful treatment of this "teleological" tradition in Reformation scholarship is provided by Brady, "Social History," 161–81. For a survey of historiographical trends in Reformation scholarship from the 1500s to the 1980s, see Dickens and Tonkin, *Reformation in Historical Thought.*

13. Thomas, *Religion and the Decline of Magic*. For a useful discussion of the influence of the Weberian paradigm on scholarship on late medieval and early modern religion, as well as the subtle ways that his view of the Reformation continues to affect the way that historians consider the problem of religious change, see Walsham, "Migrations of the Holy," 241–80.
14. See van Dülmen, "Reformation und Neuzeit," 1–25.
15. For an excellent overview of this scholarship, see Boettcher, "Social Impact of the Lutheran Reformation," 305–59.
16. According to Susan Boettcher, research since the 1970s "suggests that Lutheranism enjoyed a much more modest effect on most areas of society than the initial claims of much earlier scholarship asserted." See Boettcher, "Social Impact of the Lutheran Reformation," 307. For examples of this scholarship, see Roper, *Household;* and Brady, *Turning Swiss.*
17. Strauss, *Luther's House of Learning.*
18. James Kittelson, for example, challenged the applicability of Strauss's findings for urban communities. See James Kittelson, "Successes and Failures in the German Reformation: The Report from Strasbourg," *Archiv für Reformationsgeschichte* 73 (1982): 153–74. See also Geoffrey Parker, "Success and Failure during the First Century of the Reformation," *Past & Present* 136 (1992): 43–82. More recently, scholars have questioned the validity of visitation reports, sources intended to catalog problems and shortcomings in parishes, for assessing the success of reforms. See, for example, Christopher Boyd Brown, *Singing the Gospel: Lutheran Hymns and the Success of the Reformation* (Cambridge, MA, 2005).
19. For an example of a work that acknowledges the role of negotiation and accommodation, rather than acculturation and domination, in Protestant reform efforts, see C. Scott Dixon, *The Reformation and Rural Society: The Parishes of Brandenburg-Ansbach-Kulmbach, 1528–1603* (Cambridge, 1996), 102–207. See also Boettcher, "Social Impact of the Lutheran Reformation," 331. Boettcher points out that rather than assuming that theology alone could change society, this scholarship recognizes the "complex negotiations between tradition, theology, and material circumstance in particular local contexts" that marked the era's reform efforts.
20. Robert W. Scribner, "The Reformation, Popular Magic and the 'Disenchantment of the World,'" *Journal of Interdisciplinary History* 23 (1993): 475–94. For an insightful examination of Scribner's contribution and its implications for historical scholarship on the Reformation, see Walsham, "Reformation and the 'Disenchantment of the World' Reassessed," 497–528.
21. See Rublach, *Reformation Europe,* 18, 184–87.
22. Barnes, *Astrology and Reformation.*
23. See Clark, *Thinking with Demons.*
24. Cameron, *Enchanted Europe.*
25. See Saler, "Modernity and Enchantment," 692, who states that "a new historiographic position, if not consensus, has emerged that presents Western modernity as 'enchanted.'"
26. Walsham, "Reformation and the 'Disenchantment of the World' Reassessed," 527–28.

1. "Idolatry and Reprobate Infidelity"

1. For attitudes about magic and witchcraft in medieval Europe, see Norman Cohn, *Europe's Inner Demons: The Demonization of Christians in Medieval Christendom,* rev. ed. (London, 1993). See also Richard Kieckhefer, *Magic in the Middle Ages* (Cambridge, 1989); Michael D. Bailey, *Battling Demons: Witchcraft, Heresy, and Reform in the Late Middle Ages* (University Park, PA, 2003), and "From Sorcery to Witchcraft: Clerical Conceptions of Magic in the Later Middle Ages," *Speculum* 76 (2001): 960–90; and Laura Stokes, *Demons of Urban Reform: Early European Witch Trials and Criminal Justice, 1430–1530* (Houndmills, Basingstoke, 2011).
2. See Broedel, *Malleus Maleficarum and the Construction of Witchcraft.* See also Herzig, "Witches, Saints, and Heretics," 25–27.
3. Kramer, *Hammer of Witches,* trans. and ed. Christopher S. Mackay, 242.
4. Kramer, *Hammer of Witches.* See Mackay's introduction, 1–17.
5. Kramer, *Hammer of Witches,* 459–60.
6. For early Christian attitudes toward divination, see Kahlos, "Early Church," in Collins, ed., *Cambridge History of Magic and Witchcraft,* 148–82.
7. For the magical beliefs of the ancient Hebrews, see Ankarloo and Clark, eds., *Witchcraft and Magic in Europe: Biblical and Pagan Societies;* and Ricks, "Magician as Outsider," in Meyer and Mirecki, eds., *Ancient Magic,* 131–43.
8. Deuteronomy 18:9–11 (Douay-Rheims Bible). Biblical quotations in this chapter are from the Douay-Rheims Bible, since it is closest to the Vulgate edition that late medieval theologians would have used. On the origins of this prohibition among the Hebrews, see also Ankarloo and Clark, eds., *Witchcraft and Magic in Europe: Ancient Greece and Rome,* 295.
9. Leviticus 20:27 (Douay-Rheims Bible). "A man, or woman, in whom there is a pythonical or divining spirit, dying let them die. They shall stone them. Their blood be upon them."
10. For early Christian attitudes toward magic, see Kahlos, "Early Church," in Collins, ed., *Cambridge History of Magic and Witchcraft,* 148–82.
11. For early Christian responses to the story of the witch of Endor, a staple in Christian treatises on necromancy and other forms of divination, see Ankarloo and Clark, eds., *Witchcraft and Magic in Europe: Ancient Greece and Rome,* 307, 346. See also Schmidt, "The 'Witch' of En-Dor," in Meyer and Mirecki, eds., *Ancient Magic and Ritual Power,* 111–29.
12. For concise treatment of divination in the ancient world, see the introduction to Johnston, *Ancient Greek Divination,* 1–32, 133–34. See also Ankarloo and Clark, eds., *Witchcraft and Magic in Europe: Biblical and Pagan Societies.*
13. Dickie, *Magic and Magicians in the Greco-Roman World,* 27–46. See also Ankarloo and Clark, eds., *Witchcraft and Magic in Europe: Ancient Greece and Rome,* 229–30.
14. Quoted in Ankarloo and Clark, eds., *Witchcraft and Magic in Europe: Ancient Greece and Rome,* 228. On the place of these spirits in Greek divination, see Johnston, *Ancient Greek Divination,* 9–12.
15. Graf, "Excluding the Charming," in Meyer and Mirecki, eds., *Ancient Magic and Ritual Power,* 29–42. For forms of divination common in ancient Greece, see Flower, *Seer in*

Ancient Greece; and Ankarloo and Clark, eds., *Witchcraft and Magic in Europe: Ancient Greece and Rome,* 286–87.

16. Fraser, "Roman Antiquity," in Collins, ed., *Cambridge History of Magic and Witchcraft,* 125–35. See also Kieckhefer, *Magic in the Middle Ages,* 25–26.
17. Dickie, *Magic and Magicians in the Greco-Roman World,* 142–61.
18. Quoted in Ankarloo and Clark, eds., *Witchcraft and Magic in Europe: Ancient Greece and Rome,* 262. For imperial Roman repression of diviners, see also Johnston, *Ancient Greek Divination,* 152–53.
19. Augury was the ancient Roman practice of reading omens through the flight of auspicious birds and other heavenly signs, while haruspicy was divination from the entrails of sacrificed animals.
20. Dickie, *Magic and Magicians in the Greco-Roman World,* 96–128.
21. Kahlos, "Early Church," 154–60.
22. See Ankarloo and Clark, eds., *Witchcraft and Magic in Europe: Ancient Greece and Rome,* 278–80.
23. See I Corinthians 10:20: "But the things which the heathens sacrifice, they sacrifice to devils, and not to God. And I would not that you should be made partakers with devils." Kahlos, "Early Church," 152–56. For the Christian invention of the devil, see Ankarloo and Clark, eds., *Witchcraft and Magic in Europe: Ancient Greece and Rome,* 296–97. See also Johnston, *Ancient Greek Divination,* 175–76.
24. Acts 16:16–24.
25. See Acts 16:19–23.
26. Early Christian authorities like Origen also condemned divination as incompatible to belief in divine providence and human free will, although they allowed for prophecies from God or his angels as described in scripture. See Ankarloo and Clark, eds., *Witchcraft and Magic in Europe: Ancient Greece and Rome,* 338–39.
27. On this Augustinian strain in medieval demonology, see Broedel, *Malleus Maleficarum,* 40–43.
28. See Ankarloo and Clark, eds., *Witchcraft and Magic in Europe: Ancient Greece and Rome,* 318.
29. Cameron, *Enchanted Europe,* 79–85. See also Bailey, "Diabolic Magic," in Collins, ed., *Cambridge History of Magic and Witchcraft,* 361.
30. Augustine, *On Christian Teaching,* trans. R. P. H. Green, 51.
31. Quoted in Ankarloo and Clark, eds., *Witchcraft and Magic in Europe: Ancient Greece and Rome,* 320–21.
32. Kieckhefer, *Magic in the Middle Ages,* 41.
33. Kahlos, "Early Church," 160–61.
34. Athanasius, *De Incarnatione Verbi Dei,* quoted in Ankarloo and Clark, eds., *Witchcraft and Magic in Europe: Ancient Greece and Rome,* 334.
35. Kahlos, "Early Church," 164–66.
36. Ankarloo and Clark, eds., *Witchcraft and Magic in Europe: Ancient Greece and Rome,* 342–43. On the *Sortes Biblicae,* see also Cameron, *Enchanted Europe,* 67–69.
37. Augustine, *The Confessions of St. Augustine,* trans. J. K. Ryan, Bk. VIII, 29–30.
38. Caesarius of Arles, *Sermons,* Vol. I *(1–80),* trans. Mary Magdalene Mueller, 265–70.

39. See Bailey, *Magic and Superstition,* 67, 74. See also Ankarloo and Clark, eds., *Witchcraft and Magic in Europe: Ancient Greece and Rome,* 280–81, 344–45.
40. Hen, "The Early Medieval West," in Collins, ed., *Cambridge History of Magic and Witchcraft,* 183–206.
41. Kieckhefer, *Magic in the Middle Ages,* 11–12, 85.
42. Quoted in Lea, *Materials toward a History of Witchcraft,* vol. 1, 179–80. On the *Canon Episcopi,* see also Waite, *Heresy, Magic, and Witchcraft,* 32–33.
43. McNeill and Gamer, ed. and trans., *Medieval Handbooks of Penance,* 329–33.
44. Kieckhefer, *Magic in the Middle Ages,* 85–88.
45. For learned ritual magic in medieval and Renaissance Europe, see Klaasen, *Transformations of Magic.* See also Kieckhefer, *Forbidden Rites.* Chap. 5, "Learning Hidden and Future Things," deals specifically with divination.
46. Thomas Aquinas, *Summa Theologiae,* II.2.95. For a lucid examination of Aquinas's views on divination, see Cameron, *Enchanted Europe,* 63–64. See also Kieckhefer, *Magic in the Middle Ages,* 12.
47. For the work's print history, see Milway, "Forgotten Best-Sellers from the Dawn of the Reformation," in Bast and Gow, eds., *Continuity and Change,* 113–42.
48. Guido of Monte Rochen, *Handbook for Curates,* trans. Anne T. Thayer, 294–95.
49. Jacopo Passavanti, *Mirror of True Penitence* (ca. 1350), in Kors and Peters, eds., *Witchcraft in Europe,* 108.
50. Passavanti, *Mirror of True Penitence,* 110.
51. Kieckhefer, *Magic in the Middle Ages,* 176–201. See also Cohn, *Europe's Inner Demons,* 24–31.
52. Bailey, *Battling Demons,* 130–36.
53. On Bernardino and the origins of witch-hunting in fifteenth-century Italy, see Mormando, *The Preacher's Demons.* See also Waite, *Heresy, Magic, and Witchcraft,* 37–40. The quotation is from Bernardino of Siena, *Saint Bernardine of Siena: Sermons,* ed. Nazareno Orlandi, trans. Helen Josephine Robins, 164.
54. Bernardino of Siena, *Saint Bernardine,* 164.
55. Bernardino of Siena, *Saint Bernardine,* 164.
56. Bernardino of Siena, *Saint Bernardine,* 165.
57. Bernardino of Siena, *Saint Bernardine,* 165.
58. Kramer, *Hammer of Witches,* 246.

2. "A Hellish Trap"

1. Luther, *Tischreden III,* no. 3618B.
2. For Mechler's account, see Baron, *Faustus on Trial,* 112–14.
3. For the Lutheran clergy's intense interest in folk magic, see Clark, "Protestant Demonology," in Levack, ed., *New Perspectives on Witchcraft, Magic, and Demonology,* 79–81.
4. In a classic 1978 work, Peter Burke explored how sixteenth-century elites—Protestant and Catholic alike—gradually withdrew from popular culture and sought to rein in its more carnivalesque excesses. See Burke, *Popular Culture.*

5. Barnes, *Astrology and Reformation.* See also Barnes, "Astrology and the Confessions," Headley, Hillerbrand, and Papalas, eds., *Confessionalization in Europe,* 131–54.
6. Barnes, *Astrology and Reformation,* 3.
7. Barnes, "Astrology and the Confessions," 131–54. See also Barnes, *Prophecy and Gnosis.*
8. For Lutheran portents, see Clark, *Thinking with Demons,* 339–40.
9. For Melanchthon's astrological beliefs, see Cameron, *Enchanted Europe,* 176–78, 211–12. See also Philip Melanchthon, *Orations on Philosophy and Education,* ed. Sachiko Kusukawa, xxi, 94; and Baron, *Doctor Faustus,* 51–53.
10. Baron, *Doctor Faustus,* 53.
11. Barnes, "Astrology and the Confessions," 139.
12. See Brann, *Trithemius and Magical Theology.* See also Collins, "Learned Magic," in idem, ed., *Cambridge History of Magic and Witchcraft,* 332–34; and Baron, *Doctor Faustus,* 23–31.
13. See Nauert, *Agrippa and the Crisis of Renaissance Thought;* and Lehrich, *Language of Demons and Angels,* 30–33. See also Waite, *Heresy, Magic, and Witchcraft,* 119–23.
14. Weeks, *Paracelsus,* 103. See also Waite, *Heresy, Magic, and Witchcraft,* 123–24.
15. Green, *Printing and Prophecy,* 55. See also Barnes, *Astrology and Reformation,* 174.
16. Baron, *Doctor Faustus,* 41.
17. Baron, *Doctor Faustus,* 42–44.
18. Baron, *Doctor Faustus,* 49.
19. Luther, *Luther's Works,* vol. 9, 190.
20. Luther, *Luther's Works,* vol. 54, 172–73.
21. Luther, *Luther's Works,* vol. 1, 45.
22. Luther, *Luther's Works,* vol. 9, 175–76.
23. Luther, *Luther's Works,* vol. 43, 17.
24. Bailey, *Magic and Superstition,* 43–44.
25. For a lucid examination of Aquinas's views on divination, see Cameron, *Enchanted Europe,* 63–64.
26. Erasmus, "Letter to Antoon Van Bergen," in Mynors and Thompson, eds., *Correspondence of Erasmus,* 9–10.
27. Bailey, *Magic and Superstition,* 196.
28. See Deuteronomy 18:10. For Protestant views on the demonic operation of common superstitious practices, based upon their expansive interpretation of Deuteronomy, see Clark, *Thinking with Demons,* 483–84.
29. Jörg Haustein, "Mensch-Prediger-Professor-Autorität," in *Hexen und Hexenverfolgung in Thüringen,* 134.
30. Luther, "A Short Exposition of the Decalogue, the Apostles' Creed and the Lord's Prayer (1520)," in Bertram Lee Woolf, ed., *Reformation Writings of Martin Luther,* vol. I, 75, quoted in Clark, *Thinking with Demons,* 490.
31. Haustein, "Mensch-Prediger-Professor-Autorität," 136. See also Clark, *Thinking with Demons,* 490–91.
32. Haustein, "Mensch-Prediger-Professor-Autorität," 138.
33. Spreter, *Hexen Büchlein.* A decade later, the Württemberg reformer Johannes Brenz also attacked divination on similar grounds; see Clark, *Thinking with Demons,* 492.

34. On judicial astrology and its ambiguous treatment in the theological literature on superstition in the Middle Ages and early modern period, see Cameron, *Enchanted Europe*, esp. 686–89, 99–100, 160, 176–77.
35. Spies, *Historia von D. Johann Fausten*, 44.
36. Spies, *Historia von D. Johann Fausten*, 45.
37. Spies, *Historia von D. Johann Fausten*, 120.

3. "Unchristian and Devilish Crimes"

1. Thüringisches Staatsarchiv Gotha, ZZ.X. Criminalia des Amts Tenneberg: 6–11, Sundhausen, 1560.
2. On Milichius and the *Zauber-Teuffel*, see Charles Zika, *The Appearance of Witchcraft: Print and Visual Culture in Sixteenth-Century Europe* (London, 2007), 96–97; and Stuart Clark, "Protestant Demonology: Sin, Superstition, and Society (c. 1520–c. 1630)," in Brian P. Levack, ed., *New Perspectives on Witchcraft, Magic, and Demonology*, vol. I (New York, 2001), 64–65. In 1562, a pair of Lutheran pastors, Mattheus Alber and Wilhelm Bidembach, published a series of sermons against divination entitled *Ein summa etlicher predigen vom Hagel und Unholden* (Tübingen, 1562). Hermann Hamelman's *Eine Predigt zu Gandersheim . . . Wider die Beschwerer, Wicker, Christallenkücker, Zeuberer, Nachweiser, und Segner* (n.p., 1572) echoed Milichius's condemnations, as did the Westphalian reformer's contribution to the demonological collection entitled *Theatrum diabolorum* (1569). On the *Teufelbücher* genre, see Heinrich Grimm, "Die deutschen 'Teufelbücher' des 16. Jahrhunderts: ihre Rolle in Buchwesen und ihre Bedeutung" (1959); Keith Roos, *The Devil in Sixteenth-Century German Literature: The Teufelsbücher* (Frankfurt am Main, 1972); and Lyndal Roper, *Oepdipus and the Devil: Witchcraft, Sexuality, and Religion in Early Modern Europe* (New York, 1994).
3. Milichius, *Der Zauber-Teuffel*, 195.
4. Milichius, *Der Zauber-Teuffel*, 327.
5. Milichius, *Der Zauber-Teuffel*, 340.
6. Milichius, *Der Zauber-Teuffel*, 343.
7. Weyer, *On Witchcraft*, ed. and trans. Kohl and Midelfort, 259–60.
8. Weyer, *On Witchcraft*, ed. and trans. Kohl and Midelfort, 259–60. Weyer's reference to "Pytho" in this passage pertains to the chthonic rites associated with the Delphic oracle in ancient Greece.
9. Witekind, *Christlich bedenken und erinnerung von Zauberey*, 22. On Witekind's career, see also Midelfort, *Witch Hunting in Southwestern Germany*, 57.
10. On this remarkable episode, see Starenko, "In Luther's Wake."
11. On the boy-prophet, Hans Tausendschön, see Beyer, *Lay Prophets in Lutheran Europe*.
12. Witekind, *Christlich bedenken und erinnerung von Zauberey*, 21.
13. On the publication history of Bodin's *Daemonomania* in Germany, see Jonathan Schüz, "Bodin's *Démonomanie* in the German Vernacular," in Howell A. Lloyd, ed., *The Reception of Bodin* (Leiden, 2013), 237–56. For Bodin as a demonologist, see Ursula Lange, *Untersuchungen zu Bodins Demonomanie* (Frankfurt am Main, 1970); Gerhild Scholz Williams, *Defining Dominion: The Discourses of Magic and Witchcraft in Early Modern France and Germany* (Ann Arbor, 1995); Stuart Clark, *Thinking with Demons:*

The Idea of Witchcraft in Early Modern Europe (Oxford, 1997), 668–82; and Jonathan Pearl, *The Crime of Crimes: Demonology and Politics in France, 1560–1620* (Waterloo, Ontario, 1999).

14. Bodin, *De magorum Daemonomania.*
15. The Ernestine custom of partitioning their lands among the surviving sons of departed rulers continued to fragment Thuringia into ever smaller principalities throughout the early modern period. In 1572, the Ernestine lands were subdivided with the Division of Erfurt. Johann Wilhelm, duke of Saxe-Weimar, gained Altenburg, Gotha, and Meiningen. When he died a year later, his eldest son, Friedrich Wilhelm I, inherited these three cities, ruling them as duke of Saxe-Altenburg. His younger brother, Johann II, was named duke of Saxe-Weimar. Meanwhile, Johann Friedrich II's young sons, Johann Casimir and Johann Ernst, received the duchy of Saxe-Coburg-Eisenach, which was governed by a regent until they came of age. In 1596, having reached their majority, the brothers agreed to another partition, splitting their patrimony into the duchies of Saxe-Coburg and Saxe-Eisenach. For the next three hundred years, the merging and splitting of these duchies dominated politics in Thuringia as the fortunes of the various branches of the Ernestine Wettins waxed and waned. On the impact of the Protestant Reformation on dynastic politics in Germany, see Fichtner, *Protestantism and Primogeniture.*
16. Christman, "The Pulpit and the Pew," in Kolb, ed., *Lutheran Ecclesiastical Culture,* 259–303.
17. Luther, *Large Catechism,* 2.
18. Luther, *Large Catechism,* 2.
19. For the difficulties the Lutheran clergy faced in carrying out their pastoral duties in the face of local resistance, see Gerald Strauss's pathbreaking work, *Luther's House of Learning: Indoctrination of the Young in the German Reformation* (Baltimore, 1978). See also Susan Karant-Nunn, *Luther's Pastors: The Reformation in the Ernestine Countryside* (Philadelphia, 1979); and C. Scott Dixon, *The Reformation and Rural Society: The Parishes of Brandenburg-Ansbach-Kulmbach, 1528–1603* (Cambridge, 1996).
20. These coercive efforts, and peasant resistance, are explored in Sabean, *Power in the Blood,* 37–60.
21. For the development of these disciplinary instruments in Lutheran Germany, see Dixon, *Reformation and Rural Society.* See also Christman, "Pulpit and the Pew."
22. Luther, *Large Catechism,* 3.
23. Thüringisches Staatsarchiv Weimar, 6-11-0035; s. 1; v. 30: Ernestinisches Gesamtarchiv, Re. li: Visitation im gesamten ernestischen Gebeit (1554–55), 10, 34.
24. Thüringisches Staatsarchiv Gotha, ZZ.X. Criminalia des Amts Tenneberg: 3. Wehrsegerin u. Zeuberi (1556–61), 1–2, Wahlwinkel, 1556.
25. Thüringisches Staatsarchiv Gotha, ZZ.X. Criminalia des Amts Tenneberg: 3–5, Gotha, 1561.
26. Quoted in Füssel, *Hexenverfolgung in Thüringer Raum,* 130.
27. *Der . . . Fürsten und Herren/Herren Friederich Wilhelms/und Herren Johansen Gebrüdern/ Hertzogen zu Sachsen/und Marggraven zu Meisen/etc. Policey und Landesordnunge/ zuwolfart/nutz und besten derselben Unterthanen und Fürstenthumb bedacht und ausgangen* (Jena, 1589).

28. For the reputation of executioners in early modern Germany as magical practitioners and witch-finders, see Thomas Robisheaux, *The Last Witch of Langenburg: Murder in a German Village* (New York, 2009), 154–55. For their social position and medical activities, see also Joel Harrington, *The Faithful Executioner: Life and Death, Honor and Shame in the Turbulent Sixteenth Century* (New York, 2013); and Kathy Stuart, *Defiled Trades and Social Outcasts: Honor and Ritual Pollution in Early Modern Germany* (Cambridge, 2006).
29. On the diagnosis of sudden illness as bewitchment, see Briggs, *Witches and Neighbors*, 62–76.
30. Stadtarchiv Erfurt, 1–16/16m 13: Hexenprozesse (1587–88).
31. See Gerald Strauss, *Luther's House of Learning: Indoctrination of the Young in the German Reformation* (Baltimore, 1978). Although Strauss's contention that the Reformation failed in its central educational mission proved controversial, in recent decades a number of scholars have also questioned the Reformation's success. See, for example, Robert W. Scribner, "The Reformation, Popular Magic and the 'Disenchantment of the World,'" *Journal of Interdisciplinary History* 23 (1993): 475–94; and Lyndal Roper, *The Holy Household: Women and Morals in Reformation Augsburg* (Oxford, 1989). For an excellent overview of the debate regarding the impact of the Reformation, see Susan R. Boettcher, "The Social Impact of the Lutheran Reformation in Germany," in Robert Kolb, ed., *Lutheran Ecclesiastical Culture, 1550–1675* (Leiden, 2008), 305–59.

4. "Heathenish and Forbidden Abominations"

1. *Von Gottes Gnaden/Wir ERNST . . . Es ist . . . bewust/welcher gestalt der Allgerechte Gott . . . mit schweren Straffen wegen der vielfältigen Ubertretungen seines Worts/ heimgesuchet/und es in die wütende Kriegs-Flammen aus gerechtem Zorn und Gerichte gesetzet . . . worden* (Gotha, 1647). See Venables, "In the Shadow of War," 190–93.
2. See Clark, "Protestant Demonology," in Levack, ed., *New Perspectives on Witchcraft*, vol. I, 179–215, who argues that Protestant demonologists, who were often pastors, formed their ideas within a pastoral tradition that emphasized the dangers of "popular magical technique."
3. Celichius, *Notwendige Erinnerung: Vonn des Sathans letzten Zornsturm* (Wittenberg, 1594), 100–102. On Celichius's apocalyptic views, see Midelfort, *History of Madness in Sixteenth-Century Germany*, 58–59. Other Lutheran demonologists of the era had also condemned popular divination, citing biblical prohibitions. See, for example, Abraham Saur, *Eine kurtze treuwe Warnung, Anzeige und Underricht: Ob auch zu dieser unser zeit unter uns Christen, Hexen, Zäuberer, und Unholden vorhanden: Und was sie außrichten können* (Marburg, 1582); and Paul Frisius, *Von deß Teuffels Nebelkappen, Das ist: Kurtzer Begriff, den gantzen Handel von der Zauberey belangend, zusammen gelesen* (Frankfurt am Main, 1583).
4. David Meder, *Acht Hexenpredigten: darinnen Von des Teuffels Mordkindern, der Hexen, Unholden, Zauberischen, Drachenleuten, Milchdieben, etc., erschrecklichen Abfalle, Lastern und Ubelthaten, dadurch die Göttliche Maiestät gelestert, und Menschen und Viehe, etc., verderblicher Schaden zugefüget* (Leipzig, 1605), 11.

5. Meder, *Acht Hexenpredigten,* 25–26. For Luther's story of the soothsayer supposedly burned in Erfurt, see chap. 2.
6. Meder, *Acht Hexenpredigten,* 108.
7. Meder, *Acht Hexenpredigten,* 117.
8. Peter Binsfeld, *Tractat von Bekanntnuß der Zauberer und Hexen* (Trier, 1590), 27. For an examination of Binsfeld's role in the witch hunts at Trier, see Dillinger, *"Evil People"*; and Voltmer, "Zwischen Herrschaftskrise, Wirtschaftsdepression und Jesuitenpropaganda," 37–107.
9. Binsfeld, *Tractat,* 16–19.
10. Binsfeld, *Tractat,* 24.
11. Abraham Scultetus, *Warnung für der Warsagerey der Zauberer und Sterngucker/ verfast in zwoen Predigten/ so uber die letzte vier Versickel deß 47. Capitels deß Propheten Jesaiae gehalten durch* (Neustadt an der Haardt, 1608), 6.
12. Scultetus, *Warnung für der Warsagerey,* 10. As evidence, Scultetus cites Acts 16:16: "Es geschah aber, da wir zu dem Gebet gingen, daß eine Magd uns begegnete, die hatte einen Wahrsagergeist und trug ihren Herren viel Gewinnst zu mit Wahrsagen."
13. Scultetus, *Warnung für der Warsagerey,* 15, 27.
14. Scultetus, *Warnung für der Warsagerey,* 8–9.
15. Scultetus, *Warnung für der Warsagerey,* 14. Compare with Isaiah 8:19: "And when they shall say unto you, Seek unto them that have familiar spirits, and unto wizards that peep, and that mutter: should not a people seek unto their God?"
16. Scultetus, *Warnung für der Warsagerey,* 30.
17. For these sorts of divining, see Bever, *Realities of Witchcraft and Popular Magic,* 222–30, 253.
18. Barnes, "Astrology and the Confessions in the Empire," in Headley, Hillerbrand, and Papalas, eds., *Confessionalization in Europe,* 131–53. See also Barnes, *Prophecy and Gnosis.*
19. See Evans, *Rudolf II and His World.*
20. Robert Scribner, "Reformation, Popular Magic and the 'Disenchantment of the World,'" 475–94. See also Rublach, *Reformation Europe,* 177, who notes that more than two hundred folk prophets have been identified in Lutheran areas during the early modern period. For the controversy surrounding the most famous of these figures, Hans Keil, a vintner who proclaimed a prophetic vision in Württemberg just before the end of the Thirty Years' War, see Sabean, *Power in the Blood.* See also Beyer, *Lay Prophets in Lutheran Europe.*
21. On judicial astrology and its ambiguous treatment in the theological literature on superstition in the Middle Ages and early modern period, see Cameron, *Enchanted Europe,* esp. 68–69, 99–100, 160, 176–77.
22. Barnes, *Astrology and Reformation,* 300–301.
23. Henning Friedrich, *Gründliche Widerlegung der Aberglaübischen Astrologorum, so ausz dem Gestirn, und desselbigen influents, prognosticiren, Geneses, oder Nativiteten stellen . . .* (Erfurt, 1624). See Barnes, *Astrology and Reformation,* 292.
24. Venables, "In the Shadow of War," 85.
25. Johnson, "Violence and Retaliation," 52. For the effects of the war on Germany, see also Theibault, "Demography of the Thirty Years War Re-revisited," 1–21. See also Theibault, *German Villages in Crisis.*

26. See Johnson, "Violence and Retaliation," 57.
27. Venables, "In the Shadow of War," 109.
28. Johnson, "Violence and Retaliation," 28.
29. Bernhard Waldschmidt, *Pythonissa Endorea: Das ist Acht und Zwantzig Hexen und Gespenst Predigten genommen auß der Histori der Zaüberin zu Endor I Sam. XXVIII. und gehalten von M. Bernhardo Waldschmidt Evangelischem Prediger Franckfurt . . .* (Frankfurt am Main, 1660).
30. Waldschmidt, *Pythonissa Endorea,* 2–3.
31. Waldschmidt, *Pythonissa Endorea,* 94–95, 100–101.
32. Waldschmidt, *Pythonissa Endorea,* 104–5.
33. Waldschmidt, *Pythonissa Endorea,* 36, 297–98, 393.
34. Waldschmidt, *Pythonissa Endorea,* 102.
35. Waldschmidt, *Pythonissa Endorea,* 396–97.
36. Waldschmidt, *Pythonissa Endorea,* 36, 43–48, 355, 376–77.
37. On Faber's role in the Esslingen witch-hunt, see Midelfort, *Witch Hunting in Southwestern Germany,* 53–54. For a detailed account of the Esslingen witch-hunt, see Jerouschek, *Hexen und ihr Prozeß.*
38. Johannes Fabri [Johann Jacob Faber], *Specimen Zeli iusti Theologici contra Maleficos & Sagas. Das ist: Muster und Prob eines recht Theologischen Eifers / wider die Zauberer und Hexen: bestehend in 6. unterschiedlichen Predigten* (1667).
39. Faber, *Specimen Zeli iusti Theologici contra Maleficos & Sagas,* 267–68.
40. Faber, *Specimen Zeli iusti Theologici contra Maleficos & Sagas,* 36, 56.
41. Faber, *Specimen Zeli iusti Theologici contra Maleficos & Sagas,* 29–30.
42. Faber, *Specimen Zeli iusti Theologici contra Maleficos & Sagas,* 8. See 2 Chronicles 33.
43. Faber, *Specimen Zeli iusti Theologici contra Maleficos & Sagas,* 11.
44. See Waite, "Sixteenth-Century Religious Reform and the Witch-Hunts," in Levack, ed., *Oxford Handbook of Witchcraft,* 487.
45. Faber, *Specimen Zeli iusti Theologici contra Maleficos & Sagas,* 12–13.
46. Faber, *Specimen Zeli iusti Theologici contra Maleficos & Sagas,* 13–14.
47. Faber, *Specimen Zeli iusti Theologici contra Maleficos & Sagas,* 31.
48. Faber, *Specimen Zeli iusti Theologici contra Maleficos & Sagas,* 36, 56.
49. Faber, *Specimen Zeli iusti Theologici contra Maleficos & Sagas,* 185.
50. Faber, *Specimen Zeli iusti Theologici contra Maleficos & Sagas,* 142.
51. Faber, *Specimen Zeli iusti Theologici contra Maleficos & Sagas,* 149–50.
52. Faber, *Specimen Zeli iusti Theologici contra Maleficos & Sagas,* 29–30.
53. Faber, *Specimen Zeli iusti Theologici contra Maleficos & Sagas,* 30.
54. On Seckendorf and his time at the court of Ernst I, see Wakefield, *Disordered Police State.*
55. For treatment of the reign of Ernst the Pious and his disciplinary efforts, see Stievermann, "Ernst der Fromme," in Jacobsen and Ruge, eds., *Ernst der Fromme;* Klinger, *Gothaer Fürstenstaat;* Albrecht-Birkner, *Reformation des Lebens;* and Venables, "In the Shadow of War."
56. Faber, *Specimen Zeli iusti Theologici contra Maleficos & Sagas,* 212.

57. Thüringisches Staatsarchiv Gotha, Oberkonsitorium Generalia. Loc. 29b Kirchli. Discipl. Nr. 4. The sermon instructions survive as an undated manuscript, in a seventeenth-century hand.
58. *Fürstliche Sächsische abermals verbesserte Landes-Ordnung/Des Durchläuchstigen/ Hochgebornen Fürsten und Herrn/Herrn Ernsten/Hertzogen zu Sachsen/Jülich/Cleve und Bergk/Landgraffen in Thüringen/Marggraffen zu Meissen/.* . . . (Gotha, 1653), 220–21. The prohibitions in Ernst I's *Landesordnung* of 1653 were repeated in slightly modified form in a revised version issued in 1667.
59. Forschungsbibliothek Gotha, *Rüge-Ordnung* (1646), 275.

5. "Born under an Unlucky Sign"

1. Thüringisches Staatsarchiv Gotha, Geheimes Archiv, EEE XI (13) e, 12–13.
2. For a fascinating discussion of this early modern ideology, see Wegert, "Social Context of State Terror in Early Modern Germany," 32–33.
3. This treatment of witchcraft prosecution in Thuringia is drawn from Füssel, *Hexenverfolgungen in Thüringer Raum.* For witch-hunting in the region, see also Wilde, *Zauberei- und Hexenprozesse in Kursachsen.* For witch-hunting in the German-speaking lands, see H. C. Erik Midelfort, *Witch Hunting in Southwestern Germany, 1562–1684: The Social and Intellectual Foundations* (Stanford, 1972); Gerhard Schormann, *Hexenprozesse in Deutschland* (Göttingen, 1981); Walter Niess, *Hexenprozesse in der Grafschaft Büdingen: Protokolle, Ursachen, Hintergründe* (Büdingen, 1982); Wolfgang Behringer, *Hexen und Hexenprozesse in Deutschland* (München, 1988); Herbert Pohl, *Hexenglaube und Hexenverfolgung im Kurfürsten Mainz: Ein Beitrag zur Hexenfrage im 16. Und beginnenden 17. Jahrhundert* (Stuttgart, 1988); Günther Jerouschek, *Die Hexen und ihr Prozeß: Die Hexenverfolgungen in der Reichsstadt Esslingen* (Esslingen, 1992); Rainer Walz, *Hexenglaube und magische Kommunikation im Dorf der frühen Neuzeit: Die Verfolgungen in der Grafschaft Lippe* (Paderborn, 1993); Gunther Franz and Franz Irsigler, *Hexenglaube und Hexenprozesse im Raum Rhein-Mosel-Saar* (Trier, 1995); Rainer Decker, *Die Hexen und ihre Henker: Ein Fallbericht* (Freiburg, 1994); Wolfgang Behringer, *Witchcraft Persecutions in Bavaria: Popular Magic, Religious Zealotry, and Reason of State in Early Modern Europe* (Cambridge, 1997); Alison Rowlands, *Witchcraft Narratives in Germany: Rothenburg, 1561–1652* (Manchester, 2003); Manfred Wilde, *Die Zauberei- und Hexenprozesse in Kursachsen* (Köln, 2003); Lyndal Roper, *Witch Craze: Terror and Fantasy in Baroque Germany* (New Haven, 2004); Rita Voltmer, *Hexenverfolgung und Herrschaftspraxis* (Trier, 2005); Johannes Dillinger, *Böse Leute: Hexenverfolgungen in Schwäbisch-Österreich und Kurtrier im Vergleich* (Trier, 1999), published in English as *"Evil People": A Comparative Study of Witch Hunts in Swabian Austria and the Electorate of Trier* (Charlottesville, 2009); and Thomas Robisheaux, *The Last Witch of Langenburg: Murder in a German Village* (New York, 2009). The best single-volume survey of the early modern witch-hunts remains Brian P. Levack, *The Witch-Hunt in Early Modern Europe* (London, 1995).
4. Bever, "Popular Witch Beliefs," in Levack, ed., *Oxford Handbook of Witchcraft,* 51.
5. For the activities of cunning folk, see Labouvie, *Verbotene Künste;* Willem de Blécourt, "Witch Doctors, Soothsayers, and Priests: On Cunning Folk in European

Historiography and Tradition," *Social History* 19 (1994): 285–303; Walter Rummel, "'Weise' Frauen und 'weise' Männer im Kampf gegen Hexerei die Widerlegung einer modernen Fabel," in Christof Dipper, Lutz Klinkhammer, and Alexander Nützenadel, eds., *Europäische Sozialgeschichte. Festschrift für Wolfgang Schieder* (Berlin, 2000), 353–75; Owen Davies, *Popular Magic: Cunning-Folk in English History* (London, 2003); Bever, *Realities of Witchcraft and Popular Magic;* and Johannes Dillinger, *Magical Treasure Hunting in Europe and North America: A History* (Houndmills, Basingstoke, 2012).

6. For the divinatory activities of hangmen in sixteenth-century Thuringia, see chap. 3.
7. Thüringisches Staatsarchiv Weimar, 6-12-4008: s. 1587; v. 1599: Eisenacher Archiv, Rechtspflege: Inquisitionsakte im Hexenprozess gegen Martha Keller aus Ostheim (1662–63) [Amt Lichtenberg].
8. Thüringisches Staatsarchiv Gotha, Justizamt Ohrdruf (vol. 89); Loc. B, Nr. 11–23: Hanns Karsten wegen Däller wegen Hexerei (1671). For the history of witch-hunting in Saxe-Gotha, see Füssel, *Hexenverfolgungen in Thüringer Raum,* 266–67, who provides summary statistics. There were 112 witchcraft cases in Saxe-Gotha between 1640 and 1680, during the reigns of Ernst I and his son, Friedrich I, who carried on his father's witch-hunting activities.
9. Thüringisches Staatsarchiv Gotha, Justizamt Ohrdruf (vol. 89); Loc. B, Nr. 11–23.
10. Thüringisches Staatsarchiv Gotha, Justizamt Ohrdruf (vol. 89); Loc. B, Nr. 11–23.
11. Thüringisches Staatsarchiv Gotha, Justizamt Ohrdruf (vol. 89); Loc. B, Nr. 11–23.
12. For the role of slander in witchcraft cases in early modern Rothenburg, see Rowlands, *Witchcraft Narratives in Germany.*
13. Thüringisches Staatsarchiv Gotha, Justizamt Ohrdruf (vol. 89); Loc. B, Nr. 11–23.
14. Thüringisches Staatsarchiv Gotha, Justizamt Ohrdruf (vol. 89); Loc. B, Nr. 11–23.
15. Describing the activities of English cunning folk working as witch-finders, Owen Davies explains that "the process was one of confirmation rather than detection." See Davies, *Popular Magic,* 107. Edward Bever examines the activities of similar cunning folk operating in early modern Württemberg. See Bever, *Realities of Witchcraft and Popular Magic,* 189–91, 221–22.
16. Thüringisches Staatsarchiv Gotha, Justizamt Ohrdruf (vol. 89); Loc. B, Nr. 11–23.
17. Thüringisches Staatsarchiv Gotha, Justizamt Ohrdruf (vol. 89); Loc. B, Nr. 11–23.
18. Thüringisches Staatsarchiv Gotha, Justizamt Ohrdruf (vol. 89); Loc. B, Nr. 11–23.
19. Thüringisches Staatsarchiv Gotha, Justizamt Ohrdruf (vol. 89); Loc. B, Nr. 11–23.
20. Thüringisches Staatsarchiv Gotha, Justizamt Ohrdruf (vol. 89); Loc. B, Nr. 11–23.
21. For the ways in which early modern villagers dealt with witchcraft suspicions and magical diagnosis through the courts or unofficial "self-help" like magical charms or violence, see Briggs, *Witches and Neighbours.* For Germany, see also Rummel, *Bauern, Herren und Hexen;* and Labouvie, *Verbotene Künste.*
22. Thüringisches Staatsarchiv Weimar, 6-12-4008: s. 1564; v. 1556, 3: Eisenacher Archiv, Rechtspflege: Untersuchung gegen Anna Reich von Unterweid wegen Hexereiverdachts (18 March 1673) [Amt Kaltennordheim].
23. Thüringisches Staatsarchiv Weimar, 6-12-4008: s. 1564; v. 1556, 10b-11: Eisenacher Archiv, Rechtspflege: Untersuchung gegen Anna Reich von Unterweid wegen Hexereiverdachts (21 April 1673) [Amt Kaltennordheim].
24. Thüringisches Staatsarchiv Gotha, Geheimes Archiv, EEE XI (13) e, 12–13.

25. For the prevalence of magical activity in response to lost or stolen goods, see Cameron, *Enchanted Europe,* 39–40.
26. For these customary responses to bewitchment, see Briggs, *Witches and Neighbours.*
27. Briggs, *Witches and Neighbours,* 174.

6. "Superstitious Activities"

1. Thüringisches Staatsarchiv Gotha, ZZ.X. Criminalia des Amts Tenneberg: 1–6, "Abergläubischer Handel" Waltershausen (1718).
2. This was not the only case of "superstitious activities" in 1718. In late December of that year, Barbara Cramerin, a widow from Sonnenberg, was accused of seeking help from a wise man. Thüringisches Staatsarchiv Gotha, Oberkonsitorium Generalia; Loc. 29b Kirchli. Discipl. Nr. 4 (23 December 1718), 32.
3. On this shift in the meaning of superstition, see Bailey, "Disenchantment of Magic," 388–89, 402. See also Clark, *Thinking with Demons,* 485–87. For these developments in an English context, see also Davies, *Witchcraft, Magic, and Culture.*
4. See Levack, "Decline and End of Witchcraft Prosecutions," in Gijswijt-Hofstra, Levack, and Porter, eds., *Witchcraft and Magic in Europe: The Eighteenth and Nineteenth Centuries,* 184–85.
5. See Füssel, *Hexenverfolgungen in Thüringer Raum.*
6. For the role of the early Enlightenment in gradually undermining belief in witchcraft and magic in Germany, through its opposition to so-called superstition, see Pott, *Aufklärung und Aberglaube.*
7. See Levack, "Crime and the Law," in Davies and Barry, eds., *Palgrave Advances in Witchcraft Historiography,* 146–63. See also Eiden and Voltmer, eds., *Hexenprozesse und Gerichtspraxis.*
8. See Levack, "Decline and End of Witchcraft Prosecutions," in Gijswijt-Hofstra, Levack, and Porter, eds., *Witchcraft and Magic in Europe: The Eighteenth and Nineteenth Centuries,* 19, 40, 43–45, and idem, "Decline and End of Witchcraft Prosecutions," in idem, ed., *Oxford Handbook of Witchcraft in Early Modern Europe and Colonial America,* 429–46. See also Porter, "Witchcraft and Magic in Enlightenment, Romantic, and Liberal Thought," in Gijswijt-Hofstra, Levack, and Porter, eds., *Witchcraft and Magic in Europe: The Eighteenth and Nineteenth Centuries,* 240.
9. For this work, see Trainer, "Incest-Theme in the Works of Tieck," 819–24.
10. See Cameron, *Enchanted Europe,* 311–12.
11. See Levack, "Decline and End of Witchcraft Prosecution," in idem, ed., *Oxford Handbook of Witchcraft in Early Modern Europe and Colonial America,* 437–38.
12. Bathasar Bekker, *Die Bezauberte Welt: Oder Eine gründliche Untersuchung des Allgemeinen Aberglaubens* (Amsterdam, 1693), 292.
13. See Cameron, *Enchanted Europe,* 264–69. See also See also Waite, *Heresy, Magic, and Witchcraft,* 198–201.
14. Christian Thomasius's *Dissertatio de Crimine magiae* (1701) is available in a modern edition under the title *Vom Laster der Zauberei—De Crimie Magiae,* trans. and ed. Rolf Lieberwirth. On Thomasius's influence, see Gestrich, "Pietismus und Aberglaube," in Lorenz and Bauer, eds., *Ende der Hexenverfolgung,* 269–88. For the influence of Pietism

in Thuringia, see Schneider, *German Radical Pietism*. See also Brecht, ed., *Geschichte des Pietismus,* vol. I; and Lehmann, Melton, and Strom, eds., *Pietism in Germany and North America.*

15. See Dorn-Haag, *Hexerei und Magie im Strafrecht,* 84–90. On Thomasius's skeptical views, see also Pott, *Aufklärung und Aberglaube,* 192–265; Hunter, *Rival Enlightenments;* and Ahnert, *Religion and the Origins of the German Enlightenment.*
16. See Thomasius, *Vom Laster der Zauberei,* 221.
17. Thomasius, *Vom Laster der Zauberei,* 221.
18. Erik Midelfort, for example, pointed out that "the trials . . . had effectively come to an end before the skeptical opponents of witchcraft had achieved any notable philosophical victories." See his *Witch Hunting in Southwestern Germany,* 6.
19. See Levack, "Decline and End of Witchcraft Prosecution," in idem, ed., *Oxford Handbook of Witchcraft in Early Modern Europe and Colonial America,* 429–46. See also Levack, "Decline and End of Witchcraft Prosecutions," in Gijswijt-Hofstra, Levack, and Porter, eds., *Witchcraft and Magic in Europe: The Eighteenth and Nineteenth Centuries,* 7, 72, 36–37. See also Easlea, *Witch Hunting, Magic and the New Philosophy.*
20. See Levack, "Decline and End of Witchcraft Prosecutions," in Gijswijt-Hofstra, Levack, and Porter, eds., *Witchcraft and Magic in Europe: The Eighteenth and Nineteenth Centuries,* 435–37.
21. See Michael Berns, *Gründliche und völlige Wiederlegung der Bezauberten Welt Balthasar Beckers* (Hamburg, 1708). The charge of fostering atheism was often levelled against thinkers deemed to be opponents of Lutheran orthodoxy during this period. See Martin Mulsow, *Enlightenment Underground: Radical Germany, 1680–1720,* trans. H. C. Erik Midelfort (Charlottesville, 2015); Winfried Schröder, *Ursprünge des Atheismus: Untersuchungen zur Metaphysik- und Religionskritik des 17. und 18. Jahrhunderts,* 2nd ed. (Stuttgart, 2011); and Hans-Martin Barth, *Atheismus und Orthodoxie: Analysen und Modelle christlicher Apologetik im 17. Jahrhundert* (Göttingen, 1971).
22. Joseph Glanvill, *Joseph Glanvill . . . Saducismus triumphatus: Oder, Vollkommener und klarer Beweiss von Hexen and Gespenstern, oder, Geister-Erscheinungen, in zween Theilen verfasset* (Hamburg, 1701). See also William Fleetwood, *Gründliche Untersuchung der Wunder-Wercke: Worinnen nicht alleine die Beschaffenheit der wahren Wunder . . . am Ende sind beygefüget M. Pascals Sonderbahre Gedancken von Wundern* (Leipzig, 1705).
23. See Cameron, *Enchanted Europe,* 298–99.
24. Johann Georg Schmidt, *Die gestriegelte Rockenphilosophie, Oder Aufrichtige Untersuchung derer von vielen Super-Klugen Weibernhochgehaltenen Aberglauben* (Chemnitz, 1718), 169–73.
25. Schmidt, *Die gestriegelte Rockenphilosophie,* 170–71.
26. Schmidt, *Die gestriegelte Rockenphilosophie,* 193.
27. de Levie, "Patriotic Sermons of Christian Ludewig Hahnzog," 36–39.
28. Christian Ludwig Hahnzog, *Predigten wider den Aberglauben der Landleute* (Magdeburg, 1784), xii.
29. Hahnzog, *Predigten wider den Aberglauben,* xiv–xv.
30. Hahnzog, *Predigten wider den Aberglauben,* 431.
31. Hahnzog, *Predigten wider den Aberglauben,* 437.
32. Hahnzog, *Predigten wider den Aberglauben,* 438.

33. Heinrich Ludwig Fischer, *Das Buch vom Aberglauben* (Leipzig, 1790), 113–14.
34. Fischer, *Das Buch vom Aberglauben,* ii.
35. *Saxe-Altenburg Landesordnung* (1705), 273.
36. Thüringisches Staatsarchiv Gotha, ZZ.X. Criminalia des Amts Tenneberg: 1–6, "Abergläubisher Handel" Waltershausen (1718).
37. Thüringisches Staatsarchiv Weimar, 6-12-4008: Eisenacher Archiv, Rechtspflege Sig. 900; v. Num. 1582: Bestrafung von Heinrich Hirsch aus Tiefenort wegen verbottener Wahrsagerei (1691–92).
38. Thüringisches Staatsarchiv Gotha, Justizamt Ohrdruf (vol. 89); Loc. A, Nr. 1–21 (27 March 1741), 17.
39. Thüringisches Staatsarchiv Gotha, Justizamt Ohrdruf (vol. 89); Loc. A, Nr. 1–21 (21 September 1759), 18b. For the term "*Hünerfängerin,*" see Jacob and Wilhelm Grimm, *Deutsches Wörterbuch* (Leipzig, 1854), vol. 10, 1879, where it is defined as "*hühnerdieb.*"
40. See Jacob and Wilhelm Grimm, *Deutsches Wörterbuch* (Leipzig, 1854), vol. 4, 1550–51.
41. Thüringisches Staatsarchiv Weimar, 6-12-3007: Rechtspflege Sig. B 2733; v. Num. 1087: Geheime Canzlei Acta D 427, B. 2733: Untersuchung gegen Johann Friedrich Ufland und Johann Nicol Gräßler aus Wipfra wegen Befragung eines Wahrsagers (Weimar, 1774).
42. See Davies and de Blécourt, eds., *Beyond the Witch Trials,* and idem, eds., *Witchcraft Continued.* See also Gijswijt-Hofstra, "Witchcraft after the Witch-Trials," in Gijswijt-Hofstra, Levack, and Porter, eds., *Witchcraft and Magic in Europe: The Eighteenth and Nineteenth Centuries,* 175–76.

Conclusion

1. Thüringisches Staatsarchiv Gotha, Gerichtsamt Nazza, Sec. III A, Loc. 15, Nr. 19c (1840).
2. Thüringisches Staatsarchiv Gotha, Gerichtsamt Nazza, Sec. III A, Loc. 15, Nr. 24b (1844).
3. Thüringisches Staatsarchiv Gotha, Gerichtsamt Nazza, Sec. III A, Loc. 15, Nr. 31–32 (1846).
4. Thüringisches Staatsarchiv Gotha, Gerichtsamt Nazza, Sec. III A, Loc. 15, Nr. 31–32 (1846). On the scientific reception of Franz Anton Mesmer's theories during the Enlightenment, see Midelfort, *Exorcism and Enlightenment.* On Mesmer's influence on elite occultism and Romantic literature in nineteenth-century Europe, see Warne, *Laboratories of Faith: Mesmerism, Spiritism, and Occultism in Modern France* (Ithaca, 2008); and Tatar, *Spellbound: Studies on Mesmerism and Literature* (Princeton, 1978).
5. Thüringisches Staatsarchiv Gotha, Gerichtsamt Nazza, Sec. III A, Loc. 15, Nr. 31–32 (1846).
6. Thüringisches Staatsarchiv Gotha, Gerichtsamt Nazza, Sec. III A, Loc. 15, Nr. 35–41 (1846).
7. Thüringisches Staatsarchiv Gotha, Gerichtsamt Nazza, Sec. III A, Loc. 15, Nr. 45–45a (1848).
8. Thüringisches Staatsarchiv Gotha, Gerichtsamt Nazza, Sec. III A, Loc. 15, Nr. 36b (1850).
9. Thüringisches Staatsarchiv Gotha, Gerichtsamt Nazza, Sec. III A, Loc. 15, Nr. 45 (1854).

10. For examples of this scholarship, see Robert W. Scribner, "The Reformation, Popular Magic and the 'Disenchantment of the World,'" *Journal of Interdisciplinary History* 23 (1993): 475–94; Labouvie, *Verbotene Künste;* Ulinka Rublach, *Reformation Europe* (Cambridge, 2005); and Bever, *Realities of Witchcraft and Popular Magic.* See also Alexandra Walsham, "Migrations of the Holy: Explaining Religious Change in Medieval and Early Modern Europe," *Journal of Medieval and Early Modern Studies* 44:2 (Spring 2014): 241–80, for an overview of this scholarship.
11. See Barnes, *Astrology and Reformation.*
12. Haustein, "Mensch-Prediger-Professor-Autorität," in *Hexen und Hexenverfolgung in Thüringen,* 134.
13. For the prevalence of negotiation in early modern law enforcement, see the collections of essays edited by Andreas Blauert and Gerd Schwerhoff, entitled *Mit den Waffen der Justiz,* and *Kriminalitätsgeschichte.*
14. Visitors in the duchy of Braunschweig-Grubenhagen in the 1580s complained about the persistence of folk magic in local parishes, but lamented that "people are thick as thieves with each other in these villages, and no one wants to tell on his neighbor." See Strauss, *Luther's House of Learning,* 279. C. Scott Dixon also highlights the prevalence of folk magic in Lutheran parishes. See Dixon, *Reformation and Rural Society,* 187.
15. Speaking of Lutheran parishioners in Württemberg, Edward Bever maintains that "the great majority of people casually employed an eclectic blend of magic and religion in their daily routines." See Bever, *Realities of Witchcraft and Popular Magic,* 339. See also Dixon, *Reformation and Rural Society,* 188–89.
16. See Cameron, *Enchanted Europe,* 9, for a discussion of these folk beliefs.
17. See Bever, "Popular Witch Beliefs and Magical Practices," in Levack, ed., *Oxford Handbook of Witchcraft in Early Modern Europe and Colonial America,* 52.
18. Scribner, "Magic and the Formation of Protestant Popular Culture," in Roper, ed., *Religion and Culture in Germany,* 338–39. Writing in the 1970s, Gerald Strauss viewed such folk beliefs as a sort of underground religion, surviving in opposition to orthodox Christianity. He contends that "ordinary people maintained a vigorous religious subculture," a "subterranean religion . . . beyond the theologian's grasp, the preacher's appeal, or the visitor's power to compel." Strauss, *Luther's House of Learning,* 303. Current scholarship tends to see popular magical customs as complementary to orthodox religiosity, since premodern peoples tended not to see a contradiction in simultaneously holding both types of supernatural beliefs.
19. Scribner, "Reformation, Popular Magic and the 'Disenchantment of the World,'" 357–58.
20. Scribner, "Reformation, Popular Magic and the 'Disenchantment of the World,'" 338–39. See also Wilson, *Magical Universe,* xxvi.
21. Strauss notes the popularity of cunning folk in Brandenburg and Meissen in the 1590s, arguing that "the church competed for the faith and allegiance of its flock" against "this underground network of wizards, crystal-gazers, soothsayers, and wise women. It was an unequal struggle." Strauss, *Luther's House of Learning,* 304–5. See also Dixon, *Reformation and Rural Society,* 162–93.

22. Gijswijt-Hofstra, "Witchcraft after the Witch-Trials," in Gijswijt-Hofstra, Levack, and Porter, eds., *Witchcraft and Magic in Europe: The Eighteenth and Nineteenth Centuries,* ix.
23. See Bailey, "Disenchantment of Magic: Spells, Charms, and Superstition," 402.
24. Cameron, *Enchanted Europe.*
25. Bever, *Realities of Witchcraft and Popular Magic,* 406. C. Scott Dixon has argued, along similar lines, that in the century after the Reformation the Lutheran clergy, through sermons, catechisms, and visitations, gradually "reconfigured" popular magical beliefs, slowly assimilating them into Protestant orthodoxy. See Dixon, *Reformation and Rural Society,* 200–202.
26. In a 2017 edited volume, Bever himself explores this turn in the scholarship on magic and modernity. See Bever and Styers, eds., *Magic in the Modern World.*
27. Walsham, "Reformation and the 'Disenchantment of the World' Reassessed," 508.
28. See Paul Kléber Monod, *Solomon's Secret Arts: The Occult in the Age of Enlightenment* (New Haven, 2013); Egil Asprem, *The Problem of Disenchantment: Scientific Naturalism and Esoteric Discourse, 1900–1939* (Leiden, 2014); Jason A. Josephson-Storm, *The Myth of Disenchantment: Magic, Modernity, and the Birth of the Human Sciences* (Chicago, 2017); and Bever and Styers, eds., *Magic in the Modern World.*
29. Walsham, "Reformation and the 'Disenchantment of the World' Reassessed," 526. See also Saler, "Modernity and Enchantment," 703.
30. Saler, "Modernity and Enchantment," 691–92.
31. Walsham, "Migrations of the Holy," 259.
32. Walsham, "Reformation and the 'Disenchantment of the World' Reassessed," 521.
33. Walsham, "Reformation and the 'Disenchantment of the World' Reassessed," 518.
34. For important examples of this scholarship, see Birgit Meyer and Peter Pels, eds., *Magic and Modernity: Interfaces of Revelation and Concealment* (Stanford, 2003); and Alex Owen, *The Place of Enchantment: British Occultism and the Culture of the Modern* (Chicago, 2007).
35. Laqueur, "Why the Margins Matter: Occultism and the Making of Modernity," 115–17.
36. Treitel, *Science for the Soul.* Other scholars have traced more unsavory aspects of such modern occultism, showing that it helped feed the Nazi movement in its early years by fostering a neo-pagan religious revival based on mystical racial purification. See Kurlander, *Hitler's Monsters.* For the neo-pagan revival in nineteenth-century Britain, see also Hutton, *Triumph of the Moon.*
37. Laqueur, "Why the Margins Matter," 131.
38. Walsham, "Reformation and the 'Disenchantment of the World' Reassessed," 517.
39. For the effects of nineteenth-century socioeconomic conditions on magical beliefs, see Labouvie, *Verbotene Künste.* See also Davies, "Urbanization and the Decline of Witchcraft: An Examination of London"; and Gijswijt-Hofstra, Levack, and Porter, eds., *Witchcraft and Magic in Europe: The Eighteenth and Nineteenth Centuries.*
40. A December 2009 Pew Research Center study reported that 1 in 4 American adults believed in astrology. According to a 2001 National Science Foundation poll, 15 percent of American respondents reported that they read their horoscopes in the newspaper every day or very often. See Johnston, *Ancient Greek Divination,* 2.

BIBLIOGRAPHY

Archival Sources

Forschungsbibliothek Gotha

Rüge-Ordnung (1646).

Stadtarchiv Erfurt

1–16/16m 13: Hexenprozesse (1587–88).

Thüringisches Staatsarchiv Gotha

Criminalia des Amts Tenneberg: ZZ.X., 3: Wehrsegerin u. Zeuberi (1556–61), Wahlwinkel, 1556.

Criminalia des Amts Tenneberg: ZZ.X., 6–11: Sundhausen, 1560.

Criminalia des Amts Tenneberg: ZZ.X., 3–5: Gotha, 1561.

Criminalia des Amts Tenneberg: ZZ.X., 1–6: "Abergläubisher Handel" Waltershausen (1718).

Geheimes Archiv, EEE XI (13) e, 12–13.

Gerichtsamt Nazza, Sec. III A, Loc. 15, Nr. 19c (1840).

Justizamt Ohrdruf (vol. 89); Loc. A, Nr. 1–21 (27 March 1741), 17.

Justizamt Ohrdruf (vol. 89); Loc. A, Nr. 1–21 (21 September 1759), 18b.

Justizamt Ohrdruf (vol. 89); Loc. B, Nr. 11–23: Hanns Karsten wegen Däller wegen Hexerei (1671).

Oberkonsitorium Generalia; Loc. 29b Kirchli. Discipl. Nr. 4 (n.d.).

Thüringisches Staatsarchiv Weimar

6-11-0035; s. 1; v. 30: Ernestinisches Gesamtarchiv, Re. li: Visitation im gesamten ernestischen Gebeit (1554–55).

6-12-3007: Rechtspflege Sig. B 2733; v. Num. 1087; Geheime Canzlei Acta D 427, B. 2733: Untersuchung gegen Johann Friedrich Ufland und Johann Nicol Gräßler aus Wipfra wegen Befragung eines Wahrsagers (Weimar, 1774).

6-12-4008: s. 1564; v. 1556, 3: Eisenacher Archiv, Rechtspflege: Untersuchung gegen Anna Reich von Unterweid wegen Hexereiverdachts (18 March 1673) [Amt Kaltennordheim].
6-12-4008: Eisenacher Archiv, Rechtspflege Sig. 900; v. Num. 1582: Bestrafung von Heinrich Hirsch aus Tiefenort wegen verbottener Wahrsagerei (1691–92).
6-12-4008: s. 1587; v. 1599: Eisenacher Archiv, Rechtspflege: Inquisitionsakte im Hexenprozess gegen Martha Keller aus Ostheim (1662–63) [Amt Lichtenberg].

Printed Primary Sources

Albrecht, Bernhard. *Magia: Das ist, Christlicher Bericht von der Zauberey und Hexerey*. Leipzig, 1628.

Amsterdam, Johannes. *Etliche wahrhafftige weissagung/und fürneme spruche des Ehrwirdigen Vaters/Hern Doctor Martini Luthers*. Magdeburg, 1552.

Anhorn, Bartholomaeus. *Magiologia: Das ist Christlicher Bericht von dem Aberglauben und Zauberey*. Basel, 1674.

Anon. *Antwort an einen Freund/Welcher Unterricht ausgebeten von der neulich zu Hall gehalten DISPUTATION, Welche erweisen soll Daß keine Hexen oder Zauberen sey . . . Daß wer solches läugne/den Weg zum Atheismo bahne*. n.p., 1703.

———. *Das Faustbuch nach der Wolfenbütteler Handschrift*. Edited by Harry Gerald Haile. Berlin: Erich Schmidt Verlag, 1969.

Aquinas, Thomas. *Summa Theologiae. Second Book*. Translated and edited by Thomas Gilby. Cambridge: Cambridge University Press, 1964.

Augustine. *The Confessions of St. Augustine*. Edited by J. K. Ryan. Garden City, NY: Doubleday, 1960.

———. *On Christian Teaching*. Translated by R. P. H. Green. Oxford: Oxford University Press, 1997.

Bekker, Balthasar. *D. Balthasar Bekkers reformierte Predigers in Amsterdam bezauberte Welt*. Leipzig, 1782.

———. *Die Bezauberte Welt: Oder Eine gründliche Untersuchung des Allgemeinen Aberglaubens*. Amsterdam, 1693.

Bernardino of Siena. *Saint Bernardine of Siena: Sermons*. Edited by Nazareno Orlandi and translated by Helen Josephine Robins. Siena: Tipographia sociale, 1920.

Berns, Michael. *Gründliche und völlige Wiederlegung der Bezauberten Welt Balthasar Beckers*. Hamburg, 1708.

Binsfeld, Peter. *Tractat von Bekanntnuß der Zauberer und Hexen*. Trier, 1590.

Bodin, Jean. *De magorum Daemonomania: Vom Aüßgelasnen Wütigen Teüffelsheer Allerhand Zauberern Hexen und Hexenmeistern Unholden Teuffelsbeschwerern Warsagern Schwartzkünstlern Vergifftern Augenverblendern etc*. Strasbourg, 1591.

Brunnemann, Jacob. *Discours von betrüglichen Kennzeichen der Zauberey*. Halle, 1727.

Buddeus, Johannes Franciscus. *Lehrsatz von der Atheisterey und dem Aberglaüben*. Jena, 1717.

Burchard of Worms. *Corrector*. In *Medieval Handbooks of Penance: A Translation of the Principal Libri Poenitentiales*, edited by John T. McNeill and Helena M. Gamer, 321–45. New York: Columbia University Press, 1990.

Caesarius of Arles. *Saint Caesarius of Arles: Sermons. Vol. I (1–80)*. Translated by Mary Magdalene Mueller. Washington, D.C.: Catholic University of America Press, 1956.

Calvin, John. *Avertissement contre l'astrologie judiciaire.* Edited by Oliver Millet. Geneva: Droz, 1985.

———. "Commentary on Daniel 1:17." *Calvin's Complete Commentary on the Bible. Vol. 4, Ezekiel to Joel.* n.p.: Delmarva Publications, 2013.

———. *"Commentary on Isaiah 65:1–25." Commentary on the Book of the Prophet Isaiah.* Vol. IV, edited by Anthony Uyl. Ingersoll, OT: Devoted Publishing, 2019.

———. *"Sermons on Deuteronomy."* n.p.: Banner of Truth Trust, 1987.

Celichius, Andreas. *Notwendige Erinnerung: Vonn des Sathans letzten Zornsturm.* Wittenberg, 1594.

Erasmus, Desiderius. "Letter to Antoon Van Bergen." In *The Correspondence of Erasmus, 1501–1514.* Translated by R. A. B. Mynors and D. F. S. Thompson. Toronto: University of Toronto Press, 1975.

Fabri, Johannes [Johann Jacob Faber]. *Specimen Zeli iusti Theologici contra Maleficos & Sagas. Das ist: Muster und Prob eines recht Theologischen Eifers/ wider die Zauberer und Hexen: bestehend in 6. unterschiedlichen Predigten.* Tübingen, 1667.

Feyerabend, Sigmund. *Theatrum Diabolorum, Das ist: Warhafte eigentliche und kurtze Beschreibung Allerley grewlicher, schrecklicher und abschewlicher Laster, so in diesen letzten, schweren und bösen Zeiten an allen Orten und Enden fast bräuchlich, auch grausamlich im schwang gehen. . . .* Frankfurt am Main, 1569.

Fischer, Heinrich Ludwig. *Das Buch vom Aberglauben.* Leipzig, 1790.

Fleetwood, William. *Gründliche Untersuchung der Wunder-Wercke: Worinnen nicht alleine die Beschaffenheit der wahren Wunder . . . am Ende sind beygefüget M. Pascals Sonderbahre Gedancken von Wundern.* Leipzig, 1705.

Friedrich, Henning. *Gründliche Widerlegung der Aberglaübischen Astrologorum, so ausz dem Gestirn, und desselbigen influents, prognosticiren, Geneses, oder Nativiteten stellen. . . .* Erfurt, 1624.

Frisius, Paul. *Von deß Teuffels Nebelkappen, Das ist: Kurtzer Begriff, den gantzen Handel von der Zauberey belangend, zusammen gelesen.* Frankfurt am Main, 1583.

Der . . . Fürsten und Herren/Herren Friederich Wilhelms/und Herren Johansen Gebrüdern/ Hertzogen zu Sachsen/und Marggraven zu Meiseen/etc. Policey und Landesordnunge/ zuwolfart/nutz und besten derselben Unterthanen und Fürstenthumb bedacht und ausgangen. Jena, 1589.

Fürstliche Sächsische abermals verbesserte Landes-Ordnung/Des Durchläuchstigen/ Hochgebornen Fürsten und Herrn/Herrn Ernsten/Hertzogen zu Sachsen/Jülich/Cleve und Bergk/ Landgraffen in Thüringen/Marggraffen zu Meissen/. . . . Gotha, 1653.

Glanvill, Joseph. *Joseph Glanvill . . . Saducismus triumphatus: Oder, Vollkommener und klarer Beweiss von Hexen and Gespenstern, oder, Geister-Erscheinungen, in zween Theilen verfasset.* Hamburg, 1701.

Gödelmann, Georg. *Von Zaüberern, Hexen und Unholden.* Frankfurt am Main, 1592.

Goldschmidt, Peter. *Verworffener Hexen- und Zauberer-Advokaten.* Hamburg, 1705.

Guido of Monte Rochen. *Handbook for Curates: A Late Medieval Manual on Pastoral Ministry.* Translated by Anne T. Thayer. Washington, D.C.: Catholic University of America Press, 2011.

Hahnzog, Christian Ludwig. *Predigten wider den Aberglauben der Landleute.* Magdeburg, 1784.

Hauber, Eberhard David, ed. *Bibliotheca, Acta et Scripta, Magica*. 3 vols. Lemgo, 1738–45.

Horst, Georg Conrad. *Damonomagie, oder Geschichte des Glaubens an Zauberei und dämonische Wunder*. Frankfurt am Main, 1818.

Keller, Ernst Urban. *Das Grab des Aberglaubens*. Stuttgart, 1775.

———. *Gegen den Aberglauben*. Stuttgart, 1786.

Kramer, Heinrich. *The Hammer of Witches: A Complete Translation of the Malleus Maleficarum*. Translated and edited by Christopher S. Mackay. Cambridge: Cambridge University Press, 2009.

Luther, Martin. *Large Catechism*. Translated and edited by Theodore G. Tappert. Philadelphia: Muhlenberg Press, 1959.

———. *Luther's Works*. Vol. 1, *Lectures on Genesis* (1535–45), edited by Jaroslav Pelikan. St. Louis: Concordia Publishing House, 1955–86.

———. *Luther's Works*. Vol. 9, *Lectures on Deuteronomy* (1523), edited by Jaroslav Pelikan. St. Louis: Concordia Publishing House, 1955–86.

———. *Luther's Works*. Vol. 43, *Personal Prayer Book* (1522), edited by Jaroslav Pelikan. St. Louis: Concordia Publishing House, 1955–86.

———. *Luther's Works*. Vol. 54, *Table Talk* (1532), edited by Jaroslav Pelikan. St. Louis: Concordia Publishing House, 1955–86.

———. *Tischreden III*, Weimarer Ausgabe. Weimar: Hermann Böhlaus, 1883–1929.

Meder, David. *Acht Hexenpredigten: Darinnen Von des Teuffels Mord Kindern, der Hexen . . . erschrecklichen Abfalle, Lastern und Ubelthaten, dadurch die Göttliche Maiestet gelestert, und Menschen und Viehe, etc. verderblicher Schaden zugefüget*. Leipzig, 1605.

Melanchthon, Philip. *Orations on Philosophy and Education*. Edited by Sachiko Kusukawa. Cambridge: Cambridge University Press, 1999.

Milichius, Ludwig. *Der Zauber-Teuffel, das ist von Zauberey, Warsagung, Beschwehren, Segen, Aberglauben, Hexerey und mancherley Wercken des Teuffels. . . .* Frankfurt am Main, 1566.

Passavanti, Jacopo. *The Mirror of True Penitence*. In *Witchcraft in Europe, 400–1700: A Documentary History*, edited by Alan Charles Kors and Edward Peters, 105–10. Philadelphia: University of Pennsylvania Press, 2000.

Praetorius, Anton. *Gründlicher Bericht Antonii Praetorii Von Zauberey vnd Zauberern deren Vrsprung, Vnterscheid, Vermögen vnd Handlungen, Auch wie einer Christlichen Obrigkeit solchem schändlichen Laster zu begegnen . . . zu hindern vnd zu straffen gebühre . . . Auß Göttlichem vnd Kayserlichem Recht*. Frankfurt am Main, 1629.

Remigius, Nicholas [Nicholas Remy]. *Daemonolatria: Das ist von Unholden und Zauber Geistern*. Speyer, 1597.

Saur, Abraham. *Eine kurtze treuwe Warnung, Anzeige und Underricht: Ob auch zu dieser unser zeit unter uns Christen, Hexen, Zäuberer, und Unholden vorhanden: Und was sie außrichten können*. Marburg, 1582.

Saxe-Altenburg Landesordnung. Altenburg, 1705.

Schmidt, Johann Georg. *Die gestriegelte Rockenphilosophie, Oder Aufrichtige Untersuchung derer von vielen Super-Klugen Weibern hochgehaltenen Aberglauben*. Chemnitz, 1718.

Schwager, Johann Moriz. *Versuch einer Geschichte der Hexenprocesse*. Berlin, 1784.

Scultetus, Abraham. *Warnung für der Warsagerey der Zauberer und Sterngucker/ verfast in zwoen Predigten/ so uber die letzte vier Versickel deß 47. Capitels deß Propheten Jesaiae gehalten durch*. Neustadt an der Haardt, 1608.

Spies, Johann. *Historia von D. Johann Fausten*. n.p., 1587.

[Spreter, Johann]. *Hexen Büchlein: das ist, ware entdeckung vnd erklärung, oder Declaration fürnämlicher artickel der Zauberey, vnd was von Zauberern, Vnholden, Hengsten, Nachtschaden, Schützen. Auch der Hexenhändel, art, thuon, lassen, wesen, buolschafften, artzeney, wohär sie erwachsen, vnd aller jhrer Machination. Item was Wechsel kind vnd Wütes här, vnd daruon zuo halten sey. Allen Vögten, Schultheyssen, Amptleüten oder Ampts verwaltern, vnd Regenten des weltlichen Schwedts vnd Regiments nutzlich zuo lessen. . . .* n.p., 1545.

Thomasius, Christian. *Vom Laster der Zauberei—De Crimie Magiae: Über die Hexenprozesse—Processus Inquisitorii Contra Sagas*. Translated and edited by Rolf Lieberwirth. 2nd ed. Munich, 1987.

Waldschmidt, Bernhard. *Pythonissa Endorea: Das ist Acht und Zwantzig Hexen und Gespenst Predigten genommen auß der Histori der Zaüberin zu Endor I Sam. XXVIII. und gehalten von M. Bernhardo Waldschmidt Evangelischem Prediger Franckfurt. . . .* Frankfurt am Main, 1660.

Weyer, Johann. *On Witchcraft: An Abridged Translation of Johann Weyer's De praestigiis daemonum*. Translated and edited by Benjamin G. Kohl and H. C. Erik Midelfort. Asheville, NC: Pegasus Press, 1998.

[Witekind, Hermann]. *Christlich bedenken und erinnerung von Zauberey*. Speyer, 1585.

Secondary Sources

Ahnert, Thomas. *Religion and the Origins of the German Enlightenment: Faith and the Reform of Learning in the Thought of Christian Thomasius*. Rochester: University of Rochester Press, 2006.

Albrecht-Birkner, Veronika. *Reformation des Lebens: Die Reformen Herzog Ernst des Frommen von Sachsen-Gotha und ihre Auswirkungen auf Frömmigkeit, Schule und Alltag im ländlichen Raum (1640–1675)*. Leipzig: Evangelische Verlagsanstalt, 2002.

Ankarloo, Bengt, and Stuart Clark, eds. *Witchcraft and Magic in Europe: Ancient Greece and Rome*. Philadelphia: University of Pennsylvania Press, 1999.

———. *Witchcraft and Magic in Europe: Biblical and Pagan Societies*. Philadelphia: University of Pennsylvania Press, 2001.

Asprem, Egil. *The Problem of Disenchantment: Scientific Naturalism and Esoteric Discourse, 1900–1939*. Leiden: Brill, 2014.

Bailey, Michael D. *Battling Demons: Witchcraft, Heresy, and Reform in the Late Middle Ages*. University Park: Pennsylvania University Press, 2003.

———. "Diabolic Magic." In *Cambridge History of Magic and Witchcraft in the West from Antiquity to the Present*, edited by David J. Collins, 361–92. Cambridge: Cambridge University Press, 2015.

———. "The Disenchantment of Magic: Spells, Charms, and Superstition in Early European Witchcraft Literature." *American Historical Review* 111:2 (2006): 388–402.

———. "From Sorcery to Witchcraft: Clerical Conceptions of Magic in the Later Middle Ages." *Speculum* 76 (2001): 960–90.

———. *Magic and Superstition in Europe: A Concise History from Antiquity to the Present*. Lanham, MD: Rowman & Littlefield Publishers, 2007.

Barnes, Robin B. "Astrology and the Confessions in the Empire, c. 1550–1620." In *Confessionalization in Europe, 1555–1700: Essays in Honor and Memory of Bodo Nischan*, edited by

John M. Headley, Hans J. Hillerbrand, and Anthony J. Papalas, 131–54. Farnham, UK: Routledge, 2004.

———. *Astrology and Reformation*. Oxford: Oxford University Press, 2016.

———. *Prophecy and Gnosis: Apocalypticism in the Wake of the Lutheran Reformation*. Stanford: Stanford University Press, 1988.

Baron, Frank. *Doctor Faustus from History to Legend*. Munich: Fink, 1978.

———. *Faustus on Trial: The Origins of Johann Spies's "Historia" in an Age of Witch Hunting*. Berlin: Walter de Gruyter, 1992.

Barry, Jonathan, Marianne Hester, and Gareth Roberts, eds. *Witchcraft in Early Modern Europe: Studies in Culture and Belief*. Cambridge: Cambridge University Press, 1996.

Barth, Hans-Martin. *Atheismus und Orthodoxie: Analysen und Modelle christlicher Apologetik im 17. Jahrhundert*. Göttingen: Vandenhoeck & Ruprecht, 1971.

Behringer, Wolfgang. *Hexen und Hexenprozesse in Deutschland*. München: Dtv, 1988.

———. *Witchcraft Persecutions in Bavaria: Popular Magic, Religious Zealotry, and Reason of State in Early Modern Europe*. Cambridge: Cambridge University Press, 1997.

———. *Witches and Witch-Hunts: A Global History*. Cambridge: Polity, 2004.

Bever, Edward. "Divination." In *Encyclopedia of Witchcraft: The Western Tradition*. Vol, 1, edited by Richard M. Golden, 285–87. Santa Barbara, CA: ABC-CLIO, 2006.

———. "Popular Witch Beliefs and Magical Practices." In *The Oxford Handbook of Witchcraft in Early Modern Europe and Colonial America*, edited by Brian P. Levack, 50–68. Oxford: Oxford University Press, 2013.

———. *The Realities of Witchcraft and Popular Magic in Early Modern Europe: Culture, Cognition, and Everyday Life*. Houndmills, Basingstoke: Palgrave Macmillan, 2008.

Bever, Edward, and Randall Styers, eds. *Magic in the Modern World: Strategies of Repression and Legitimation*. University Park: Pennsylvania State University Press, 2017.

Beyer, Jürgen. *Lay Prophets in Lutheran Europe (c. 1550–1700)*. Leiden: Brill, 2017.

———. "A Lübeck Prophet in Local and Lutheran Context." In *Popular Religion in Germany and Central Europe 1400–1800*, edited by Robert Scribner and Trevor Johnson, 166–82. Houndmills, Basingstoke: Palgrave Macmillan, 1996.

Blauert, Andreas, and Gerd Schwerhoff, eds. *Kriminalitätsgeschichte: Beiträge zur Sozial- und Kulturgeschichte der Vormoderne*. Konstanz: UVK, 2000.

———. *Mit den Waffen der Justiz: Zur Kriminalitätsgeschichte des späten Mittelalters und der Frühen Neuzeit*. Konstanz: Fischer, 1993.

Boettcher, Susan R. "The Social Impact of the Lutheran Reformation in Germany." In *Lutheran Ecclesiastical Culture, 1550–1675*, edited by Robert Kolb, 305–59. Leiden: Brill, 2008.

Brady, Thomas A., Jr. "Social History." In *Reformation Europe: A Guide to Research*, edited by Steven Ozment, 161–81. St. Louis: Center for Reformation Research, 1982.

———. *Turning Swiss: Cities and Empire, 1450–1550*. Cambridge: Cambridge University Press, 1985.

Brann, Noel L. *Trithemius and Magical Theology: A Chapter in the Controversy over Occult Studies in Early Modern Europe*. Albany: SUNY Press, 1999.

Brecht, Martin, ed. *Geschichte des Pietismus: Der Pietismus vom siebzehnten bis zum frühen achtzehnten Jahrhundert*. Vol. I. Göttingen: Vandenhoeck & Ruprecht, 1993.

Briggs, Robin. *Witches and Neighbours: The Social and Cultural Context of European Witchcraft*. London: Viking, 1996.

Broedel, Hans Peter. *The Malleus Maleficarum and the Construction of Witchcraft: Theology and Popular Belief.* Manchester: Manchester University Press, 2003.

Brown, Christopher Boyd. *Singing the Gospel: Lutheran Hymns and the Success of the Reformation.* Cambridge, MA: Harvard University Press, 2005.

Burke, Peter. *Popular Culture in Early Modern Europe.* New York: New York University Press, 1978.

Cameron, Euan. *Enchanted Europe: Superstition, Reason, and Religion, 1250–1750.* Oxford: Oxford University Press, 2010.

Christman, Robert. "The Pulpit and the Pew: Shaping Popular Piety in the Late Reformation." In *Lutheran Ecclesiastical Culture, 1550–1675,* edited by Robert Kolb, 259–303. Leiden: Brill, 2008.

Clark, Jonathan. "Providence, Predestination and Progress: Or, did the Enlightenment Fail?" *Albion* 35 (2003): 559–89.

Clark, Stuart, ed. *Languages of Witchcraft: Narrative, Ideology, and Meaning in Early Modern Culture.* Houndmills, Basingstoke: Macmillan Press, 2001.

———. "Protestant Demonology: Sin, Superstition, and Society (c. 1520–c. 1630)." In *New Perspectives on Witchcraft, Magic, and Demonology.* Vol. I, *Demonology, Religion, and Witchcraft,* edited by Brian P. Levack, 179–215. New York: Routledge, 2001.

———. *Thinking with Demons: The Idea of Witchcraft in Early Modern Europe.* Oxford: Oxford University Press, 1997.

Cohn, Norman. *Europe's Inner Demons: The Demonization of Christians in Medieval Christendom.* 2nd rev. ed. Chicago: University of Chicago Press, 2000.

Collins, David J., ed. *Cambridge History of Magic and Witchcraft in the West from Antiquity to the Present.* Cambridge: Cambridge University Press, 2015.

———. "Learned Magic." In *Cambridge History of Magic and Witchcraft in the West,* edited by idem, 332–60. Cambridge: Cambridge University Press, 2015.

Cryer, Frederick H., and Marie-Louise Thomsen, eds. *Witchcraft and Magic in Europe. Vol. 1, Biblical and Pagan Societies.* Philadelphia: University of Pennsylvania Press, 2001.

Davies, Owen. *Popular Magic: Cunning-Folk in English History.* London, 2003.

———. "Urbanization and the Decline of Witchcraft: An Examination of London." *Journal of Social History* 30 (1997): 597–617.

———. *Witchcraft, Magic, and Culture, 1736–1951.* Manchester: Manchester University Press, 1999.

Davies, Owen, and Willem de Blécourt, eds. *Beyond the Witch Trials: Witchcraft and Magic in Enlightenment Europe.* Manchester: Manchester University Press, 2004.

———, eds. *Witchcraft Continued: Popular Magic in Modern Europe.* Manchester: Manchester University Press, 2004.

de Blécourt, Willem. "Witch Doctors, Soothsayers, and Priests: On Cunning Folk in European Historiography and Tradition." *Social History* 19 (1994): 285–303.

Decker, Rainer. *Die Hexen und ihre Henker: Ein Fallbericht.* Freiburg: Herder, 1994.

de Levie, Dagobert. "The Patriotic Sermons of Christian Ludewig Hahnzog, Germany 1785." *Journal of Modern History* 26:1 (March 1954): 36–39.

Dickens, A. G., and John M. Tonkin. *The Reformation in Historical Thought.* Cambridge, MA: Harvard University Press, 1985.

Dickie, Matthew W. *Magic and Magicians in the Greco-Roman World.* London: Routledge, 2001.

Dillinger, Johannes. *"Evil People": A Comparative Study of Witch Hunts in Swabian Austria and the Electorate of Trier.* Charlottesville: University of Virginia Press, 2009.

———. *Magical Treasure Hunting in Europe and North America: A History.* Houndmills, Basingstoke: Palgrave Macmillan, 2012.

Dixon, C. Scott. "Popular Astrology and Lutheran Propaganda in Reformation Germany." *History* 84 (1999): 403–18.

———. *The Reformation and Rural Society: The Parishes of Brandenburg-Ansbach-Kulmbach, 1528–1603.* Cambridge: Cambridge University Press, 1996.

Dorn-Haag, Verena J. *Hexerei und Magie im Strafrecht: Historische und dogmatische Aspekte.* Tübingen: Mohr Siebeck, 2016.

Easlea, Brian. *Witch Hunting, Magic and the New Philosophy.* Brighton: Humanities Press, 1980.

Edwards, Kathryn A., ed. *Everyday Magic in Early Modern Europe.* Farnam, Surry: Routledge, 2015.

Eiden, Herbert, and Rita Voltmer, eds. *Hexenprozesse und Gerichtspraxis.* Trier: Paulinus, 2002.

Evans, R. J. W. *Rudolf II and His World: A Study in Intellectual History, 1576–1612.* Oxford: Oxford University Press, 1973.

Fichtner, Paula Sutter. *Protestantism and Primogeniture in Early Modern Germany.* New Haven: Yale University Press, 1989.

Flower, Michael Attyah. *The Seer in Ancient Greece.* Berkeley: University of California Press, 2008.

Franz, Gunther, and Franz Irsigler. *Hexenglaube und Hexenprozesse im Raum Rhein-Mosel-Saar.* Trier: Paulinus, 1995.

Fraser, Kyle A. "Roman Antiquity." In *Cambridge History of Magic and Witchcraft in the West from Antiquity to the Present,* edited by David J. Collins, 115–47. Cambridge: Cambridge University Press, 2015.

Füssel, Ronald. *Die Hexenverfolgung in Thüringer Raum.* Hamburg: DOBU, 2003.

Gestrich, Andreas. "Pietismus und Aberglaube: Zum Zusammenhang von popularem Pietismus und dem Ende der Hexenverfolgung im 18. Jahrhundert." In *Das Ende der Hexenverfolgung,* edited by Sönke Lorenz and Dieter Bauer, 269–86. Stuttgart: Franz Steiner, 1995.

Gijswijt-Hofstra, Marijke. "Witchcraft after the Witch-Trials." In *Witchcraft and Magic in Europe. Vol. 5, The Eighteenth and Nineteenth Centuries,* edited by Marijke Gijswijt-Hofstra, Brian P. Levack, and Roy Porter, 95–189. London: The Athlone Press, 1999.

Ginzburg, Carlo. *The Cheese and the Worms: The Cosmos of a Sixteenth-Century Miller.* Translated by John and Anne Tedeschi. Baltimore: Johns Hopkins University Press, 1992.

———. *Ecstasies: Deciphering the Witches' Sabbath.* Translated by Raymond Rosenthal. Chicago: University of Chicago Press, 1991.

Gordon, Bruce. "'God killed Saul': Heinrich Bullinger and Jacob Ruef on the Power of the Devil." In *Werewolves, Witches, and Wandering Spirits: Traditional Belief and Folklore in Early Modern Europe,* edited by Kathryn A. Edwards, 155–79. Kirksville, MO: Truman State University Press, 2002.

Graf, Fritz. "Excluding the Charming: The Development of the Greek Concept of Magic." In *Ancient Magic and Ritual Power,* edited by Marvin Meyer and Paul Mirecki, 29–42. Leiden: Brill, 2001.

Green, Jonathan. *Printing and Prophecy: Prognostication and Media Change, 1450–1550.* Ann Arbor: University of Michigan Press, 2012.

Grimm, Heinrich. "Die deutschen Teufelbücher des 16. Jahrhunderts: Ihre Rolle in Buchwesen und ihre Bedeutung." *Archiv für Geschichte des Buchwesens* 16 (1959): 1733–90.

Harrington, Joel. *The Faithful Executioner: Life and Death, Honor and Shame in the Turbulent Sixteenth Century.* New York: Farrar, Straus, and Giroux, 2013.

Haustein, Jörg. "Mensch-Prediger-Professor-Autorität: Martin Luther und die Hexenverfolgung." In *Hexen und Hexenverfolgung in Thüringen: Herausgegeben von den Meininger Museen,* 128–47. Meiningen und Bielefeld: Verlag für Regionalgeschichte, 2003.

Heckmann, Hermann, ed. *Thüringen: Historische Landeskunde Mitteldeutschlands.* Würzburg: Weidlich Verlag, 1991.

Hen, Yitzhak. "The Early Medieval West." In *Cambridge History of Magic and Witchcraft in the West,* edited by David J. Collins, 183–206. Cambridge: Cambridge University Press, 2015.

Herzig, Tamar. "Witches, Saints, and Heretics: Heinrich Kramer's Ties with Italian Women Mystics." *Magic, Ritual, and Witchcraft* 1, no. 1 (Summer 2006): 24–55.

Hunter, Ian. *Rival Enlightenments: Civil and Metaphysical Philosophy in Early Modern Germany.* Cambridge: Cambridge University Press, 2001.

Hutton, Ronald. *The Triumph of the Moon: A History of Modern Pagan Witchcraft.* Oxford: Oxford University Press, 1999.

Jerouschek, Günther. *Die Hexen und ihr Prozeß: Die Hexenverfolgungen in der Reichsstadt Esslingen.* Esslingen: Stadtarchiv Esslingen, 1992.

Johnson, Evan. "Violence and Retaliation: Civilian Agency in Thuringia in the Thirty Years' War." M.A. Thesis, University of Georgia, 2014.

Johnston, Sarah Iles. *Ancient Greek Divination.* Malden, MA: Wiley-Blackwell, 2008.

Jolly, Karen, Catharina Raudvere, and Edward Peters, eds. *Witchcraft and Magic in Europe: The Middle Ages.* London: The Athlone Press, 2002.

Josephson-Storm, Jason A. *The Myth of Disenchantment: Magic, Modernity, and the Birth of the Human Sciences.* Chicago: University of Chicago Press, 2017.

Kahlos, Maijastina. "The Early Church." In *The Cambridge History of Magic and Witchcraft from Antiquity to the Present,* edited by David J. Collins, 148–82. Cambridge: Cambridge University Press, 2015.

Karant-Nunn, Susan. *Luther's Pastors: The Reformation in the Ernestine Countryside.* Philadelphia: American Philosophical Society, 1979.

Kieckhefer, Richard. *Forbidden Rites: A Necromancer's Manual of the Fifteenth Century.* University Park: Pennsylvania State University Press, 1997.

———. *Magic in the Middle Ages.* Cambridge: Cambridge University Press, 1990.

Kittelson, James. "Successes and Failures in the German Reformation: The Report from Strasbourg." *Archiv für Reformationsgeschichte* 73 (1982): 153–74.

Klaasen, Frank. *The Transformations of Magic: Illicit Learned Magic in the Later Middle Ages and Renaissance.* University Park: Pennsylvania State University Press, 2013.

Klinger, Andreas. *Der Gothaer Fürstenstaat: Herrschaft, Konfession und Dynastie unter Herzog Ernst dem Frommen.* Husum: Matthiesen, 2002.

Kurlander, Eric. *Hitler's Monsters: A Supernatural History of the Third Reich.* New Haven: Yale University Press, 2017.

Labouvie, Eva. *Verbotene Künste: Volksmagie und ländlicher Aberglaube in den Dorfgemeinschaften des Saarraumes (16.–19. Jahrhunderts)*. St. Ingert: Röhring, 1992.

Lange, Ursula. *Untersuchungen zu Bodins Demonomanie*. Frankfurt am Main: V. Klostermann, 1970.

Laqueur, Thomas. "Why the Margins Matter: Occultism and the Making of Modernity." *Modern Intellectual History* 3:21 (2006): 115–35.

Lea, Henry Charles. *Materials toward a History of Witchcraft*. Arranged and edited by Arthur C. Howland. Intro. by George Lincoln Burr. Vol. 1. New York: T. Yoseloff, 1957, c1939.

Lehmann, Hartmut, James Van Horn Melton, and Jonathan Strom. *Pietism in Germany and North America, 1680–1820*. New York: Routledge, 2016.

Lehrich, Christopher I. *The Language of Demons and Angels: Cornelius Agrippa's Occult Philosophy*. Leiden: Brill, 2003.

Levack, Brian P. "Crime and the Law." In *Palgrave Advances in Witchcraft Historiography*, edited by Owen Davies and Jonathan Barry, 146–63. Houndmills, Basingstoke: Palgrave Macmillan, 2007.

———. "The Decline and End of Witchcraft Prosecutions." In *The Oxford Handbook of Witchcraft in Early Modern Europe and Colonial America*, edited by idem, 429–49. Oxford: Oxford University Press, 2013.

———. "The Decline and End of Witchcraft Prosecutions." In *Witchcraft and Magic in Europe. Vol. 5, The Eighteenth and Nineteenth Centuries*, edited by Marijke Gijswijt-Hofstra, Brian P. Levack, and Roy Porter, 1–94. London: The Athlone Press, 1999.

———, ed. *The Oxford Handbook of Witchcraft in Early Modern Europe and Colonial America*. Oxford: Oxford University Press, 2013.

———. *The Witch-Hunt in Early Modern Europe*. London: Routledge, 1995.

Maxwell-Stuart, P. G., ed. *The Malleus Maleficarum*. Manchester: Manchester University Press, 2007.

———. "Rational Superstition: The Writings of Protestant Demonologists." In *Religion and Superstition in Reformation Europe*, edited by Helen Parish and William G. Naphy, 170–82. Manchester: Manchester University Press, 2002.

McNeill, John T., and Helena M. Gamer, eds. and trans. *Medieval Handbooks of Penance: A Translation of the Principal Libri Poenitentiales*. New York: Columbia University Press, 1990.

Meyer, Birgit, and Peter Pels, eds. *Magic and Modernity: Interfaces of Revelation and Concealment*. Stanford: Stanford University Press, 2003.

Midelfort, H. C. Erik. *Exorcism and Enlightenment: Johann Joseph Gassner and the Demons of Eighteenth-Century Germany*. New Haven: Yale University Press, 2005.

———. *A History of Madness in Sixteenth-Century Germany*. Stanford: Stanford University Press, 1999.

———. *Witch Hunting in Southwestern Germany, 1562–1684: The Social and Intellectual Foundations*. Stanford: Stanford University Press, 1972.

Milway, Michael. "Forgotten Best-Sellers from the Dawn of the Reformation." In *Continuity and Change: The Harvest of Late Medieval and Reformation History*, edited by Robert J. Bast and Andrew C. Gow, 113–42. Leiden: Brill, 2000.

Monod, Paul Kléber. *Solomon's Secret Arts: The Occult in the Age of Enlightenment*. New Haven: Yale University Press, 2013.

Mormando, Franco. *The Preacher's Demons: Bernardino of Siena and the Social Underworld of Early Renaissance Italy*. Chicago: University of Chicago Press, 1999.

Mulsow, Martin. *Enlightenment Underground: Radical Germany, 1680–1720*. Translated by H. C. Erik Midelfort. Charlottesville: University of Virginia Press, 2015.

Nauert, Charles. *Agrippa and the Crisis of Renaissance Thought*. Urbana: University of Illinois Press, 1965.

Niess, Walter. *Hexenprozesse in der Grafschaft Büdingen: Protokolle, Ursachen, Hintergründe*. Büdingen: Geschichtswerkstatt Büdingen, 1982.

Nipperdey, Thomas. "The Reformation and the Modern World." In *Politics and Society in Reformation Europe: Essays for Sir Geoffrey Elton on his Sixty-Fifth Birthday*, edited by E. I. Kouri and Tom Scott, 535–52. Houndmills, Basingstoke: Palgrave Macmillan, 1987.

Owen, Alex. *The Place of Enchantment: British Occultism and the Culture of the Modern*. Chicago: University of Chicago Press, 2007.

Parker, Geoffrey. "Success and Failure during the First Century of the Reformation." *Past & Present* 136 (1992): 43–82.

Pearl, Jonathan. *The Crime of Crimes: Demonology and Politics in France, 1560–1620*. Waterloo, Ontario: Wilfrid Laurier University Press, 1999.

Pohl, Herbert. *Hexenglaube und Hexenverfolgung im Kurfürsten Mainz: Ein Beitrag zur Hexenfrage im 16. und beginnenden 17. Jahrhundert*. Stuttgart: Fritz Steiner Verlag, 1988.

Poley, Jared. *The Devil's Riches: A Modern History of Greed*. New York: Berghahn, 2016.

Porter, Roy. "Witchcraft and Magic in Enlightenment, Romantic, and Liberal Thought." In *Witchcraft and Magic in Europe. Vol. 5, The Eighteenth and Nineteenth Centuries*, edited by Marijke Gijswijt-Hofstra, Brian P. Levack, and Roy Porter, 191–282. London: The Athlone Press, 1999.

Pott, Martin. *Aufklärung und Aberglaube: Die deutsche Frühaufklärung im Spiegel ihrer Aberglaubenskritik*. Tübingen: Niemeyer, 1992.

Potter, Mary. "A Warning against Judicial Astrology." *Calvin Theological Journal* 18 (1983): 157–89.

Racaut, Luc. "A Protestant or Catholic Superstition? Astrology and Eschatology during the French Wars of Religion." In *Religion and Superstition in Reformation Europe*, edited by Helen Parish and William G. Naphy, 154–69. Manchester: Manchester University Press, 2002.

Ricks, Stephen D. "The Magician as Outsider in the Hebrew Bible and New Testament." In *Ancient Magic and Ritual Power*, edited by Marvin Meyer and Paul Mirecki, 131–43. Leiden: Brill, 2001.

Robisheaux, Thomas. "The German Witch Trials." In *The Oxford Handbook of Witchcraft in Early Modern Europe and Colonial America*, edited by Brian P. Levack, 179–98. Oxford: Oxford University Press, 2013.

———. *The Last Witch of Langenburg: Murder in a German Village*. New York: W. W. Norton, 2009.

Roos, Keith. *The Devil in Sixteenth-Century German Literature: The Teufelsbücher*. Frankfurt am Main: Herbert Lang, 1972.

Roper, Lyndal. *The Holy Household: Women and Morals in Reformation Augsburg*. Oxford: Oxford University Press, 1989.

———. *Oedipus and the Devil: Witchcraft, Sexuality, and Religion in Early Modern Europe*. London: Routledge, 1994.

———. *Witch Craze: Terror and Fantasy in Baroque Germany*. New Haven: Yale University Press, 2004.

Rowlands, Alison. *Witchcraft Narratives in Germany: Rothenburg, 1561–1652*. Manchester: Manchester University Press, 2003.

Rublach, Ulinka. *Reformation Europe*. 2nd ed. Cambridge: Cambridge University Press, 2017.

Ruggiero, Guido. *Binding Passions: Tales of Magic, Marriage, and Power at the End of the Renaissance*. New York: Oxford University Press, 1993.

Rummel, Walter. *Bauern, Herren und Hexen: Studien zur Sozialgeschichte sponheimischer und kurtrierische Hexenprozesse 1574–1664*. Göttingen: Vandenhoeck & Ruprecht, 1991.

———. "'Weise' Frauen und 'weise' Männer im Kampf gegen Hexerei die Widerlegung einer modernen Fabel." In *Europäische Sozialgeschichte. Festschrift für Wolfgang Schieder*, edited by Christof Dipper, Lutz Klinkhammer, and Alexander Nützenadel, 353–75. Berlin: Duncker & Humblot, 2000.

Sabean, David Warren. *Power in the Blood: Popular Culture and Village Discourse in Early Modern Germany*. Cambridge: Cambridge University Press, 1984.

Saler, Michael. "Modernity and Enchantment: A Historiographical Review." *American Historical Review* 111:3 (2006): 692–716.

Schmidt, Brian B. "The 'Witch' of En-Dor, 1 Samuel 28, and Ancient Near Eastern Necromancy." In *Ancient Magic and Ritual Power*, edited by Marvin Meyer and Paul Mirecki, 111–29. Leiden: Brill, 2001.

Schneider, Hans. *German Radical Pietism*. Translated by Gerald T. MacDonald. Lanham, MD: Scarecrow Press, 2007.

Schormann, Gerhard. *Hexenprozesse in Deutschland*. Göttingen: Vandenhoeck & Ruprecht, 1981.

Schröder, Winfried. *Ursprünge des Atheismus: Untersuchungen zur Metaphysik- und Religionskritik des 17. und 18. Jahrhunderts*. Stuttgart: Frommann, 1998.

Schüz, Jonathan. "Bodin's *Démonomanie* in the German Vernacular." In *The Reception of Bodin*, edited by Howell A. Lloyd, 237–56. Leiden: Brill, 2013.

Scribner, Robert W. "Magic and the Formation of Protestant Popular Culture in Germany." In *Religion and Culture in Germany (1400–1800)*, edited by Lyndal Roper, 323–46. Leiden: Brill, 2001.

———. "Reformation and Desacralisation: From Sacramental World to Moralised Universe." In *Problems in the Historical Anthropology of Early Modern Europe*, edited by R. Po-Chia Hsia and R. W. Scribner, 75–92. Wolfenbütteler Forschungen, Vol. 78. Wiesbaden: Harrassowitz, 1997.

———. "The Reformation, Popular Magic and the 'Disenchantment of the World.'" *Journal of Interdisciplinary History* 23 (1993): 475–94.

Sheehan, Jonathan. "Enlightenment, Religion, and the Enigma of Secularization: A Review Essay." *American Historical Review* 108 (2003): 1057–60.

Spierenburg, Pieter. *The Broken Spell: A Cultural and Anthropological History of Preindustrial Europe*. Houndmills, Basingstoke: Palgrave Macmillan, 1991.

Starenko, Peter. "In Luther's Wake: Duke John Frederick II of Saxony, Angelic Prophesy, and the Gotha Rebellion of 1567." Ph.D. Dissertation, University of California, Berkeley, 2002.

Stievermann, Dieter. "Ernst der Fromme: Möglichkeiten und Grenzen eines Landesfürsten in der frühen Neuzeit." In *Ernst der Fromme (1601–1675): Staatsmann und Reformer*, edited by Roswitha Jacobsen and Hans-Jörg Ruge, 9–24. Jena: Quartus-Verlag, 2002.

Stokes, Laura. *Demons of Urban Reform: Early European Witch Trials and Criminal Justice, 1430–1530*. Houndmills, Basingstoke: Palgrave Macmillan, 2011.

Strauss, Gerald. *Luther's House of Learning: Indoctrination of the Young in the German Reformation*. Baltimore: Johns Hopkins University Press, 1978.

———. "Success and Failure in the German Reformation." *Past and Present* 67 (1975): 30–63.

Stuart, Kathy. *Defiled Trades and Social Outcasts: Honor and Ritual Pollution in Early Modern Germany*. Cambridge: Cambridge University Press, 2006.

Tambiah, Stanley Jeyaraja. *Magic, Science, Religion and the Scope of Rationality*. Cambridge: Cambridge University Press, 1990.

Tatar, Maria. *Spellbound: Studies on Mesmerism and Literature*. Princeton: Princeton University Press, 1978.

Theibault, John. "The Demography of the Thirty Years War Re-revisited: Günther Franz and His Critics." *German History* 15, no. 1 (1997): 1–21.

———. *German Villages in Crisis: Rural Life in Hesse-Kassel and the Thirty Years War, 1580–1720*. Highlands, NJ: Humanities Press, 1995.

Thomas, Keith. *Religion and the Decline of Magic: Studies in Popular Beliefs in Sixteenth- and Seventeenth-Century England*. New York: Charles Scribner's Sons, 1971.

Trainer, James. "The Incest-Theme in the Works of Tieck." *Modern Language Notes* 76, no. 8 (December 1961): 819–24.

Treitel, Corinna. *A Science for the Soul: Occultism and the Genesis of the German Modern*. Baltimore: Johns Hopkins University Press, 2004.

van Dülmen, Richard. "Reformation und Neuzeit: Ein Versuch." *Zeitschrift für Historische Forschung* 14 (1987): 1–25.

———. *Religion und Gesellschaft. Beiträge zu einer Religionsgeschichte der Neuzeit*. Frankfurt am Main: Ort Verlag, 1989.

Venables, Mary Constance Noll. "In the Shadow of War: The Reign of Ernst the Pious in Seventeenth-Century Saxony." Ph.D. Dissertation, Yale University, 2004.

Vogler, Bernhard. "Die Enstehung der Protestantischen Volksfrömmigkeit in der rheinischen Pfalz zwischen 1555 und 1619." *Archiv für Reformationsgeschichte* 72 (1981): 158–95.

Voltmer, Rita. *Hexenverfolgung und Herrschaftspraxis*. Trier: Paulinus, 2005.

———. "Zwischen Herrschaftskrise, Wirtschaftsdepression und Jesuitenpropaganda. Hexenverfolgungen in der Stadt Trier (15.–17. Jahrhundert)." *Jahrbuch für westdeutsche Landesgeschichte* 27 (2001): 37–107.

Waite, Gary K. *Heresy, Magic, and Witchcraft in Early Modern Europe*. Houndmills, Basingstoke: Palgrave Macmillan, 2003.

———. "Sixteenth-Century Religious Reform and the Witch-Hunts." In *The Oxford Handbook of Witchcraft in Early Modern Europe and Colonial America*, edited by Brian P. Levack, 485–506. Oxford: Oxford University Press, 2013.

Wakefield, Andre. *The Disordered Police State: German Cameralism as Science and Practice*. Chicago: University of Chicago Press, 2009.

Walsham, Alexandra. "Migrations of the Holy: Explaining Religious Change in Medieval and Early Modern Europe." *Journal of Medieval and Early Modern Studies* 44:2 (Spring 2014): 241–80.

———. *Providence in Early Modern England*. Oxford: Oxford University Press, 1999.

———. "The Reformation and the 'Disenchantment of the World' Reassessed." *The Historical Journal* 51:2 (2008): 497–528.

Walz, Rainer. *Hexenglaube und magische Kommunikation im Dorf der frühen Neuzeit: Die Verfolgungen in der Grafschaft Lippe*. Paderborn: Schöningh Verlag, 1993.

Warne, Monroe John. *Laboratories of Faith: Mesmerism, Spiritism, and Occultism in Modern France*. Ithaca: Cornell University Press, 2008.

Weber, Max. *The Protestant Ethic and the Spirit of Capitalism*. Translated and edited by Peter Baehr and Gordon C. Wells. New York: Penguin, 2002. First English ed. 1930.

———. *The Sociology of Religion*. Translated by Ephraim Fischoff. Boston: Beacon Press, 1963.

Weeks, Andrew. *Paracelsus: Speculative Theory and the Crisis of the Early Reformation*. Albany: SUNY Press, 1997.

Wegert, Karl. "The Social Context of State Terror in Early Modern Germany." *Canadian Journal of History* 26 (1991): 21–42.

Wilde, Manfred. *Die Zauberei- und Hexenprozesse in Kursachsen*. Köln: Böhlau, 2003.

Williams, Gerhild Scholz, *Defining Dominion: The Discourses of Magic and Witchcraft in Early Modern France and Germany*. Ann Arbor: University of Michigan Press, 1995.

Wilson, Stephen. *The Magical Universe: Everyday Ritual and Magic in Pre-Modern Europe*. London and New York: Hambledon and London, 2000.

Zika, Charles. *The Appearance of Witchcraft: Print and Visual Culture in Sixteenth-Century Europe*. London: Routledge, 2007.

INDEX

Recent books in the series
Studies in Early Modern German History

The Devil's Art: Divination and Discipline in Early Modern Germany
Jason Philip Coy

Four Fools in the Age of Reason: Laughter, Cruelty, and Power in Early Modern Germany
Dorinda Outram

The Executioner's Journal: Meister Frantz Schmidt of the Imperial City of Nuremberg
Translated by Joel F. Harrington

Hometown Religion: Regimes of Coexistence in Early Modern Westphalia
David M. Luebke

Enlightenment Underground: Radical Germany, 1680–1720
Martin Mulsow, translated by H. C. Erik Midelfort

Crossing the Boundaries of Belief: Geographies of Religious Conversion in Southern Germany, 1648–1800
Duane J. Corpis

Crime and Culture in Early Modern Germany
Joy Wiltenburg

The Witch in the Western Imagination
Lyndal Roper

The Fuggers of Augsburg: Pursuing Wealth and Honor in Renaissance Germany
Mark Häberlein

"Evil People": A Comparative Study of Witch Hunts in Swabian Austria and the Electorate of Trier
Johannes Dillinger, translated by Laura Stokes

Witchcraft and the Papacy: An Account Drawing on the Formerly Secret Records of the Roman Inquisition
Rainer Decker, translated by H. C. Erik Midelfort